Developing Writing 3-13

Roger Beard

Hodder & Stoughton

A MEMBER OF THE HODDER HEADLINE GROUP

Orders: please contact Bookpoint Ltd, 130 Milton Park, Abingdon, Oxon OX14 4SB.
Telephone: (44) 01235 827720. Fax: (44) 01235 400454. Lines are open from 9.00 – 6.00,
Monday to Saturday, with a 24 hour message answering service.
Email address: orders@bookpoint.co.uk

British Library Cataloguing in Publication Data
A catalogue record for this title is available from The British Library.

ISBN 0 340 655 607

First published 2000
Impression number 10 9 8 7 6 5 4 3 2
Year   2005 2004 2003 2002

Typeset by Transet Limited, Coventry, England
Printed in Great Britain for Hodder & Stoughton Educational, a division of Hodder Headline Plc,
338 Euston Road, London NW1 3BH by The Bath Press, Bath

Contents

Acknowledgements

I am deeply indebted to the following colleagues for helping with the typing of the manuscript: Nicky Hutchinson, Pat Russell, Kal Suri and Sarah Warm.

The author and publishers would also like to thank the following for permission to use material in this book:
Basic Skills Agency for examples from Children's Writing on pp 66 and 71; Blackwell Publishers for the diagram on p.91; Longman Group UK for the table on p.147; NFER-Nelson for the Figures on p.176; the Office for Standards in Education for the extracts from school inspection reports on pp. 11–12; Open University Press for the table on p.76; and the Qualifications and Curriculum Authority for the extracts from National Curriculum Statements of Attainment and Level Descriptions on p.6, the Figure on p.169 and the extracts from the Standard Assessment Tasks marking guide on p.197.

Every effort has been made to trace and acknowledge ownership of copyright. The author and publishers will be glad to make suitable arrangements with any copyright holders whom it has not been possible to contact.

Introduction

Time present and time past are both perhaps present in time future.
(T.S. Eliot)[1]

This chapter

- summarises the contents of *Developing Writing 3–13*
- outlines some of the main developments in the field in recent years
- reviews the recent centralisation of British education
- identifies some strengths and weaknesses of current school practices.

The World of the 'Second R'[2]

Across the world, the ability to write is acclaimed as one of the twin peaks of literacy and as one of the central gains from education. This worldly acclaim is fully warranted. Being able to read and write brings great benefits. Reading and writing are justifiably referred to as central parts of 'the basics' and these basics are the tools of further learning.[3] Writing helps to bring permanence and completeness to communication. These qualities give literacy certain advantages over oracy for communicating across space and time. Literacy is also widely seen as promoting valuable ways of thinking about and of understanding the world and ourselves. As a consequence, our ability to write can form a central part of our educational self-image. This self-image will be further driven by the confidence in being able to communicate with anyone we please, when we choose and wherever they are. The advent of the word processor in millions of locations has further reinforced our ability to communicate in this way. Indeed, the ICT[4] revolution has restructured our awareness of the forms such communications can take.

This book explores the nature of writing and how it develops in the 3–13 age-range, drawing on research from many parts of the world. It is written for teachers, student teachers and others who have an interest in children's writing. Parents, in particular, should also be able to make use of this book. It discusses issues that are of interest to anyone who cares for and works with children.

During the years between 3 and 13, writing skill can be transformed from the early scribbles of the pre-school child to the weekly production of dozens of pages of notes, essays, poetry and prose. This achievement by so many young people is easy to under estimate. It represents growth along several linguistic dimensions: of broadly understanding the relationship between language and literacy, and of specifically fusing together spelling, vocabulary and grammar into a range of texts. Each type of text will have its socially valued features and traditions.

Research into writing has made considerable progress in recent years. Writing is now seen as involving several processes, as the text is composed, encoded and read by the writer, with a view to improving it. The significance of early scribbles and emergent writing is now better understood. Researchers have investigated the demands of different literary and factual types of text and have indicated how these genres may be more effectively taught. The roles of efficient handwriting and confident spelling have been established. Many studies have looked at what word processing can offer the young writer. New questions have been raised about the relatively poor writing performance of boys.

Looking Back and Looking On

Developing Writing 3–13 has been written to replace an earlier book, *Children's Writing in the Primary School*,[5] that was first published in 1984. This earlier book drew on my own work as a teacher and on research and publications in education. The book covered a number of topics, including: the key components of writing; different kinds of writing; how writing develops over time and what can be done to promote it. These discussions were linked to others on the structure of language and the nature of the wider curriculum. The structure of *Developing Writing 3–13* can be partly explained by such a look back. The research and practice of the ensuing years are thrown into sharper relief. Looking back helps to identify the research findings that remain under-exploited in practice. A retrospective analysis also helps in looking forward to the educational implications for the new millennium.

The structure of language and the nature of the curriculum have become even more topical issues in British education in the last decade. In *Developing Writing 3–13*, the later sections of **Chapter 1** outline the introduction of a National Curriculum in varying degrees in England, Wales, Scotland and Northern Ireland and how this has influenced the wider context in which writing is being taught. There is now also greater emphasis in teacher training on subject knowledge related to the structure of language. This structure is outlined in **Chapter 2**.

There has been much continuing research on the various processes of writing, including the composing and re-drafting of texts, and these are discussed in **Chapter 3**. This chapter also draws attention to the limitations of what is often called 'process writing' and discusses some alternatives.

Recent years have also seen a great deal of research interest in children's pre-school literacy experiences. A number of influential publications have focused on various aspects of emergent and early writing. These are discussed in **Chapter 4**, which also deals with the role of spelling and handwriting in writing development. Spelling is further discussed in **Chapter 8.**

It has becoming increasingly recognised that pupils and students write more effectively if there is an authentic context. Young writers benefit from having a clear purpose for writing and from being helped to draw upon appropriate content. The different ways of organising writing have also continued to attract attention. These issues are discussed in **Chapter 5**, on range in writing.

There is now much more interest in the role of grammar, as the central organising structure of language and as a tool in understanding growth and variety in writing. **Chapters 6** and **7** and part of **Chapter 8** are devoted to these important areas.

Children's Writing in the Primary School looked closely at the ways in which children's writing develops over time. This is the focus of **Chapters 8** and **9**, together with the implications for assessment. **Chapter 9** also deals with some other developments in the field which were only beginning to attract interest at the time when the earlier book was being written. For instance, word processors have become widely used in schools, although it is not easy to find evidence that their use in the 3–13 age-range improves the quality of writing. Furthermore, the gap between the general writing attainment of boys and girls has widened. A range of ideas for helping to close this gender gap are set out in **Chapter 9.**

Finally, **Chapter 10** is very similar to the final chapter of *Children's Writing in the Primary School*. The recommendations for school policies on writing seemed to have a enduring quality which defies substantial amendment. What has changed indelibly, however, is the wider context in which such policies are drawn up.

The New Centralised Context

Children's Writing in the Primary School did not anticipate the huge centralisation of the British education system that was to come about in the 1988 Education Reform Act. Looking back to the early 1980s, however, it is possible to detect signs of what the future was to hold. There were recurrent concerns about the inconsistencies in the education system in what was offered in the curriculum as a whole. Since the large-scale demise of selection of children for different kinds of schools at age 11, schools and local education authorities (LEAs) had developed very different patterns of curriculum provision.[6] Writers such as Colin Richards[7] had pointed out that such inconsistencies were incompatible with a genuinely 'comprehensive' system. The implications were that a more centralised, national curriculum was required.

What followed from the late 1980s onwards was an increasing centralisation in British education, under the general banner of the need to raise standards. As the following chart shows, in every year since the publication of *Children's Writing in the Primary School*, there have been centralised developments that were intended to influence the content, assessment methods or teaching approaches in literacy education or, more generally, to shape how schools are organised and managed.

1985	National Writing Project, set up by the Schools Curriculum Development Committee in various English and Welsh LEAs (until 1989)
1986	Committee of Inquiry into the Teaching of English Language announced
1987	Consultation Report on a National Curriculum
1988	Report of the Committee of Inquiry into the Teaching of English Language (the Kingman Committee)
	Report of the National Working Party on the National Curriculum for English (The Cox Committee)
1989	National Curriculum taught for the first time in England, Wales and N. Ireland
1990	Central evaluations of National Curriculum begun
1991	Standard Assessment Tasks (SATs) for 7 year olds used for the first time
	Commissioned external evaluation of the National Curriculum begun
	National Curriculum for Scotland published
1992	Standard Assessment Tasks (SATs) for 11 year olds used for the first time
	Decision taken to revise the National Curriculum
	New inspection body set up for England, the Office for Standards in Education (Ofsted)
1993	External evaluation of the National Curriculum in England and Wales published
1994	Report on the Revised National Curriculum (the Dearing Review) published
1995	Revised National Curriculum taught for first time
1996	Literacy Task Force set up
	National Literacy Project begun in 15 English LEAs
1997	Preliminary and Final Reports from the Literacy Task Force
1998	National Literacy Strategy *Framework* taught for first time
1999	Second Revision of National Curriculum available for consultation
2000	Second Revision of National Curriculum taught for the first time

As the above shows, the last 15 years of the twentieth century saw British schools increasingly influenced by central government through a National Curriculum, new statutory assessment arrangements at 7, 11 and 14 and increased inspection arrangements. The last two years of the century also saw central government encouraging schools to teach literacy in particular ways, through a National Literacy Strategy.[8]

Although the United Kingdom has a central government, some aspects of educational (and other) policies are administered by separate government offices (and, increasingly since 1999, devolved Assemblies in Scotland, Wales and Northern Ireland). The different outcomes from the increased centralisation in education are summarised in Table 1.1. As can be seen, each country has been affected differently, with the most far-reaching changes occurring in England.

Table 1.1

	England	**Wales**	**Scotland**	**N. Ireland**
Curriculum Content	National Curriculum Programmes of Study *(Statutory)*	National Curriculum Programmes of Study *(Statutory)*	Curriculum and Assessment National Guidelines	National Curriculum Programmes of Study *(Statutory)*
Assessment	Standard Assessment Tasks (SATs) *(Statutory)*	Standard Assessment Tasks (SATs) *(Statutory)*	National tests when teachers decide (currently under review)	Teacher Assessment at 7 and 11 External tests at 14 (*All Statutory*)
School Inspection	Office for Standards in Education	Her Majesty's Inspectorate	Her Majesty's Inspectorate	Education and Training Inspectorate
Teaching approach	National Literacy Strategy *(Recommended)*	Schools to decide	Schools to decide	Schools to decide

It may also be helpful to spell out some of the main differences in a little more detail and how the increased centralisation has changed the context in which literacy is being taught. Whether this succession of government initiatives actually has raised literacy standards is a more difficult question to answer.

The National Curriculum and its Revisions

Since 1989, England, Wales and Northern Ireland have had statutory Programmes of Study. Scotland has developed a separate and less centralised framework. In the field of English, this was based on national guidelines for curriculum and assessment, *English Language 5–14*.[9]

The first version of the ten-subject National Curriculum for England and Wales was revised in 1995 after being in force since 1989. The original[10] was based on a Statements of Attainment model, with one component for speaking and listening, one for reading and three for writing (conveying meaning, spelling and handwriting). Evaluations suggested that some Statements of Attainment were pitched at the wrong level and some gaps between Levels were too wide.[11]

The revised National Curriculum that was introduced in 1995 had a different format as well as reduced content.[12] The basis of assessment was changed from formulaic Statements of Attainment to broader Level Descriptions. Among the changes to the sections on writing, literacy skills were set out in greater detail and the three components of writing were merged into one. The extent of the 1995 revision is neatly captured in the extracts from Levels 1 and 5 (roughly spanning the 'national expectations' for 5–6 year olds and 12–13 year olds).

Table 1.2

	1989 **Statements of Attainment**	**1995 and 2000** **Level Descriptions**
Level 1	Pupils should be able to: a) use pictures, symbols or isolated letters, words or phrases to communicate meaning; b) begin to show an understanding of the difference between drawing and writing, and between numbers and letters; c) write some letter shapes in response to speech sounds and letter names; d) use at least single letters or groups of letters to represent whole words or parts of words; d) begin to form letters with some control over the size, shape and orientation of letters or lines of writing.	Pupils' writing communicates meaning through simple words and phrases. In their reading or in their writing, pupils begin to show awareness of how full stops are used. Letters are usually clearly shaped and correctly orientated.
Level 5	Pupils should be able to: a) write in a variety of forms for a range of purposes and audiences, in ways which attempt to engage the interest of the reader; b) produce, independently, pieces of writing in which the meaning is made clear to the reader and in which organisational devices and sentence punctuation, including commas and the setting out of direct speech, are generally accurately used; c) demonstrate increased effectiveness in the use of Standard English (except in contexts where non-standard forms are needed for literary purposes) and show an increased differentiation between speech and writing; d) assemble ideas on paper or on a VDU, individually or in discussion with others, and show evidence to an ability to produce a draft from them and then to revise and redraft as necessary; e) show in discussion the ability to recognise variations in vocabulary	Pupils' writing is varied and interesting, conveying meaning clearly in a range of forms for different readers, using a more formal style where appropriate. Vocabulary choices are imaginative and words are used precisely. Simple and complex sentences are organised into paragraphs. Words with complex patterns are usually spelt correctly. A range of punctuation, including commas, apostrophes and inverted commas, is usually used accurately. Handwriting is joined, clear and fluent and, where appropriate, is adapted to a variety of tasks.

according to purpose, topic and
audience and whether language
is spoken or written, and use them
appropriately in their writing;
f) spell correctly, in the course of
their own writing, words of greater
complexity;
g) check final drafts of writing
for misspelling and other errors
of presentation;
h) produce clear and legible
handwriting in printed and
cursive styles.

The 1995 National Curriculum Progammes of Study were structured under three broad strands: Range; Key Skills; Standard English and Language Study. In the 2000 version, Range was incorporated into Breadth of Study. Key Skills and Standard English and Language Study were all incorporated into Knowledge, Skills and Understanding.[13] The basic structure of the 2000 version for the 5–11 age-range is set out in Table 1.3.[14]

Table 1.3

Speaking and Listening	Reading	Writing
Knowledge, Skills and Understanding	**Knowledge, Skills and Understanding**	**Knowledge, Skills and Understanding**
Speaking	Reading strategies	Composition
Listening	• phonemic awareness	Planning and drafting
Group discussion	and phonic knowledge	Punctuation
and interaction	• word recognition and	Spelling
Drama	graphic knowledge	• spelling strategies
Standard English	• grammatical awareness	• checking spelling (5–7)
Language variation	• contextual understanding	• morphology (7–11)
	Reading for information	Handwriting and presentation
	Literature	• handwriting
	Language structure and	• presentation
	variation	Standard English
		Language structure
Breadth of Study	**Breadth of Study**	**Breadth of Study**
Speaking	Literature	Range of purposes
Listening	Non-fiction and non-literary	Writing for remembering and
Group discussion	texts	developing ideas
and interaction		Range of readers for writing
Drama activities		Range of forms of writing

The structure clearly reflects a concern with the 'why, who for and how' of writing, leaving the 'what' to the decisions of teachers and pupils in the context of the wider curriculum and personal experience. The National Curriculum encourages the continued teaching of key skills like spelling and handwriting. It also maintains an emphasis on purposeful variety that helped schools to provide for a broader range of writing than had been reported from the observational and inspection evidence of the 1970s and 1980s. The structure also recognises that pupils' life chances are likely to be greatly enhanced if they learn to write in the vocabulary and grammar of Standard English. Standard English is the most prestigious of the dialects of English and the one used in most written language.

In comparison, the presence of the sections on Language structure and Language variation in the National Curriculum represents a more cautious approach to the teaching of grammar. This is an aspect of literacy education where research findings are less conclusive. The Report of the Committee of Inquiry into the Teaching of English Language (the Kingman Committee) in 1988 reviewed these findings in detail.[15] As a result, the committee did not recommend a return to the more formal Latin-based approaches which had been widely used until the late 1960s.[16] Instead, it recommended that pupils should be encouraged to reflect 'disinterestedly and illuminatingly' on a range of questions, observations and problems that crop up in everyday language use.[17] This whole issue is discussed at length in Chapters 6 and 7.

The Curriculum and Assessment Guidelines for Scotland have similar strands representing range, skills and 'knowledge about language'. The setting up of different forms of National Curriculum in British schools has drawn upon the insights provided by research and scholarly publications in the field, as well as, no doubt, the introspections of literate professionals.

It seems unlikely that the National Curriculum or its revised version significantly raised standards of literacy. The first version of the National Curriculum was massively overcrowded. Teachers had potentially to grapple with several hundred statements of attainment per pupil. The revised version of the National Curriculum was intended to be more manageable. Nevertheless, its more explicit details of 'key skills' gave the new order added complexity which teachers found hard to translate directly into practice. There also remained the perennial ambiguity of English as a separate subject and English as a medium through which other subjects are taught. This was an ambiguity that left English in danger of being marginalised by the demands of several other subjects. Their more content-based programmes of study made them easier to 'deliver' and to warrant specific curriculum space.[18] As the programmes of study of the other, 'foundation', subjects were slotted into curriculum plans, alongside those for the detailed content areas of mathematics and science, English remained at risk. The influences of centralisation went further, however, by introducing a programme of national testing in England and Wales. In time, this contributed to a new target-setting culture in education, with annual published league tables of schools' performance.

Standard Assessment Tasks (SATs)

The increasing centralisation in England and Wales brought with it Attainment Targets for ten levels of attainment and an annual programme of national criterion-referenced testing of children aged 7, 11 and 14. The SATs system took on an additional significance in 1997. A national target was set by the incoming government that, by 2002, 80 per cent of 11 year olds should reach the standard expected for their age in English (Level 4) in the National Curriculum tests.[19] The proportion reaching this standard in 1996 was 57 per cent. Individual schools were requested to agree related interim targets with their Local Education Authorities (LEAs).

Writing is notoriously difficult to assess in a comparative way, perhaps more so than reading, because of the significance in writing of highly variable contextual factors ('why, who for', and so on). The same is true of speaking and listening, although in the SATs the latter is assessed by Teacher Assessment and not by externally written test formats. When comparing the two modes of literacy, it is interesting to note that the International Association for Educational Achievement[20] has established the validity of conducting international comparisons of reading performance, but not of writing. The use of SATs evidence by central government to monitor changes in local or national standards raises additional issues, compounded by the change in the assessment framework in 1995. Such issues include the following:

- the criterion-referenced tests have to be re-written each year
- the main reference points, the level descriptions, are rather generalised
- the assessment has concentrated on the observable aspects of writing, in a relatively narrow range of tasks, undertaken in a limited time

Whether the national testing in itself has helped to raise standards is an open question. Research by Julie Davies and Ivy Brember at Manchester University has shed doubt on whether the introduction of the National Curriculum as a whole has led to any such rise, at least in reading.[21] At the same time, there are indications from several studies carried out by Caroline Gipps and her colleagues at London University that being involved in administering the national SATs has substantially increased teachers' professional knowledge of educational assessment.[22] Perhaps the most valuable spin-off from the national SATs has been the unprecedented amount of data generated on children's school attainment. Annual national reports on Key Stage tests in English provide clear implications for teaching and learning.

For instance, in the 1998 report,[23] there were several aspects of writing that showed the need for substantial attention on a large scale across England in the 7–14 age-range:

- When given the choice, pupils prefer to write narrative but show relatively little progress in their use and range of narrative conventions.

- The structure and organisation of pupils' non-narrative writing is less secure than that of narrative. Pupils need to be taught ways of organising ideas in sentences and paragraphs in order to sustain discussion, analysis and comment.
- The highest incidence of error in the writing of 7–14 year olds tends to be for punctuation within the sentence. Understanding of punctuation is linked to understanding of sentence and clause structure.
- Spelling is weak at all ages and the writing of significant numbers of pupils at the lower levels shows a range of spelling errors that impairs communication.
- In writing about what they have read, pupils are better at identifying the effects of language used in the text than commenting on how these effects are achieved. Pupils need to be taught how to comment explicitly on language.

School Inspections

Until 1992, British schools were occasionally inspected by Her Majesty's Inspectorate (HMI) or its equivalent. After 1992, and the setting up of the Office for Standards in Education (Ofsted), schools in England were inspected more often, initially every four years. Table 1.4 gives an indication of the main points about children's writing that were made in the 1990s in annual reviews of inspection evidence by Her Majesty's Inspectorate and subsequently by Ofsted (see Table 1.4).

These extracts provide interesting snap-shots of current practices. Some extracts suggest that the effective practices of the 1970s and 1980s have been consolidated and built upon. There are clear indications of the importance of the supporting classroom context, of how literature can generate writing and of effective use of ICT. Teacher knowledge seems to play an important part in all this. Other extracts suggest that earlier weaknesses are still very evident, including the over-use of de-contextualised exercises, the under-use of persuasive or discursive tasks and the lack of diagnostic teaching support. There is recurrent evidence of relative underachievement in pupils' writing compared with achievements in the other language modes. This underachievement is substantially greater in boys.

Whether the increase in school inspections has influenced literacy standards is a matter of some debate. However, inspection evidence on such a scale does provide unique glimpses of what is going on in schools. As such, it can form a helpful backcloth to what follows in this book, giving the contents of the book a sense of proportion and its practical suggestions a real sense of relevance.

Table 1.4

HER MAJESTY'S INSPECTORATE (1991) *English Key Stage 1: A Report by HM Inspectorate on the First Year, 1939–90,* London: HMSO.	350 classes containing Y1 pupils; supporting evidence from 360 other KS1 classes.	'The most effective writing... was often preceded and supported by discussion, so that children began... with a clear idea of what they wished to communicate, the conventions they should follow, and how they might gain further support.' (p.15)
HER MAJESTY'S INSPECTORATE (1992) *English Key Stages 1, 2 and 3: A Report by HM Inspectorate on the Second Year 1990–91,* London: HMSO.	1134 lessons in 258 primary schools and 366 lessons in 137 secondary and 26 middle schools.	'... high attainment in writing was infrequent and in Key Stage 2 it was clear that opportunities for writing were often too constrained (p.14). [In Key Stage 3] some excellent drafting using IT was seen, but the processes of drafting were generally insufficiently understood by teachers and pupils alike, with the result that drafting seldom touched upon such matters as readership or style, or the construction of an argument.' (p.17)
OFFICE FOR STANDARDS IN EDUCATION (1993a) *English: Key Stages 1, 2 and 3: Third Year 1991–2,* London: HMSO.	1209 KS1 and KS2 classes in 450 primary schools; 548 classes in 149 secondary and 21 middle schools.	'Standards in all three Key Stages were weaker than in the other ATs [Attainment Targets], especially with regard to drafting and spelling...' (p.2); '[In Key Stage 3] much of the best work was linked with good literature, for example in the writing of poetry inspired by pupils' reading of other poets' work. There were still too many schools where written exercises, intended to develop pupils' writing generally but in fact not related to their specific needs, were used.' (pp.13–14)
OFFICE FOR STANDARDS IN EDUCATION (1993b) *English: Key Stages, 1, 2, 3 and 4: Fourth Year 1992–3,* London: HMSO.	629 lessons in 107 primary phase schools and 645 lessons in 133 secondary schools	'Standards of writing... were weaker in Key Stage 2 than in Key Stage 1... Much remains to be done to improve the writing competence of pupils of all ages.' (p.2)
OFFICE FOR STANDARDS IN EDUCATION (1995) *English: A review of inspection findings 1993/94,* London: HMSO.	122 full inspections in primary phase schools; 545 visits to primary schools and 685 visits to secondary schools.	'Good standards of writing are evident in only one in seven schools [at Key Stage 2]... There is too much use of decontextualised and undemanding exercises' (p.8); 'An essential ingredient of high-quality teaching [at Key Stages 3 and 4] is the teacher's confident knowledge about knowledge about language, understanding of the concept of literary genres, and acquaintance with a broad range of literary and non-fiction texts.' (p.12)
OFFICE FOR STANDARDS IN EDUCATION (1996a) *The Annual Report of Her Majesty's Chief Inspector of Schools: Standards and Quality in Education 1994/95,* London: HMSO.	1500 primary phase schools and 2050 secondary phase schools; Section 9 inspections in 2397 primary/nursery phase schools and 902 secondary phase schools.	'... the good start made prior to and in KS1 is often not sustained in KS2 where many pupils make slower progress than they should... particularly in writing' (p.9); 'Where standards are highest in Key Stages 3 and 4, proof-reading, so that there is increasing evidence both of purposeful drafting and of final pupils improve the quality of the organisation of ideas in their writing and learn systematically to eliminate errors. Pupils in Key Stage 3 are required to write too much narrative and too little discussion and argument.' (p.19)

Reference	Sample	Findings
OFFICE FOR STANDARDS IN EDUCATION (1996b) *Subjects and Standards: Issues for school development arising from OFSTED inspection findings 1994–5: Key Stages 1 & 2*, London: HMSO.	3476 primary, secondary and special schools.	'The teaching of writing is the weakest aspect [of teaching quality].....It is important for schools to ensure that pupils progress in writing as well as they do in reading, speaking and listening; and that a better balance is struck between the development of content, style and presentation. The relationship between the teaching of reading and writing needs greater emphasis.' (pp.2–3)
OFFICE FOR STANDARDS IN EDUCATION (1996c) *Subjects and Standards: Issues for school development arising from OFSTED inspection findings 1994–5: Key Stages 3 & 4 and Post-16*, London: HMSO.	3476 primary, secondary and special schools.	'Standards of writing are lower than for speaking, listening and reading, both in English and across the curriculum....Teachers... are giving growing attention to the quality and variety of vocabulary in pupils' writing and to purposeful redrafting. However, they do not always provide sufficient variety of writing, particularly in Key Stage 3 where there is too little discursive writing, and generally there is insufficient use of writing as a tool for thinking and intellectual development.' (p.2)
OFFICE FOR STANDARDS IN EDUCATION (1997a) *The Annual Report of Her Majesty's Chief Inspector of Schools: Standards and Quality in Education 1995/6*, London: The Stationery Office.	HMI inspections of 950 primary schools and 1350 secondary schools; Section 10 inspections of 4077 primary schools and 853 secondary schools.	'There is... too little direct teaching in many primary schools.... Too much teaching time... continues to be wasted on unduly complex organisational arrangements' (p.6); '[In the 11–14 age range] the weakest aspect of English.... is writing.' (p.19)
OFFICE FOR STANDARDS IN EDUCATION (1997b) *Standards in English 1995–6: Primary Schools*, London: Ofsted.	4077 primary phase schools.	'Standards in writing remain weaker than in the other Attainment Targets' (p.1); '[In secondary schools] many pupils need more systematic help with grammar, spelling and punctuation... Pupils are rarely given opportunities to analyse their own and other people's writing.' (pp.6–7)
OFFICE FOR STANDARDS IN EDUCATION (1998a) *The Annual Report of Her Majesty's Chief Inspector of Schools: Standards and Quality in Education 1996/97*, London: The Stationery Office.	HMI inspections of 2275 schools; Section 10 inspections of 6027 primary schools and 955 secondary schools.	'Too many pupils are unable to produce sustained, accurate writing in a variety of forms. This has been a pervasive weakness in many primary schools, which should be addressed more urgently' (p.19); '... in several subjects, particularly in Key Stage 3, standards in writing are constrained by pupils' limited technical ability and drafting skills and by the narrow range of styles that they use.' (p.32)
OFFICE FOR STANDARDS IN EDUCATION (1998b) *Standards in Primary English*, London: Ofsted.	5864 primary phase schools.	'Writing skills are weaker than those in reading and speaking and listening.' (p.3)
OFFICE FOR STANDARDS IN EDUCATION (1999) *The Annual Report of Her Majesty's Chief Inspector of Schools: Standards and Quality in Education 1997/98*, London: The Stationery Office	Section 10 inspections of 6218 primary schools and 645 secondary schools.	'[In primary schools] ... achievement in writing remains weaker than in reading or speaking and listening. Boys' writing shows much greater variation in standards than that of girls. Too few boys are able to produce sustained accurate writing and their handwriting skills are weak.' (p.23)

The National Literacy Strategy

The National Literacy Strategy (NLS) was established in 1997 by the incoming UK government to raise standards of literacy in English primary schools over a five- to ten-year period. The NLS was the result of the work of a Literacy Task Force that had been set up by the Shadow Secretary of State for Education and Employment, David Blunkett, in May 1996. The Task Force published a preliminary consultation report in February 1997[24] and a final report in August 1997.[25] In its final report, the Task Force set out the details of a 'steady, consistent strategy' for raising standards of literacy that could be sustained over a long period of time and be made a central priority for the education service as a whole. The main strands of the NLS include:

1 A national target that, by 2002, 80 per cent of 11 year olds should reach the standard expected for their age in English (Level 4) in the National Curriculum tests for Key Stage 2 (7–11 year olds). The proportion reaching this standard in 1996 was 57 per cent. Again, boys were found to be performing significantly less well than girls. Individual schools were requested to agree related interim targets with their Local Education Authorities (LEAs).

2 A *Framework for Teaching*[26] which:
    (i) set out termly teaching objectives for the 5–11 age range. The objectives focus on three broad dimensions of literacy: word-level work (phonics, spelling and vocabulary and also including handwriting); sentence-level work (grammar and punctuation); text-level work (comprehension and composition) The *Framework* draws attention to the importance of linking children's reading and writing, at word, sentence and text levels.
    (ii) provided a practical structure of time and class management for a daily Literacy Hour. The structure of the Literacy Hour is divided between approximately 30 minutes of whole-class teaching, 20 minutes of group and independent work and 10 minutes for whole-class review, reflection and consolidation.

The *Framework* was derived from materials developed in the National Literacy Project, which was set up by the previous government to raise standards in a selected number of LEAs. Every primary school was encouraged to adopt the *Framework* unless it could demonstrate that its own approach was at least as effective. The *Framework* notes that further literacy work should be productively linked to other curriculum areas and that additional time may also be needed for:

- reading to the class (e.g. in end of day sessions);
- pupils' own independent reading (for interest and pleasure);
- extended writing (especially for older pupils).

The NLS also included a programme of professional development for all primary teachers and other community-based aspects (including a media campaign and Literacy Summer Schools). The strategy was first implemented in England in 1998. Of all the centralising developments in British education in the final years of the twentieth century, the NLS may in time be seen to have been the most successful in raising literacy standards. There is a certain irony in this because it is the only one of the developments discussed here that was not a statutory requirement. However, the main reason for any such success may also be explained by the fact that the NLS targeted how teachers teach.

School Effectiveness

The Literacy Task force and the National Literacy Project were both clearly influenced by the accumulating international evidence on school effectiveness. Much of this has been built upon the seminal study of 50 London primary schools by Peter Mortimore and his colleagues in the late 1980s.[27] Before discussing school effectiveness at greater length, there are some important cautions about school effectiveness evidence, which Mortimore outlines in a subsequent publication:[28]

- school effectiveness is generally gauged by the further progress that pupils make than might be expected from consideration of the school's intake;
- the measures used are normally derived from attainment in basic subjects, especially reading, numeracy and examination results;
- the most valid research is longitudinal, so that one or more cohorts can be followed over time, and a school's consistency and stability can be investigated;
- the outcomes from this research are inappropriate for the production of 'blue-print' schools and practices. The analyses used are often correlational, using multi-level statistical techniques; they do not pertain to identify causal relationships. However, the studies provide valuable background and insights for those concerned with school improvement, as there is a core of consistency to be found across a variety of studies in several different countries.

Jaap Scheerens, of the University of Twente in the Netherlands, provides a clear summary of these factors in a meta-analysis of research from across the world.[29] Two characteristics of school effectiveness have 'multiple empirical research confirmation':

1 Structured teaching i.e:
   - making clear what has to be learnt;
   - dividing material into manageable units;
   - teaching in a well-considered sequence;
   - the use of material in which pupils make use of hunches and prompts;
   - regular testing for progress;
   - immediate feedback.

2 Effective learning time: this factor is partly related to the first, in that whole-class teaching can often be superior to individualised teaching because in the latter the teacher has to divide attention in such a way that the net result per pupil is lower. Other aspects of effective teaching time are 'curricular emphasis', the time spent on certain subjects, and the need to inspire, challenge and praise so as to stimulate the motivation to learn. These aspects also indirectly increase net learning time.

There is a similar meta-analysis of research into the effective classroom by Bert Creemers, of the University of Gronigen. In this case there are several more factors that have 'strong empirical evidence' as characteristics of effective teaching.[30]

Curriculum
> Explicitness and ordering of goals and content
> Advanced organisers, relating what pupils already know to what they have to learn next
> Evaluation of pupil achievements
> Feedback

Grouping procedures
> For Mastery Learning (mastering the learning of one unit of learning before moving onto the next)
> Evaluation

Teacher behaviour
> Management/Orderly and quiet atmosphere
> Homework
> Structuring the content by advance organisers
> Questioning
> Evaluation

There are tensions between such combinations of practice and what has been long been held to be 'good primary practice' in British primary schools. For the last 30 years, this notion has often been associated with individualised approaches, in which classes of children have tackled several different subject areas at the same time in various kinds of 'integrated day'. The role of whole-class teaching in good primary practice has been an uncertain one.

The notion of 'good practice' is in any case problematic. As Robin Alexander[31] has pointed out, the term can reflect a number of dimensions, reflecting pragmatic, empirical or political statements or statements of personal belief. Even more importantly, though, a succession of research findings have warned about the related quality control issues in individualised or integrated teaching approaches. It is very difficult for teachers simultaneously to monitor so many different aspects of learning across several subject areas.[32] The difficulties created by excessive individualisation are compounded if several different subjects are running concurrently. Pupil industry is lower, noise and pupil movement greater, teachers spend more time on routine matters and behaviour control, communications between teachers and pupils are reduced and pupil progress is less. Research has consistently suggested that teachers are often unable to cope satisfactorily with the myriad of demands made upon them.

Researchers in this area also stress that their findings do not imply the need for unadulterated traditional class teaching. Their data indicate the value of flexible approaches that can blend class and group interaction with independent work as is appropriate. Nor does the focus on one (or at most two) curriculum areas imply that the pupils should do exactly the same work. Effects were most positive when the teacher geared the level of work to pupils' needs but not where all pupils worked individually on exactly the same piece of work.

In fact, it is interesting to note that the authors of some of these research studies have reported that their findings were often welcomed by heads and teachers. Experienced and skilful teachers, whose normal practice was to limit the curriculum focus of their lessons, had been led to feel guilty about their failure to manage more diverse activities. Yet alternative approaches to the integrated day have been slow to gain status.

Evaluating the NLS

The NLS, with its Literacy Hour, gives greater attention to how literacy is taught, with a more conscious use of direct teaching of classes and groups and independent work, together with focused plenary sessions.[33] Its potential for raising standards is underlined by the findings from the evaluation of the National Literacy Project that was undertaken by the National Foundation for Educational Research.[34] Data were collected from 250 schools on children's progress in reading between October 1996 and March 1998, using a variety of reading and English tests (comprehension, spelling and punctuation).

The test results revealed a significant and substantial improvement over the 18-month period. Final test scores had improved by approximately six standardised score points for 7/9 year old pupils and 9/11 year old pupils. This is equivalent to 8 to 12 months progress *over and above* what is expected in these ages. For 5–7 year olds, the increase was nearly twice as large again, at 11.5 standardised score points.

Girls had higher average scores than boys and made more progress during the project. Children eligible for free school meals, those with special educational needs and those learning English as an additional language had lower scores. However, all these groups also made statistically significant progress. All ethnic groups benefited equally.

Much To Do About Writing

Despite the promise of the National Literacy Strategy, several questions remain to be resolved in the years ahead about its potential for promoting large scale improvement in children's writing:

- the evaluation of the National Literacy Project concentrated on improvements in reading – in writing, only spelling and punctuation were directly measured;
- much will depend on what is done to link Literacy Hour work to the rest of the curriculum and the remainder of the day;
- there are considerable demands on teachers' professional knowledge in translating the National Curriculum-based objectives into shared and guided literacy teaching and related independent work.

Looking Forward

Developing Writing 3–13 reflects these many developments by discussing them in detail and by bringing together the insights from related research in countries across the world. It also goes on to outline the practical possibilities which emanate from greater use of the shared and guided teaching approaches that have been promoted by the National Literacy Strategy.

The age-range covered by *Developing Writing 3–13* has been extended in both directions from its predecessor for several reasons. A 3–13 focus allows better coverage of the significant developments referred to above. The age-range spans the extremes of British education where a general class teacher approach is used, from 3–5 nurseries to 9–13 middle schools. It also brings the book into line with another of my books, *Developing Reading 3–13*.

Some readers of this book may argue that it might be more appropriate to deal with literacy in a more holistic way. However, devoting a book largely to writing enables the topic to be discussed in far more detail than would otherwise be possible. There are recurrent references to links between writing, reading, speaking and listening. The next chapter provides a general look at language, spoken and written.

Spoken Language and Written Language

Language is the dress of thought.
(Samuel Johnson)[1]

This chapter

- outlines the importance of spoken language and some of its uses
- illustrates how social context influences language use
- explains some of the main elements of spoken language
- briefly discusses social variation in language use
- summarises the basis of different systems of writing.

The Foundations of Language

Writing is one of the four modes of the system of human communication that we call language. Language is a capacity that, together with speaking, listening and reading, sets people clearly apart from other creatures of the earth on the evolutionary scale. Literacy learning normally builds on the foundations of early language development. An understanding of the functions and elements of language can help make these foundations firm and supportive.

Even creatures as small as bees can communicate with each other on, for example, the nature, direction and distance of a food source. They do this by dancing in ways instinctively programmed for them by their nervous system.[2] The more complex nervous systems of humans allow a far greater range of communication. This is partly because humans have more means of communication available to them (i.e. sounds and words). More particularly, this range comes from the open-ended quality of human language. It is a quality that allows the finite means of sounds and words to be used in infinite combinations to produce a limitless range of meanings.

The Importance of Spoken Language

Human language is essentially a symbolic system of communication by which we represent the world to ourselves. Human beings can also represent the world in other ways, particularly by actions or images.[3] Children come to understand how to tie shoe laces by actually tying them; when using construction toys, they may be guided by the illustrations. It is language, though, that provides the most flexible means of representing the world, at first by speech and later by writing. The accumulated representations act as a storehouse of past experience. They also create expectations of what may yet happen to us. In this way, language helps us to construct a sense of the past and the future which can guide current actions and thinking.[4]

However, some of the most influential psychologists of the twentieth century have disagreed on how central language is to thinking abilities. The Russian psychologist, Alexandr Luria, for example, saw language as central to cognitive growth.[5] For the Swiss psychologist, Jean Piaget, activity and experience were more important.[6] In recent years, educational research has been more influenced by another Russian psychologist, Lev Vygotsky. Much of his work only became known in the West well after his death in 1934.[7] His ideas have since been further developed by Jerome Bruner at Harvard University.[8]

Vygotsky saw language as a sophisticated kind of tool. It helps us represent the world to ourselves. It helps us organise and improve upon human activities in general. He saw much learning as social in origin. Learning comes about when things first done collaboratively are internalised for future individual use. Vygotsksy coined the term 'zone of proximal development' to account for the distance between the someone's actual development level and what they can achieve with the guidance or collaboration of someone more capable.

Like Vygotsky, Bruner sees language as a key tool for cognitive growth, building on the early preoccupation of young children to represent the world to themselves, through actions, images and symbols. Bruner suggests that children's innate predisposition to learn language, through what Noam Chomsky and others describe as a LAD (a *Language Acquisition Device*) was fostered by a LASS (a *Language Acquisition Support System*). In pre-school children, the LASS was provided primarily by the parent, guiding and supporting the child's early utterances. Bruner suggests that the interactive support from the parent could be seen as a kind of 'scaffolding' of language and understanding. This kind of scaffolding is nicely shown in Figure 2.1:[9]

Figure 2.1

John (3½) and his mother are waiting together in the head teacher's room. The researcher has left a box of assorted toy vehicles with them and suggested that John might like to play with the toys whilst they wait for a few minutes.

John:	Look at this – it's for pulling trains.
Mother:	Yes, it is – are there some carriages, do you think?
John:	No, I can't find some. This is a funny train.
Mother:	Why do you think it's funny?
John:	It's not like the Huddersfield one.
Mother:	The Huddersfield one? Isn't it? What was that like?
John:	It hadn't got one like this – not with chimneys;
Mother:	Chimneys – the funnels, you mean. Do you know what they were for?
John:	For smoke – smoke comes out – out of here.
Mother:	That's right – why does that kind of engine need funnels, I wonder?
John:	'Cos of fires – fires inside.

	Yes – I'd nearly forgotten. Doesn't the Huddersfield train have fires?
John:	No – no – it's not got one like this – it's not got funnels.
Mother:	Do you remember going to Huddersfield?
John:	Yes – we went over a long bridge – a long one – high – right over.
Mother:	Did we? A viaduct do you mean?
John:	It went high over a road and I see-ed the cars.

The passage shows how learning can be promoted whenever adults see possibilities for encouraging children's 'oracy', their self-expression in speech:[10]

- starting from something which attracts the child's attention;
- taking account of the child's previous knowledge and own way of referring to things;
- encouraging the child to offer suggestions and explanations;
- providing support and clarification that builds on the child's tentative understanding.

It is not difficult to see how such interactive kinds of language can be used constructively in early literacy learning. They can build on children's early responses to environmental print, picture books and early attempts to represent and communicate through scribbles. Eventually such scaffolded support can be extended to shared and guided teaching approaches with texts of all kinds. The importance of the context in language use – and especially in the teaching and assessment of writing – runs through much of the remainder of this book.

Language, Literacy and the Classroom Context

Several studies have highlighted the influence of the classroom context in fostering productive links between language and literacy learning. Gordon Wells has drawn particular attention to the role of reading, hearing and sharing stories in this.[11] He points out that listening to stories helps children to:

- gain experience of the meaning-building organisation of written language;
- vicariously extend the range of their experience beyond their immediate surroundings;
- develop a vocabulary with which to talk about these extended experiences;
- use collaborative talk with adults to explore the significance of what is recounted;
- develop their own inner 'storying'.

Wells provides an example of a parent and child sharing John Vernon Lord's *The Giant Jam Sandwich* together, to illustrate these language and learning processes at work. Such processes can flourish whenever adults, children and texts are brought together

Figure 2.2

[*David is sitting next to Mother on the sofa so that he can see the book.*]

David:	The Giant Sandwich [*4-second pause*]
Mother:	Who's this here on the first page?
David:	The wasps.
Mother:	The wasps are coming. [*Turns the page*] Here's some more, look. Wow! [*Reads*]
	One hot summer in Itching Down
	Four million wasps flew into town.
David:	I don't like wasps … flying into town.
Mother:	Why's that?
David:	Because they sting me.
Mother:	Do they?
David:	Mm. I don't like them.
Mother:	They'll only sting you if they get angry. If you leave them alone they won't sting you. But four million would be rather a lot, wouldn't it? They'd get rather in the way. [*Reads*]
	They drove the picnickers away …
[Later]	
David:	[*looking at the illustration on the next page, which shows three male inhabitants of Itching Down, each attempting in his own way to get rid of the wasps*]: Is that a spray to shoo them away? Is that a spray to shoo them away?
Mother:	Yes. It's probably some sort of insecticide — to get rid of them. And what's that net for, do you think? [A butterfly net]
David:	It's for catching them with.
Mother:	It doesn't seem much good though, does it?
David:	No. They come out the holes.
Mother:	[*laughs*]: The holes are too big, aren't they? And what about this man? What's he got?
David:	He's—What's he got?
Mother:	What's that?
David:	A note. What does the note say?
Mother:	A note on a stick, is it? Is that what you think?
David:	Actually it's a sound.
Mother:	A what?
David:	A sound. What's it called on the—on the stick? What is it? What's that man got?
Mother:	Well you know, um—
David:	Yes…Sign.

Mother:	You think it's a sign? Yes it looks very **like** a sign with writing on, doesn't it?
David:	Yes.
Mother:	But it isn't. It's like Mummy's—um—fish slice [slotted spatula].
David:	What is it?
Mother:	It's a swatter. He's going to hit the wasp with it.
David:	How d'you hit wasps with .otters?
Mother:	[*checking*]: Swatters? Well, they're made of plastic usually—
David:	Yes.

Elizabeth Grugeon and her colleagues at De Montford University in Bedford have brought together a range of valuable practical suggestions for increasing the amount and range of talk in primary school classrooms.[12] Many of these suggestions offer promising possibilities for linking language and literacy learning. The suggestions include:

5–7 year olds

News and circle times (shaping and sharing experiences)

Story-telling, including the use of puppets (learning to speak clearly for an audience)

Problem-solving games (classifying things in different ways; inventing animals etc).

Rhymes and other word play (extending children's awareness of the rhythms and sounds of language)

Role play (listening and responding in particular contexts)

7–11 year olds

Teacher-directed discussion (interactive explaining, questioning and informing)

Talk partners (pupils talk through answers to a teacher's question in pairs)

Teaching listening skills (e.g. making notes on what is known about a topic before and after an educational video)

Brainstorming (assembling, recording and reporting ideas on a topic)

Hot seating (explaining actions and answering questions while assuming the role of another person)

One of the most difficult kinds of talk to establish on a large scale is 'exploratory talk', in which small groups engage critically but constructively with each other's ideas. Neil Mercer's research at the Open University suggests that, without the establishment of 'ground rules', children often interact in uncooperative, competitive ways, which generate 'disputational' talk. Where they do cooperate, they tend to share and build information in an uncritical way, in 'cumulative' talk. The natural incidence of 'exploratory' talk, in fact, is very low.[13]

Mercer's subsequent research shows how the quality of children's reasoning and collaborative activity may be improved.[14] This may be done by developing children's awareness of language use and by promoting certain ground rules for talking together in small groups of two or three pupils. The ground rules drawn up by one group, for instance, included the following:

1. Discuss things together. That means:
   - ask everyone for their opinion;
   - ask for reasons why;
   - listen to people.
2. Be prepared to change your mind.
3. Think before you speak.
4. Respect other people's ideas – don't just use your own.
5. Share all the ideas and information you have.
6. Make sure the group agrees after talking.

These suggestions provide useful indicators of how collaborative speaking and listening may be more productively encouraged in many primary classrooms. With the introduction of various forms of National Curriculum in British Schools, there have been understandable concerns that the time given to oracy might have been reduced. The above section may help to assuage some concerns, particularly if the potential of different kinds of context is appreciated. Indeed, the context of literacy learning can itself be very productive in encouraging talk, for instance by focusing on the 'make-up' of language, its sounds, words and rules.

The Make-Up of Spoken Language

As speech is normally developed well in advance of writing skills, it can be useful to consider how it is made up. This can assist the understanding of how the one can build on the other. Speech has a number of elements, including pronunciation, grammar and meaning. It is helpful to take note of the nature and development of spoken language in these elements. Their role in early literacy learning can then be better appreciated in subsequent chapters. David Crystal has outlined the structure of language in the following way.[15] Figure 2.3 also includes examples of each element and the main areas of linguistic study.

PRONUNCIATION

In the following sections, technical words are in **bold**.

Phonology is concerned with the study of the system of sounds in English. The production and transmission of these sounds are studied in **phonetics**. The English language has approximately 40 speech sounds, more specifically called **phonemes.** The phonemes of language are acquired from about the age of nine months,[16] as children begin to perceive the differences between sounds and produce them within their normal speech patterns. Evidence suggests that this process of acquisition normally takes until at least the age of 7. Several consonant phonemes are often the last to be acquired, including: /sh/ (as in *sh*op); /ch/ (as in *ch*in); /j/ (as in *j*ump); /th/ (as in *th*ink); /th/ (as in *th*em) and /zh/ (as in mea*s*ure).[17]

Figure 2.3

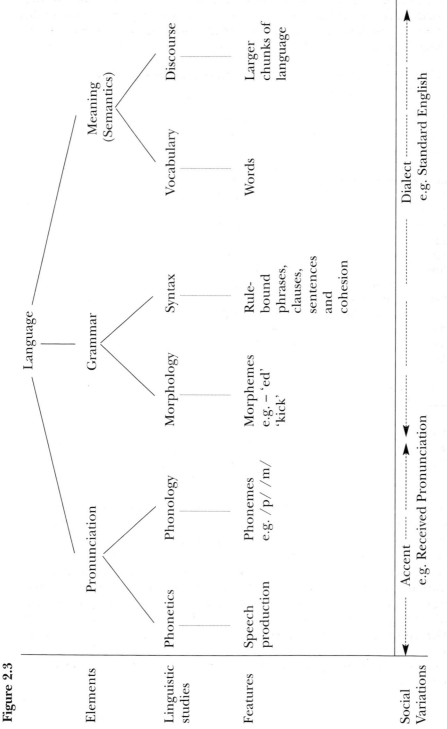

(After Crystal, 1993)

The precise number of phonemes to be acquired will vary according to the **accent** used. Accents may in turn be influenced by the region where a child grows up and by the way his or her friends speak. The regionless accent known as **Received Pronunciation** (RP) has 44 phonemes and these are set out below.

20 vowel phonemes	**24 consonant phonemes**
12 'pure vowels'	
1. *a*pple	1. *b*at
2. *e*gg	2. *c*at
3. *i*nk	3. *d*in
4. *o*range	4. *f*ish
5. *u*mbrella	5. *g*o
6. unstressed vowel (e.g. *a*bout)	6. *h*ave
7. b*ee*	7. *j*ump
8. m*oo*n	8. *l*et
9. b*oo*k	9. *m*an
10. s*aw*	10. *n*et
11. c*ar*	11. *p*at
12. h*er*	12. *r*un
8 diphthongs	13. *s*et
(two vowel-sounds pronounced	14. *t*ap
as one syllable)	15. *v*iolin
13. p*ay* ⎫	16. *w*ant
14. p*ie* ⎬ the second sound is /*i*/	17. *y*et
15. b*oy* ⎭	18. *z*oo
16. t*oe* ⎫ the second sound	19. *sh*op
17. c*ow* ⎭ is /*oo*/ as in t*oo*k	20. *ch*in
18. th*ere* ⎫ the second sound	21. *th*e
19. *ear* ⎬ is the unstressed	22. *th*ink
20. l*ure* ⎭ vowel	23. si*ng*
	24. mea*s*ure

RP is often used as a kind of yardstick in spoken language study. Because of its associated status, RP may be felt to be the 'best' or most desirable accent. There is a certain snobbishness about accent differences in Britain that has little parallel in many other parts of the world. Nevertheless, from an educational (as opposed to social) point of view, accent differences in themselves are relatively unimportant. RP may be easier to understand than some regional accents. This is probably because we are more used to hearing it on radio and television, rather than because of any inherent features of RP itself. Whatever their accent, children's store of phonemes provides them with an important early resource in learning to read and write. This is because the English writing system is largely based on its phonemes, as will be shown later in this chapter.

WORDS AND MEANINGS (SEMANTICS)

As well as a system of sounds, language comprises a system of meanings, the study of which is called **semantics**. In this system, vocabulary is widely recognised as playing a central role. There is less agreement among linguists on how other aspects of meaning can be systematically studied within and between sentences and larger language units. Teachers of young children understandably use signs of vocabulary growth as important evidence of language development, especially in written work. What is perhaps not always appreciated is the patterned nature of this growth.

From the early months of children's lives, they are involved in an incremental process of building a store of words. Children often begin by over-extending the application of word labels to the phenomena in the world around them, calling all four-legged creatures 'dog', for instance, and every man 'da-da'. From these uncertain beginnings, vocabulary development progresses in a variety of ways, with understanding often being in advance of use. Children understand words before actually using them consistently in their own speech. They use words in their speech before they use them in their writing. At a time when there is national concern to raise standards of literacy, it is important not to lose sight of the personal resources for writing that are developed through the use of spoken language.

The estimation of vocabulary growth in numerical terms is full of difficulties. Estimates of normal vocabulary size in children of particular ages vary enormously. Different criteria can be used, including words spoken, words recognised, words understood, or words defined. According to some estimates,[18] the average child acquires nearly a thousand words by the age of three.

Another aspect of vocabulary growth is the range of senses which words can communicate. We need to take account of the shades of meaning that can be attributed to words and to distinguish between different words. These shades of meaning can be seen to be playing an important role in homonyms, polysemes, synonyms and antonyms.

Homonyms are words that have identical features of pronunciation, spelling and syntactical equivalence, such as the nouns 'sound' (noise) and 'sound' (an anchorage). Pure homonyms are relatively rare. More common are specific kinds of homonyms – homographs and homophones.

homonyms
identical features of pronunciation, spelling and syntactical equivalence,
e.g. 'sound' (*noise*) and 'sound' (*an anchorage*)

homophones	*homographs*
words that are sounded in the same way, but which have different meanings (whether or not they differ in spelling), such as 'hear' and 'here'	words that are spelled identically, but which have different meanings (whether or not they are sounded the same), such as 'spoke' (*said*) and 'spoke' (*of a wheel*)

Homonyms occur widely in English. One linguist has suggested that the most common 500 words in the language have between them over 14,000 meanings,[19] thus providing a rich source of exploitation in jokes of all kinds. Experience of such word play may be of valuable assistance in what Michael Halliday has called 'learning how to mean'.[20]

Polysemes and **synonyms** provide opportunities for additional development in vocabulary.

polysemes	*synonyms*
words with more than one meaning, as with:	words that are virtually identical in meaning and therefore easily interchangeable:

'coat'	garment		consume
	layer of paint	eat	devour
	animal fur		feed on
	membrane		tuck into

The various senses of the same principal meaning can be varied for figurative effect. In children this can indicate their linguistic maturity.	In a sense, absolute synonyms are likely to cause redundancy, leading to one or more of the alternatives becoming obsolete, and are relatively uncommon.

Words that are closely similar, though, are frequently found and may need careful selection within the social context of what is being said or written. Note how two of the above synomyms for '*eat*' seem to fit more or less appropriately into the following sentences:

Food is not to be consumed in this library.
Food is not to be devoured (?) in this library.
The lions consumed (?) the carcass.
The lions devoured the carcass.

Antonyms are words that contrast. Peter Gannon and Pam Czerniewska point out that antonyms often have sharper qualities than the rather vague relationship of synonym.s.[21]

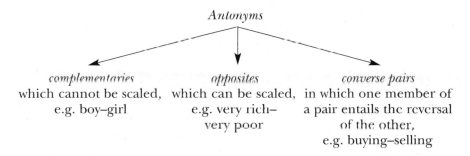

Antonyms

complementaries	*opposites*	*converse pairs*
which cannot be scaled, e.g. boy–girl	which can be scaled, e.g. very rich–very poor	in which one member of a pair entails the reversal of the other, e.g. buying–selling

The appreciation of such relationships between meanings can form an important part of a child's growth in understanding the world. It can also be a means by which teachers can introduce children to the intricate structure of semantic links that stem from single words.

Finally, we also need to take account of the patterns of meaning to be found in the larger chunks of text that we call discourse.

Discourse refers to a unit or piece of connected speech or writing that is longer than a sentence.[22] Patterns of meaning within a discourse are more diffuse and difficult to trace than those attributed to individual words. As will be seen later in Chapter 5, in recent years literacy education has been particularly influenced by Michael Halliday's work. His 'systemic' linguistics has emphasised the social functions of language and the thematic structure of writing. He has linked purposes of communication, the relationships between the participants and channels of communication to the phrase and sentence grammar of the text.

GRAMMAR

Grammar is the third principal component of language. Grammar is the set of rules that structure the sequences within and between words. Within words, there are rules of **morphology** that govern the possible combinations of **morphemes**, the minimum units of meaning. **Free form** morphemes are **root** words, such as 'view' or 'help'; to these, **bound form** morphemes, which are only part-words, can be added, e.g:

Free form morphemes	*Bound form morphemes*
view	*pre*view, *inter*view (*prefixes*)
help	help*er,* help*s* (*suffixes*)

Between words, there are rules of **syntax** in phrases, clauses, sentences and larger stretches of language. In English, for example, a reporter at a tennis match might say, 'Hingis served an ace'. In Malagasy a different set of rules govern the position of subject, verb and object in a sentence and a reporter would be likely to say, 'Served an ace Hingis'.[23] These syntactic rules of a language are largely learned by listening to and interacting with others. From such early interactions, children construct their own version of the grammatical system of the language, perhaps overgeneralising certain rules on the way ('goed' ['*went*'], 'mans' ['*men*'], 'badder' ['*worse*']).

There are two distinctive features of this process of grammar construction. Firstly, the 'pre-programmed' nature of the human brain may be responsible for some deep-seated grammatical structures being common to all human languages. Secondly, children are able to generate utterances that they have not heard before.

David Crystal[24] suggests that children learn syntax through a series of stages:

9–18 months	single-element	e.g. 'dada'
		'gone'
		'more'

18 months – 2 years	two-element	e.g.	'Where daddy?' 'Gone car.' 'More milk.'
2–2½ years	four- or more-element sentences	e.g.	'Daddy going to work today.'
3–3½ years	complex sentence structures of more than one clause	e.g.	'Daddy gone in the car and taked his coat.'

Other stages follow in which other complexities are developed. These include the pronoun system, auxiliary verbs (although understanding the full subtleties of meaning of 'may' or 'should' takes several years), a whole range of irregular verbs and nouns, passive forms, sentence connectors (e.g. 'actually', 'however') and so on. This framework is particularly helpful in studying children whose language is unusually slow to develop and it has been extended into a diagnostic framework for studying language disability.[25]

Social Variation in Language

In recent years, linguists have come to recognise the importance of inter-personal relationships in fostering language development and the supportive elements of gesture, facial expression and intonation. There has also been much interest in differences in dialect and the educational implications of these differences. A **dialect** is a variation of the same language in a particular region or social group. It includes variation in vocabulary, grammar and, if spoken, accent. The predominant dialect in the United Kingdom is **standard English**, which is the dialect normally used in published writing materials. This can be spoken in a variety of accents. Non-standard dialect features are found in the various geographical regions of the country. For instance, the standard English form 'I saw her', can be heard in Cornish dialect as 'I saw she'. The standard English form 'Yesterday, she ran across the road' can be heard in Gloucestershire dialect as 'Yesterday, her runs across the road'.

Variations of standard English, especially in syntax, have been linked to educational under-achievement, particularly in users of Black English Vernacular (BEV).[26] BEV may vary from standard English in phonology, vocabulary and grammar. Grammatical variation, for example, may include:

- omitting the *s* in plurals ('six boy') or in the present tense ('he talk');
- past tense forms ('they go');
- omitting the verb 'be' as a link in the present tense ('they real happy');
- use of 'it' instead of 'there' ('It's a gale of wind blowing outside') etc.;
- use of double negatives at the beginning of sentences ('Won't nobody do nothing about that?').

These kinds of variations have been discussed at some length by a series of central government and academic publications. There is general agreement among linguists that BEV is a well-developed language, with a sound system, grammar and vocabulary of its own. It is capable, like other forms of English, of being used expressively and richly. Detailed analyses of British Black English by Viv Edwards, David Sutcliffe and others have undermined assumptions about language deficits or dialect interference.[27] Instead, linguists have suggested a repertoire model of social variation. This model develops a sharper awareness of different language forms that children can use. It focuses on what children can do and the linguistic strengths which children bring to the classroom.[28] Some related research studies are reported in **Chapter 7**.

The practical implications of a repertoire model include the following:

- extensive shared reading, guided reading and independent reading, to introduce a variety of written styles and content;
- ensuring that texts are appropriate for the children, taking special account of the problems created by ethnocentric, racist and tokenist texts;
- being sympathetic to miscues in oral reading and non-standard grammar in writing, especially variations in plurals and tense forms that do not reflect any lack of understanding of the text;
- shared and guided writing which involve explicit teaching about the value of anticipating and rehearsing sequences of words and meanings.

Whether non-standard dialects are the 'equal' of standard English is the source of much debate. However, there is little doubt that children need to incorporate into their writing many of the grammatical structures of standard English in order to cope with the demands of the school curriculum and many of the demands of the world beyond school. These demands are examined in the next and subsequent chapters. To end this brief look at the forms of language, we need to take note of the nature of the writing system itself.

Writing and Writing Systems

Although there has been a great deal of attention to language in teacher education, until recently less attention has been given to the nature of writing systems, the province of **graphology**. In linguistics, graphology is the study of the systems of symbols (*graphemes*) that are used to communicate language in written form. Its use in teacher education can be particularly illuminating. It allows the basis of the English writing system to be highlighted by comparing it with other systems, as is shown in Figure 2.4:[29]

The Forms of Writing

English has a phonological writing system, based on sound–symbol relationships. There are 26 letters that represent approximately 44 phonemes. Most major countries use a phonological system, although China and Japan use predominantly logographic systems, where the main symbols or characters

Figure 2.4

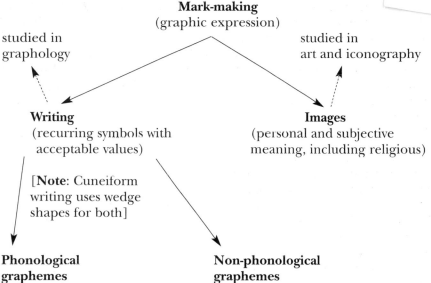

Mark-making
(graphic expression)

studied in
graphology

studied in
art and iconography

Writing
(recurring symbols with
acceptable values)

Images
(personal and subjective
meaning, including religious)

[**Note**: Cuneiform
writing uses wedge
shapes for both]

**Phonological
graphemes**
(based on symbol–sound
relationships)

**Non-phonological
graphemes**
(based on pictures, ideas
or whole words)

1 **Syllabic** graphemes,
e.g. consonant – vowel pairs,
Japanese Katakana
(used to add foreign words
to Japanese)

1 **Pictographs** (recognisable pictures),
e.g. some road signs.

2 **Ideographs** (abstract or
conventional meanings),
e.g. other road signs.

2 **Alphabetic** graphemes
i.e. direct correspondence
between phonemes and
and graphemes,
e.g. Gujarati, English

3 **Logographs** (symbols represent
words), e.g. Chinese, Japanese
Japanese Kanji,
+ – × = etc.

[**Note**: Some alphabets are
made up of consonants
with optional diacritical
marking for vowels.]

[**Note**: Hieroglyphics contain
ideographs and 'phonographs',
symbols standing for consonants]

represent whole words. English also makes some use of logographs in
mathematics, ideographs in road signs and pictographs where information
has to be conveyed quickly and unambiguously.

This kind of variety is a reminder that writing is a social convention; the nature and range of the symbols used is part of a social context. The 26 alphabetic letters can be traced back through the centuries, through Roman, Etruscan and Greek and Phoenician forms, to their early North Semitic roots in Palestine and Syria nearly 4,000 years ago. Early forms of the English alphabet were devised by missionaries who used the Roman alphabet to represent the sounds of Anglo-Saxon as well as they could. They had to devise extra letters for letters and sounds that were not used in Latin including the letter W and letters for the sound /th/.

The major advantage is that the use of just 26 letters, rather than the thousands of characters in logographic writing systems, makes English an economical system. Just a small number of symbols can be used flexibly to create an infinite number of words.

There are also problems with the the English spelling system. The relationships between the phonology (approximately 44 speech sounds) and the graphology (26 alphabet letters) are highly variable.

	sounds	letters
vowels	20	5
consonants	24	21

Indeed, the English spelling 'system' is not really one system, but a system of systems, including influences of the following:

- Many French features have come from the period following the 1066 Norman invasion (e.g. *qu* replaced *cw*, as in *qu*estion; *gh* replaced *h* in enou*gh*; *ch* for *c* in *ch*urch; *ou* for *u* in h*ou*se; *c* before *i* in *c*ircle or before *e* in *c*ell; *o* for *u* in l*o*ve);
- Many 'loan' words from other languages (e.g. yacht, cocoa);
- Some words are spelled to show their Latin origin (e.g. debt–debitum; doubt–dubitare);
- Some 'silent letters' were pronounced when printing presses were invented (e.g. *k*nee, nam*e*);
- Printing presses were invented at a time of big changes in English pronunciation, especially in vowel sounds. If these changes had occurred before the invention of printing, English spelling might have been more regular.

English Sounds and Letters

Despite its reputation for irregularity, linguists have shown that written English has many patterned consistencies. Many phonemes have close and stable relationships with certain letters, as Table 2.1 and 2.2 show. Our knowledge of the English spelling system is now much better informed because of the authoritative work at Manchester University by Ted Carney.[30]

Tables 2.1 and 2.2 are based on his work.

Table 2.1 The highs and the lows of English CONSONANT phoneme–grapheme relationships

Above 95%	Above 90%
/b/ as in bed	/f/ as in fan (including ff)
/d/ as in dog	/g/ as in gun
/h/ as in hen	j/ as in television
/m/ as in mop	/l/ as in log (including ll and -le)
/n/ as in net	/z/ as in zoo (as the initial sound
/p/as in pup	in words)
/r/ as in rod (including rr)	
/t/ as in tub	
/v/ as in van (including -ve)	
/th/ as in then	
/th/ as in thumb	

Between 50% and 90%	Below 50%
79% /s/ as in sun (including ss)	/sh/ as in shop (37%)
alternatives c (15%) (also science,	alternatives: sugar, possession,
psychology, sword, waltz)	magician, dictation, repulsion, ocean,
75% /ng/ as in ring	conscious (totalling 55%)
alternatives thank	/y/ as in yak (19%)
73% /j/ as jet as an initial sound	alternatives: use; behaviour; Majorca
65% /ch/ as in champ	ALSO
alternatives tch (10%); question,	/j/ as in jet (29% when not an initial sound)
statue etc.	/z/ as in buzz (5% when not at the
64% /w/ as in wig	beginning of words)
alternatives qu (kw) 27%; wh (5%);	alternatives possess, because
u as in penguin (4%)	
59% /c/ as in cat	(Note: These percentages are based on lexical frequency. Some figures are
alternatives k (21%); ck (6%);	significantly different when high frequency function words (e.g. the or there)
ch (2%); also 9% in x or qu	are omitted from the analysis (see page 136).)

Table 2.2 The highs and the lows of English VOWEL phoneme–grapheme relationships

Above 95%	Above 90%
/a/ as in cat	/o/ as in dog
	/ow/ as in cow

Between 50% and 90%	Below 50%
84% /e/ as in hen	/ee/ as in bee (also e...e or -e) 38%
alternatives ea (6%); ai (1%); a (4%)	alternatives ee (26%); ea (25%); ie (5%)
80% /ie/ as in pie (including	/oo/ as in moon (39%)
i...e, -ie, -y) alternatives igh (13%)	alternatives u, u...e, ue (27%);
75% /oe/ as in toe	o, o...e, ue (15%); ew (9%); ou (7%)
(including o, o...e, -oe)	/er/ (r) in her (39%)

alternatives *ow* (18%); *oa* (4%)
65% /*a*/ as in l*a*te
alternatives *ay* (18%); *ai* (12%)
64% /*oo*/ as in b*oo*k
alternatives *u* (32%)
63% /*u*/ as in *u*mbrella
alternatives *o* (27%); *ou* (8%)
61% /*i*/ as in k*i*d
alternatives *y* (20%); *e* (16%);
ee (br*ee*ches), *ie* (s*ie*ve), *o* (w*o*men),
u, *ui* (total 2%)
61% /*aw*/ as in s*aw* (non -*r* spellings,
including *al*) (34%) *au* (9%) *aw* (9%)
alternatives *r*- spellings (39%,
including *or*, *ore*, *ar*, *our*)
61% /*oi*/ as in c*oi*n
alternatives *oy* (39%)
60% /*ar*/ as in c*ar*
alternatives *a* (34%); also *ear* (h*ear*t);
er (cl*er*k) *al* (h*al*f) (total 6%)

alternatives *ur* (r) (17%); *ir* (r) (18%);
or (r) (17%); *ear* (8%)
/*ere*/ as in th*ere* (37%)
alternatives *are* (24%); *eir* (22%);
air (12%); *ear* (4%)
/*ear*/ as in sp*ear* (28%)
alternatives *ea* (12%); *er*, *ere* (12%);
ia (10%); *eer* (4%) and many others
/*ure*/ as in l*ure*
alternatives *u* plus another vowel,
often unstressed
unstressed vowel as in *a*bout (35%)
alternatives *er* (15%); *e* (13%);
o (19%).

It can be seen that seven of the most unreliable correspondences are found in the vowel phonemes. These include three of the diphthongs (*ear* as in sp*ear*, *ere* as in th*ere* and *ure* as in l*ure*) and the unstressed vowel (see p. 25).

The greater variation between letters and sounds in vowels is related to the changes in pronunciation that occurred in English between *c*.1400 and 1600 and which has become known as 'the great vowel shift'. Many of these changes occurred after spelling had become stabilised by the invention of printing. According to Tom McArthur, before the shift (around the time of Chaucer), some of the vowel pronunciations were as follows:[31]

the /*ay*/ in f*a*me	was pronounced like	the /*ar*/ in f*a*ther
the /*ee*/ in s*ee*		the /*ay*/ in s*a*me
the /*ie*/ in f*i*ne		the /*ee*/ in f*ee*
the /*oe*/ in s*o*		the /*aw*/ in s*aw*
the /*oo*/ in t*o*		the /*oe*/ in t*oe*
the /*ow*/ in cr*o*wd		the /*ue*/ in cr*u*de

Patterns for Teaching and Learning

The legacy of what was called 'the great vowel shift' is not such an unreliable system as might have been expected. Generalisations about the pronunciations of individual vowels and vowel digraphs may be relatively low. However, there is much greater reliability within *rimes*, the part of a syllable that contains the vowel and any consonants that come after it. Any preceding consonant is referred to as the *onset*. The rime of the single syllable word 'beat' is -*eat*; the onset is *b*-. Sensitivity to rimes can be encouraged by informal rhyming word play of all kinds. Sensitivity to onsets can be encouraged by 'I-Spy' and 'odd-one-out' and other alliterative games. There have been successive studies by Rebecca Treiman in the USA and Peter Bryant, Usha Goswami and others in the UK that have confirmed that rimes play an important role in children's early phonological development.[32]

This area of literacy education has been subjected to substantial debate in recent years, although the links between research findings and the implications for practice now seem reasonably clear.[33] There is more on this in **Chapters 3**, **4** and **8**.

1 Children's spontaneous ability to detect rhyme and alliteration is associated with their later reading development.
2 Sensitivity to onsets and rimes seems to provide an important step towards becoming aware of the individual phonemes.
3 Phonemic awareness greatly assists learning to read in alphabetic writing systems such as English, but it seems to depend more on direct teaching and may be assisted by early writing ('invented spelling').
4 Early literacy development benefits from children being taught to identify and segment the phonemes in words and to blend them together.
5 Many children seem to turn intuitively to individual phonemes in certain stages of their early writing, in using the phonetic spelling that can characterise this writing.
6 Phonemic awareness is further developed as reading experience becomes more sustained and more wide-ranging
7 Phonemic awareness also further supports the use of rime units in reading and writing.
8 Rime units are especially helpful as early reading and writing get under way. These units provide greater reliability in vowel–letter correspondences. This reliability helps children to use analogies in generalising from one spelling pattern to another.

The last point was shown some thirty years ago in Richard Wylie's and Donald Durrell's research in Boston.[34] They found that the 286 rimes found in children's early reading books were 95% reliable. The 272 stable rimes were all found in children's speaking vocabularies. 500 words could be derived from only 37 rimes:

-ack	-ail	-ain	-ake	-ale	-ame	-am
-ank	-ap	-ash	-at	-ate	-aw	-ay
-eat	-ell	-est	-ice	-ick	-ide	-ight
-ill	-in	-ine	-ing	-ink	-ip	-ir
-ock	-oke	-op	-ore	-or	-uck	-ug
-ump	-unk					

This chapter has outlined some of the main functions and elements of spoken language and the basis of different writing systems. It has stressed the importance of understanding context and social variation in human communication. The chapter has indicated how the elements of vocabulary, grammar and spelling are patterned in different ways. The next chapter examines how these elements are used in the processes of writing.

The Processes of Writing:
Skills in Context

How do I know what I think until I see what I say?
(E.M. Forster)[1]

This chapter

- explores the differences between talking and writing
- considers what processes are involved in writing
- outlines some basic teaching approaches

From Talking to Writing

The last chapter has shown that children normally develop a wide-ranging linguistic competence in the early years of their lives, a competence on which the development of writing can be based. This competence has been summarised by Roger Brown[2] in a celebratory way. He reports that most children, by the time they are ready to begin school, know the full contents of an introductory book in transformational grammar. One such text is a bit more than 400 pages long and it covers declaratives and interrogatives, affirmatives and negatives, actives and passives, simple sentences, conjoined sentences and some kinds of embedded sentences, even though this knowledge may not be explicit. Children are not able to 'formulate' their grammatical knowledge or necessarily do it justice in acts of communication. However, what they develop remarkably quickly is an underlying knowledge of language that can be tapped and built upon in literacy learning.

Brown's words are borne out by the findings of the ten-year study of the language development of 120 Bristol children undertaken by Gordon Wells. The most impressive finding from the Bristol research was the amount that all children had learned about communicating through language by the time they went to school. Almost all the children had mastered the basic meanings and grammar of the language of their community. They were using language for a variety of purposes with the people in their immediate surroundings.[3]

Writing builds upon this competence. Early writing draws upon the sounds, words and grammar of speech and modifies them in specific ways. Initially, however, it may be helpful to discuss what is involved in writing and to summarise the main differences between speaking and writing. There is more on early writing in **Chapter 4**.

Differences Between Speaking and Writing

Writing differs from speech in very specific ways and makes particular demands. The differences are related to each other in complex ways, but point towards some of the difficulties which children as speakers may experience in becoming writers:

- In English, speech sounds (phonemes) have to be turned into spelling patterns.
- Writing often involves a more deliberate use of vocabulary and grammar, in order to meet the social contexts in which writing is being used.
- Writing follows certain conventions of space and direction: in English normally left to right, down the page.
- Writing uses various kinds of punctuation that compare, in a limited way, with pauses in speech.
- Writing is more time-consuming than speech, perhaps by a factor of five, even for skilled writers and typists.
- Writing involves forming and using 43 letter shapes, a process that has no equivalence in speech.
- Writing is often an individual act, for an audience who may be distant in both space and time, whereas speech normally involves a face-to-face interaction.

These are differences which have profound implications for children learning to write. The written symbols which represent sounds and words have to be made up by putting together the 43 shapes of the upper and lower-case alphabet. These words will have to be arranged in formally constructed phrases and sentences with appropriate spacing. The writer is likely to be communicating without the support of a conversational partner. Anyone who writes faces a piece of paper or screen that may be read in another place at some future time. Writing stands, or falls, by itself. It is not, like spontaneous speech, inextricably bound to the context in which it occurs.

All this indicates the need for the *purpose* of any writing task to be stressed in work with children, so that they come to appreciate the reasons for writing. Purposes for writing are discussed at greater length in **Chapter 5**.

Reflecting on the purpose of writing, and its influence on an audience, can help to motivate children and young people to take on the demand of writing. Such reflection may help them to recognise the rewards that writing can bring – and the functions it can perform.

The Functions of Writing

Frank Smith[4] suggests that 'writing can do everything that language in general can do'. It is also worth asking whether writing can fulfil any special functions or at least some functions especially well. Some writers have suggested that this kind of communication over space and time does bestow upon writing specific functions. These functions may even influence the nature of thinking itself. From his studies at Harvard University of the influence of school on cognitive growth, Jerome Bruner[5] emphasises that writing is the training in the use of linguistic contexts that are 'independent of the immediate referents'. In other words, when we write we have to learn to do without the prompts and direct support of other speakers and the shared context that they create.

Margaret Donaldson has developed this view by arguing that language written down is 'cut loose' or disembedded from the context of ongoing activities and feelings in which speech functions and on which speech thrives. This makes literacy particularly apt for the development and expression of certain kinds of thought. How do birds find their way when they migrate? Why does concrete set hard? Reading enables us to learn from people we cannot personally know. Writing helps us to sustain and order thought.[6]

Writing as a Whole

Writing is not so much a single phenomenon, but more an integration of several processes. These processes draw upon various 'key skills' in order for written language to be produced effectively. It can be helpful to consider three basic and interrelated processes:

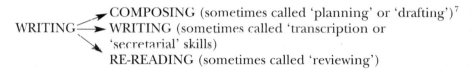

WRITING
- COMPOSING (sometimes called 'planning' or 'drafting')[7]
- WRITING (sometimes called 'transcription or 'secretarial' skills)
- RE-READING (sometimes called 'reviewing')

In turn, re-reading can be used to revise what has been written. This revision can be either larger scale re-drafting or smaller-scale editing and correcting:

RE-READING
- editing – correcting spelling and punctuation, changing word order
- re-drafting – substantially changing structure or content

The links between these processes are shown in Figure 3.1.

Figure 3.1

```
                        (redrafting)
       ┌─────────────────────────────────────────┐
       │                                          │
       │                    (editing)             │
       │             ┌──────────────────────┐     │
       ▼             ▼                       │     │
  COMPOSING ───────▶ WRITING ──────────▶ RE-READING
```

Such diagrams can provide a helpful framework for considering teaching and learning in schools, although several extra points need to be kept in mind (the points come from the successive studies of writing by John Hayes and Linda Flower at Carnegie Mellon University)[8]:

- the interactions between each process;
- the writer's working memory;
- the use of diagrams and illustrations to support the writing;
- the writer's motivation;
- the social environment (the audience, anyone collaborating etc.).[9]

What is more, any diagram will never quite do justice to the highly variable and idiosyncratic ways in which some individuals write, including professional writers, whose views are considered later in the chapter. However, studies of the writing of nearly 30,000 children in the USA have led to some interesting findings. Children who simply wrote first drafts performed no better than those who did not write plans or drafts. The children who did best were those whose planning involved lists, outlines or diagrams.[10] The explanation for these findings may lie in a comparison of writing and speaking.

Planning and Composing the Writing

Research into the composing of text has recognised the psychological demands of writing compared to talking. If we write, we have to shift from 'conversation to composition'.[11] This shift involves three important adjustments:

1 from using sounds in the air to using marks on the page or screen;
2 from communicating 'here and now' to communicating over time and space;
3 from interacting with a conversational partner to producing language alone.

Research into composing by Carl Bereiter and Marlene Scardamalia in Ontario has concentrated on the third of these adjustments.[12] There have been some helpful findings into how young writers can help themselves to overcome some of the lack of support from the conversational partner. They can do this by learning how to prompt themselves as they struggle to compose the text. These prompts can be of two main kinds:

- to call up the necessary content from memory ('content knowledge');
- to structure the text into a story, a poem, information etc. ('discourse knowledge').

The researchers have investigated a number of procedures which young writers can use in 'facilitating' the composing process:

- listing words;
- brainstorming;
- setting out the main points of the planned text;
- deciding an ending sentence very early on in a story (which otherwise can drift).

The value of these procedures will obviously vary, according to a whole range of circumstances. Composing procedures can help to relieve the pressure to produce a text, even a rough first draft, until the necessary support has been assembled. Adults might anticipate the usefulness of quite elaborate diagrams and schemes. Research has shown, however, that many children benefit from just being encouraged to assemble a list of words that they feel they are likely to need. Having these 'resources for writing' accessed and available for use can improve the young writer's confidence.[13]

Karin Dahl and Nancy Farnan have provided a helpful summary of American classroom research into how children's planning strategies change with age. Younger pupils in the 3–13 age-range are likely to transcribe their plans straight into their texts. Older children in this age-range tend to transform their notes into a text that maintains no resemblance to the original note-making.[14]

Such procedures can relieve the pressure on children to produce a text, even a rough first draft, until they have assembled the support that they need. In using pencil or pen, a double-page spread can be helpful, with the words, lists, draft sentences and other such prompts on the left and the emerging main text on the right:

Planning/Composing	Main text
Title Weather Hail beating on the window Snow about thingking outside Cold the howling storm grass thunder Storm laying	Weather As I am laying in bed at night I hear the howling wind and the beating on the window. As I am thinking about the cold I hear the grass running along as if it was in a race. then I remembered I was dreaming all the time.

In word processing software, various kinds of 'scratch pad' facilities provide similar opportunities for initial ideas to be jotted down and to be revisited and amended as the main text is developed. Planning and writing provide mutual support for each other as words and sentences are composed, ordered and re-read. Yet the main influence in refining the overall shape of what is written is likely to be a text-level one. The likely effectiveness of a text will depend on its overall organisation. This organisation will come from the writer's use of 'discourse knowledge' (this is discussed further in **Chapter 5**). Bereiter and Scardamalia make a distinction between two approaches to composing, one of which makes little use of discourse knowledge and another that is carefully structured:

'Knowledge-telling'	'Knowledge-transforming'
The writer churns out a relatively unstructured text, perhaps along the lines of 'everything I can think of about this subject'.	The writer grapples with the text and structures it according to her/his knowledge of different types of text organisation: registers, modes or genres.

There is limited evidence on how this knowledge grows in children. It is likely to be helped by wide and thoughtful reading of a range of texts. Shared reading and shared writing are also likely to help, as they can be used to help draw attention to the distinctive features of different kinds of text. Such approaches will also encourage them to 'read with a writer's alertness to technique'.[15] Guided writing can also help to support and extend such learning and this will be discussed later in the chapter.

Writing the Writing

Effectively putting pen to paper or fingers to keyboard has been called a 'tapestry of transcription'.[16] It involves decisions on word choice, spelling and grammatical arrangement, as well as the application of handwriting or typing skill. As the previous chapter shows, the words, spelling and grammar draw upon the main strands of language.

Figure 3.2

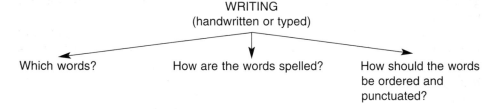

WRITING
(handwritten or typed)

Which words?   How are the words spelled?   How should the words be ordered and punctuated?

Transcription involves the weaving together of several strands of language development. If difficulties occur, there is a clear need to partition the problem, without losing sight of the underlying communicative purpose.

Which Words?

Children's vocabulary has consistently been found to be closely related to various indicators of language attainment. Limited vocabulary inhibits fluency, range and development in young people's writing.[17] Much vocabulary growth occurs informally as words and expressions are introduced into conversation as part of what Gordon Wells called the 'shared construction of reality'.[18] If the reality is sufficiently interesting and if the expression seems sufficiently helpful, then the words are likely to be taken up and used by other people. Catherine Snow at Harvard University has reported this process at work in parents and their pre-school children.[19] Research by Warwick Elley in New Zealand shows how reading to children can also be a significant source of vocabulary growth. This growth is especially helped by teacher explanation of unfamiliar words. Such assistance can double the rate of vocabulary acquisition.[20]

In the United Kingdom, successive central government initiatives have stressed the importance of reading to children and of encouraging sustained reading by children themselves. The Kingman Report argued that wide reading is essential to the full knowledge of the range of possible patterns of thought and feeling that are made accessible by the power and range of language. The report pointed out that responsive reading provides a storehouse for use in subsequent writing.[21]

The National Literacy Strategy in England has put shared reading in a prominent position in its Literacy Hour, in which teacher and pupils simultaneously read aloud a large format text. The effectiveness of shared reading compared with 'round-robin' reading has been systematically researched by Lloyd Eldredge, Ray Rentzel and Paul Hollingsworth at Brigham Young University. In two matched groups 78 seven year olds received either round-robin or shared reading teaching for thirty minutes a day for four months. The same books were used for both groups. After four months, the shared reading group had significantly higher scores on tests of reading fluency, vocabulary acquisition and comprehension. There was evidence that the supported reading experience of the shared reading group had the greatest impact on the word recognition abilities of the pupils who initially were the poorest readers.[22]

The question 'Which words?' raises central issues about the personal resources that are needed for writing. Mina Shaughnessy, after 15 years work with basic literacy students in New York, concludes that vocabulary looms as perhaps the most formidable and discouraging obstacle in the development of advanced literacy.[23]

How are the Words Spelled?

Spelling is another key skill in writing development. The sooner children can make spelling largely unconscious and automatic for a large number of words, the more attention can be devoted to the shaping of the structure of the text and its effective communication. Research into spelling provides a great deal of encouragement for teachers and parents because a variety of findings show how influential they can be. Not surprisingly, verbal ability influences success in spelling in primary school children. Carefulness in writing is also important. Children are more likely to 'catch' spelling if they are helped to develop a swift and well-formed style of handwriting. The hand movements of handwriting provide valuable kinaesthetic support to learning words through visual means. Spelling is an eye–hand skill.

Reading is also a key influence on spelling skill. Reading tacitly provides an awareness of word meanings, word structures and letter strings. What is not so widely understood is the fact that early spelling may influence early reading skill, as well. Research into early literacy development indicates that links need to be forged between reading and spelling, links that are part of a two-way 'cross-over'.

The Literacy Cross-Over: Reading–Spelling Links

In learning to read, children need to learn about how letters represent speech sounds in order to tackle the reading of unfamiliar words. As they move on to more demanding texts, whole word recognition and contextual cues become relatively less helpful.[24] In learning to read, sound is our preferred sense. If we do not know how to read a word, we sound it out and check if it makes sense.

In learning to spell, children may intuitively try to represent their speech sounds in what is sometimes called 'invented spelling' ('ov' for *of*; 'sed' for *said* etc.). Most fundamentally in learning to spell, vision is our preferred sense. If we do not know how to spell a word, we write it down to see if it looks right.

In this way, learning to be literate involves a kind of 'cross-over' between reading and spelling, as Figure 3.3 shows.

Figure 3.3

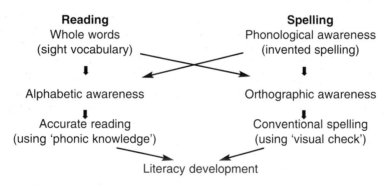

Figure 3.3 indicates how effective teaching of spelling means being able to make constructive diagnosis of children's spelling approximations and to devise needs-related teaching.

- Children need to learn from writing in order to develop reading accuracy.
- Children need to learn from their reading in order to develop their spelling accuracy.

All this is supported by the use of spoken language to explore, discuss and reflect upon how speech is mapped on to what is written. Children also need to be helped to look at the patterns of the English spelling system.[25] Success in spelling involves the conscious use of the other two language strands which were introduced in Chapter 2, grammar and vocabulary. An understanding of grammar helps in the spelling of 'pushed' with the past tense *-ed* ending, rather than a final *t* ('pusht'). Words are sometimes spelled to show their grammatical function (min*ce* or mint*s*). An understanding of vocabulary helps in the spelling of words like 'medicine'/'medical', rather than the form based on phonology ('medisin'). Words are sometimes spelled to show their origin (the silent *b* in bom*b* is to show its link to bom*b*ardier).

As John Mountford has illustrated, written English is far more than phoneme–grapheme (sound–spelling) correspondences. The spelling system organises the morphemes in written English in a visible form.[26] The spelling status of a letter like 't' is different in 'the' from what it is in 'trees'. The difference is shown in Figure 3.4:

Figure 3.4

The role of alphabet letters in the spelling system is determined by their membership of several overlapping sets. The role of a letter is determined in a grapheme, in a morpheme, in a word! The letter 't' plays two different roles in the above diagram. In 'the', it is part of the grapheme <th>.[27] In 'hothouse' and in 'trees', 't' represents the grapheme <t>. Its role in 'hothouse' is not the same as its role in 'the', even though 't' precedes 'h' in both words. We can only be sure of the boundaries of the graphemes by taking the morphemes into account. There is more on spelling development in **Chapters 4** and **8**.

How Should The Words Be Ordered?

Teachers and parents can only exert a subtle influence on the development of the grammatical aspects of children's writing. While the patterns of the spelling system are conventionally structured, the patterns of word order are infinite. As will be shown in **Chapter 9**, large-scale studies of collections of children's writing have shown clear patterns of progression, from simple, literal, affirmative sentences through to more elaborate syntax and cohesion. Curriculum development projects across the world indicate that children are likely to benefit from:

- reading and having read to them a range of text types throughout the primary years, to experience their distinctive features;
- writing of continuous passages from an early age, so that they can grapple with the coherent structuring of texts;

- undertaking a range of writing tasks, where different syntactic structures are needed;
- being helped to identify any features of non-standard dialect and to consider standard alternatives.

There is more on grammar in **Chapters 6** and **7**.

How Should the Words be Punctuated?

Unfortunately, the teaching of punctuation has rarely figured in recent educational publications on the writing process. In fact, it is interesting to note that one of the few recent books to discuss punctuation carefully has come from one of the professional writers who were members of the central government Kingman Committee in 1988. Keith Waterhouse seems to have been motivated to write *English Our English* by a sense of frustration that educational writers were not addressing the teaching of grammar with the conviction that he felt was needed.[28]

Of all the various features of punctuation, the one that may benefit children most is the orthodox use of the full stop in signalling sentence boundaries. Sentences play a key role in much written communication. Sentences are the largest linguistic units within which grammatical rules systematically operate. However, learning to write in sentences may involve, in itself, a major adjustment in children's language development. As Gunther Kress has shown, in general we do not talk in sentences but rather in chains of clauses. The formal structure of sentences is part of written language (we can easily detect someone reading aloud on the radio).[29] This is a further indication of how children's early writing development is inspired by their learning to read with an alertness to the 'how' as well as the 'what', 'why' and 'who for' writing.

The learning of punctuation has to reach out beyond sentence boundaries in several dimensions, as indicated in Figure 3.5.

It is salutary to note that the use of punctuation marks in books for children is often inconsistent from one author to another. The use of exclamation marks, dashes and some commas can depend on the whims of the writer. The devices used to show direct speech in early reading books can also be very variable. Katharine Perera's research at Manchester University has shown very different approaches in authors' practices in whether they use reporting clauses to attribute speech. If they do use these clauses, there are very different practices in where they are placed in lines or sentences. The use of inverted commas (none, single or double) and capital letters also varies. Children are likely to come across very different conventions as they move from book to book or between series of books. These variations are accompanied by marked differences in how several grammatical structures are presented, including the use of pronouns and reduced forms ('I'll' etc.).[30]

Figure 3.5

Children need to learn how to use full stops to mark sentence boundaries. They may need to be alerted to how an abbrevn. is also indicated by a full stop. Furthermore, there aren't any alternatives to using an apostrophe to show where a letter has been omitted or to show that you are referring to someone's possessions.

The use of the question mark is also surely essential if the asking of a question is to be confirmed? On the other hand, the decision to use an exclamation mark is a more open one. There are other ways of indicating the change of tone! For instance, letters can be written in **CAPITALS**.

Frank Smith [1994, p. 158] declares a relative dislike of exclamation marks — but admits to a relative indulgence in dashes. According to Keith Waterhouse, dashes have become less common as hyphenated words have been increasingly re—written as compound words, like 'rewritten'.

Paragraph boundaries are other instances of where 'poetic licence' is often apparent in some publications. It is more difficult to deny the old slogan that 'Speech marks must be used to show exactly what someone has said'. The use of the comma can be more subjective, although it seems to be frequently misused for linking two simple sentences when no conjunction is present. In contrast, the semicolon seems to be under-used in the writing of children and students; it can be helpful in contrasting two simple sentences. The uses of the colon also seem under-valued: in setting out the advance organisers of a long text; in grouping the items within a long list; and as an alternative to a comma immediately before direct speech.

Schools need to have a firm policy for deciding when and how these conventions are to be explained to children. Such teaching will benefit from being related to the context of the writing and the more creative use of punctuation (including underlining *and brackets) when opportunities allow.*

Recent investigations by Nigel Hall and Anne Robinson at Manchester Metropolitan University have highlighted how little is known about how punctuation is taught and learned. Their work has revealed the ways in which punctuation is highly dependent upon a number of social conventions.[31] After studying the teaching and learning of punctuation in a case study classroom, Nigel Hall suggests three ways of helping to overcome children's unconscious resistance to the use of full stops in punctuating sentences:

1 **Demarcation**: as soon as possible, encourage children to write two or more sentences, rather than one, and to arrange them continuously on the page.
2 **Explanation**: use explanatory concepts, rather than labelling and procedural teaching. These explanatory concepts are likely to make effective use of intonation and to reflect the authentic communication of meaning in writing.

3 **Information**: emphasise what punctuation does for a text in informing the reader, rather than concentrating on rules or rituals.[32]

The use of punctuation is closely tied to the grammar of written language, but the effective learning of punctuation is likely to be fostered by a supportive, communicative context. In the words of Alfred, Lord Tennyson, this 'use in measured language lies'; without a communicative context, punctuation risks becoming a 'sad mechanic exercise'.[33]

Writing, Handwriting and Typing

Any study of handwriting will illustrate another instance of the interrelationships of the processes involved in writing. Research indicates a close link between the development of a swift, well-formed style of handwriting and success in spelling. The hand movements involved in reproducing common letter strings help to consolidate the learning of these spelling patterns. This learning brings with it an increased self-concept.

As Rosemary Sassoon points out, handwriting is a taught skill, the visible trace of hand movement; there is little that is 'natural' about it. Moreover she warns, in order to lay the foundations for swift, automatic writing, the strokes of the basic letters must start at the correct point and move in the right direction. Re-learning is not easy once wrong hand movements have become automatic.[34]

Research suggests the following priorities in teaching:

- establish correct letter formation early;
- ensure a clear and consistent school policy for handwriting;
- maintain opportunities for regular practice.

Handwriting is taken up in greater detail in **Chapter 4**.

There seems to be little research on typing skills which children need to develop in order to make fast and effective use of word processing. British and American studies indicate that word processing itself does not make children write better, prompt them to revise more or teach them new writing strategies.[35] However, word processing seems to help create new social contexts for teachers and children to work together. In these contexts, children may learn new strategies and, more particularly, develop greater efficiency in using the strategies they already have. Curiously, though, there has been little discussion of how and when to develop ten-finger, as opposed to two-finger, typing skills in children and young people. A wide-scale improvement in typing skills could make transcription more efficient. Word processing is discussed in greater detail in **Chapter 9**.

Re-Reading the Writing

Integrating all the processes involved in writing can be an intimidating task for anyone. It is very difficult to get everything right first time, especially if there is some importance attached to what is written or to how the audience might respond. In recent years, interest has focused on the re-reading by children of what they have written and on the use of a draft as a resource for teaching and learning. It seems undeniably good practice to re-read what has been written and to consider the possibilities for editing and redrafting it in some way. Yet, this is a lesson many pupils find difficult to learn. It is important that they tackle writing where the advantages of re-reading become self-evident.

This re-reading can be approached in a variety of ways. Children can be encouraged to:

1 look back over their work in the light of what they intended;
2 read what they have written quietly to themselves;
3 read what they have written to someone else;
4 ask a series of useful questions, such as:

LOOK (Is this right?)

LISTEN (Is this what I meant to write?)

THINK (Is this what I meant?)

As they increase their experience of the range and possibilities of texts, children can be helped to adopt increasingly sophisticated editorial checks. They can be helped to use some of the basic proof-reading marks. In some kinds of writing this can be a healthy precursor to some form of publishing, which will in itself provide a particular sense of satisfaction and reward.

Figure 3.6

⊢——⊣	delete
⋏	insert
- - - - -	check spelling
⫣ ⫤	change capitals to lower case or vice versa
~~	consider alternative wording
‖	begin new paragraph
⊂——⊃	link up ('run on')

Writing as 'Design'

Mike Sharples suggests that writing can be seen as a process of 'design', a skill that is grounded in the way we use our intelligence to create and share things in the world. Crucial to this view is a recognition of a set of internal and external constraints. These constraints are not restrictions on writing. Instead, they are a means of focusing attention and channelling mental resources. Learning, experience and environment work together to shape the activity of writing.[36]

Parallels between writing and design include the following:

- their open-endedness – only broad goals are possible;
- their potential endlessness – when to end is a matter of judgement;
- there is no infallibly correct approach – there are many equally successful ones;
- they involve finding, as well as solving, problems – a number of simultaneous constraints have to be juggled;
- they inevitably involve subjective judgements – considerations of 'quality' are bound up with values.

More deep-seated parallels exist in the roles of 'primary generators' and 'design languages'. A 'primary generator' is a key underlying idea that opens up some possibilities and closes off others. Sharples points out that teachers are very much in control of primary generators in the topics that they ask their pupils to write about. These topics can have resonances that provoke questions ('An evening at Fat Franco's'); these topics can also summon up mundane writing ('What I did on my holidays').

Design languages provide a meta-language for talking about the processes of writing and the properties of texts. This meta-language provides for collections of elements, sets of organising principles and collections of qualifying situations. This parallel will become evident later in this book in **Chapters 6**, **7** and **8**. There are different elements within sentences (subject, verb, object etc.). These elements can be ordered and shaped in different kinds of sentence structure. The appropriateness of different kinds of sentence structure is linked in turn to the genre features of different types of text. All this can be unambiguously discussed if there is a meta-language available, in this case grammatical terminology. Another instance of a design language in writing also runs through this chapter, reflecting a growth of interest in recent years: the terminology of planning, composing, reviewing, redrafting and so on. An important contributor to this growth has been the promotion of 'process writing'.

Writing Processes and 'Process Writing'

One of the most important influences on the reviewing and redrafting aspects of writing has been Donald Graves.[37] Graves' work has promoted a journalistic model of the writing process, often referred to as 'process writing'. It embraces writing with a real audience in mind, drafting and re-drafting, seeking child-centred advice from the teacher and from peers, and eventual publication. Through extended experience of this process, it is suggested that children find a voice and a sense of ownership in what they have produced. The collaboration that this brings can invigorate and enliven the communicative contexts of classrooms, in various kinds of 'writing workshop' approaches.[38] The approach influenced various local initiatives in the National Writing Project that ran in England and Wales between 1985 and 1989.

At the same time, there are some uncertainties about Graves' work and influence, particularly its research base, its appropriateness in different contexts and some of its underlying assumptions. Remarkably, for a project of such influence, the research base is very limited and very vague. Some critics have suggested that his work is more evangelical 'reportage' than research. Graves' doctoral thesis was based on the study of four classes of children in a middle-class community.[39]

In a review of 11 subsequent papers by Graves and his colleagues, Peter Smagorinsky notes that only 30 children are referred to. One child (Andrea) is referred to on 41 pages. Only one other child is referred to on more than ten pages (Sarah, on 15 pages). Given the case study framework of Graves' work, questions arise about the significance of what is reported and what is not reported.[40] As Myra Barrs points out, nowhere in Graves' principal book is there an example in all its successive drafts.[41] In contrast, it is striking to note how cautious Carl Bereiter and Marlene Scardamalia are when discussing the outcomes from over 100 experimental studies of writing in the 8–13 age-range. The researchers note that children find their first drafts 'highly salient' and that encouragement to re-draft can lead to superficial tinkering that may threaten to diminish the overall effectiveness of the text.[42]

Other uncertainties arise about the extent to which process writing is appropriate in different contexts. Michael Rosen argues that 'process writing' can erode the 'feeling' from children's original words and that the subsequent re-drafted and conferenced texts can lack authentic individual expression.[43] Graves' journalistic model may be more applicable to the production of a classroom newspaper or information books for other children. It may not be so applicable to the 'emotion recalled in tranquillity' that can distinguish individual children's poetry, compared with the collaborative enterprise which Graves recommends. Similarly, it is difficult to accommodate conferencing and redrafting within the more personal kinds of 'expressive writing' to which James Britton and the Bullock Committee drew attention.[44] Such writing may initially involve a search for meaning within the self rather than 'publication' within the school.

Pam Gilbert has also argued that the 'ownership' of process writing can raise a range of issues about the content of what is written about. She reports how a group of Queensland boys collaborated to produce a violent story with crude, stereotypical characters based on disparaging views of other members of the class.[45] Gilbert reminds us that what pupils choose to write about in school inevitably reflects broader social factors. In creating and negotiating contexts for writing, teachers have to mediate between a variety of influences and expectations. This mediation may involve a delicate balance between pupils' interests and what is *in* pupils' interest. As the rest of the chapter will show, this is likely to go beyond unproblematic views of process writing.

The significance of Donald Graves' work as a whole has been well discussed by Dominic Wyse at Liverpool John Moores University in a book that provides detailed reports on the use of process writing in several schools. It also discusses some of the critiques referred to above.[46] Donald Graves' work has certainly drawn a healthy attention to how children can benefit from looking back over what they have written. It has broadened understanding of the kinds of context that support writing and of the repertoire to which writers can resort, including those who write professionally.

What Writers Tell Us About Writing

Generalisations about 'real writing' and how 'real writers' write are not easy to make from the published accounts of writers at work. Some of these accounts shed a dubious light on any nebulous notion of what 'the writing process' comprises. Lucy Calkins, for example, refers in several publications to William Faulkner's description of the way he wrote novels as an illustration of the way most professional writers work. He took a character and let the story develop spontaneously – '...all I do is trot along behind him [sic] with pencil and paper, trying to keep up...'.[47] Rosemary Harthill's collection, *Writers Revealed*, shows how unrepresentative this kind of generalisation can be. Iris Murdoch wrote nothing until she knew how the story would develop ('I plan in enormous detail down to the last conversation before I write the first sentence. So it takes a long time to invent it'). Piers Paul Read outlines the plot of each book on a single page. Brian Moore might rewrite the opening two or three pages of his books 'maybe forty, fifty times'.[48]

There are similarly huge contrasts in other aspects of how professional writers write: Tom Sharpe writes entirely on a word processor; Iris Murdoch preferred pen and paper and having the whole script to hand '...apt and ready for the eye: easily accessible'.[49] A number of professional writers speak favourably about being taught grammar formally at school and of the teachers who showed them how the language worked as a system. The late Poet Laureate, Ted Hughes, and the award-winning novelist, Jan Mark, are examples of writers who have expressed such views.[50] Some writers need quiet and solitude.[51] Others admit that there is no spur quite like a deadline.[52] Overall, it could be said that the writing processes of professional writers are as variable as the products which result from their efforts.

Writing Processes and Classroom Practices

Different classroom practices make different assumptions about the nature of writing processes and how they are learned. George Hillocks at the University of Chicago has undertaken major reviews of research on the teaching of writing and has identified three broad teaching approaches.[53] Their particular features are set out in Table 3.1.

Table 3.1

Approach	Published example	Teacher's role	Writing topics	Particular teaching strategies
'Presentational'	Many English course books	Imparting knowledge prior to writing	Assigned by teacher	Setting tasks and marking outcomes
'Natural Process'	Graves (1983) Calkins (1986)	Engaging pupils in writing and fostering positive dispositions	Chosen by pupils	Providing general procedures, e.g. multiple drafts and peer comments
'Guided writing' (what Hillocks calls an 'environmental' approach)	Scardamalia (1981) Martin (1989)	Inducing and supporting active learning of complex strategies that pupils are not capable of using on their own	Negotiated	Developing materials and activities to engage pupils in task-specific processes

Hillocks reports a meta-analysis of research that compares the three approaches, using specific linguistic indicators of pupils' learning. From 73 comparable studies, Hillocks reports that the guided writing approach was two or three times more effective than the natural process approach and over four times more effective than the presentational approach.

WHY IS THE PRESENTATIONAL APPROACH ONLY MINIMALLY EFFECTIVE?

It involves telling pupils what is strong or weak in writing performance, but it does not provide opportunities for pupils to learn procedures for putting this knowledge to work, e.g. showing pupils an information text and fastidiously marking pupil errors, but not teaching procedures to help pupils write information texts.

WHY IS THE PROCESS APPROACH ONLY MODERATELY EFFECTIVE?

It prompts ideas and plans for incorporation in particular pieces of writing, but it does not ensure that pupils develop their own ideas and plans autonomously. This is especially so in the organisation of different kinds of writing, e.g. encouraging pupils to draft, discuss and receive feedback on information texts, but not procedures for correcting or avoiding problems.

WHY IS THE GUIDED WRITING APPROACH MORE EFFECTIVE?

It presents new forms, models and criteria and facilitates their use in different writing tasks. Problems are tackled in a spirit of inquiry and problem-solving, e.g. drawing pupils' attention to information texts, helping them to identify the distinctive features of such texts and providing tasks in which they can apply this knowledge in their own independent writing.

The Supporting Role of Shared Writing

Several cautions need to be added to these conclusions. They are drawn from carefully designed research studies rather than ongoing classroom contexts. Teachers may use a judicious mix of the three approaches. They may support any of them by using shared writing, the joint construction of a text by teacher and pupils. The effectiveness of shared writing is difficult to assess in research studies because of its interactive and diverse nature. Nevertheless, shared writing builds upon psychological research that has revealed the complexity of the writing process and the potential value of teachers modelling writing and channelling children's suggestions. After many experimental studies into the psychological aspects of writing, Carl Bereiter and Marlene Scardamalia make a number of recommendations that are built around the possibilities of shared writing:[54]

- pupils (and teachers) need to be made aware of the full extent of the composing process;
- the thinking that goes on in composition needs to be modelled by the teacher;
- pupils will benefit from reviewing their own writing strategies and knowledge;
- pupils need a supportive and congenial writing environment, but will also benefit from experiencing the struggles that are an integral part of developing writing skill;
- pupils may also benefit from using various 'facilitating' techniques to help them through the initial stages of acquiring more complex processes (e.g. listing words, points that may be made, the wording of final sentences etc.), in advance of tackling the full text.

Anne Browne, of the University of East Anglia, provides a helpful discussion of the value of shared writing with younger children and the tacit lessons that may accompany more explicit ones.[55] The success of shared writing is likely to reflect the teacher's skill in using dialogue to provide scaffolded understanding of what is involved.[56] 'Scaffolding' refers to a process that enables pupils to solve a problem or carry out a task that would be beyond their unassisted efforts. A key resource in this process is pupils' experience as readers.

Lessons to be Learned

It is interesting to note that the British Government, in pursuit of its goal to raise standards, has supported a combination of shared and guided writing in its National Literacy Strategy. This appears to be a promising combination, although long-term success will depend on the quality of the tasks that are provided for guided writing and how they are linked to more sustained writing.

Hillocks' review is of additional help here. His meta-analysis also looked at particular teaching strategies. The most effective ones were the following, set out here in rank order of effectiveness (most effective first):

- **Inquiry**: producing/acquiring information, analysing it, planning how to use it, using text level criteria for composing and reviewing what is written.
- **Scales**: critically analysing texts by using specific criteria (particularly organisation and the text as a whole) and then writing new texts in the same genre while bearing these criteria in mind.
- **Sentence-combining**: constructing new sentences from already-formed sentences, although has little effect on text-level and organisation performance.
- **Models**: demonstrating exemplary pieces of writing, although does not help students learn the underlying structure or to experience the composing process.
- **Free writing**: pupils tend to use a 'what next' strategy, without developing an overall sense of text structure or focusing on overall purpose.
- **Grammar**: traditional grammar teaching (e.g. sentence-parsing); seems to have little or no effect on writing improvement.

Several of these strategies are discussed further in later chapters. At this point, it may be helpful to take a closer look at the kinds of task that may be incorporated into guided writing.

A Closer Look at the Guided Writing Approach

Curriculum development work by Marlene Scardamalia and her colleagues in Ontario has trialled a number of tasks that are closely related to the first two of these strategies. These include 'planning' and 'revision' tasks.[57] Others are referred to in **Chapters 6** and **8**.

Table 3.2

---

a) Planning tasks

Three sentences (9+)

1 Pupils each choose three sentences from a book, magazine or newspaper, which follow each other and convey a complete thought unit.
2 They copy out the three sentences and label each sentence A, B and C.
3 They write new A and C sentences, retaining the same B sentence (the thought unit need not be the same as the original).
4 The two sets of sentences are read aloud to the class.
5 The class try to decide which were the original three. (The writer is successful if they cannot.)

Plan ahead (10+)

1 The teacher presents two to four plans for writing about a certain topic by writing them on the board and reading them aloud (copies of plans may also be given out).
2 Pupils choose one plan and write a paragraph (or more, as appropriate) on the topic.
3 Paragraphs are read to the class and the class suggest which plan was used.

Extension: Paragraphs from the same plan are compared for effectiveness.

---

b) Revision tasks

Change your sentence (9+)

1 The teacher uses shared writing to elicit reasons (intentions) why a sentence might need to be changed (e.g. to make it more interesting, frightening, sad etc.; to communicate to an older, younger, unknown person; to make it easier to understand; to appeal to emotion etc.)
2 Each pupil writes a sentence describing an action.
3 Each pupil then chooses one of the intentions listed on the board and writes their sentence again but changing it to fit the intention.
4 Pupils read both of their sentences out loud and the others decide which was the original and which intention was followed.
5 The teacher draws out in class discussion how the different intentions were achieved.

Extension: Increase the number of intentions and the similarity between them.

Learning to paraphrase (11+)

1 Each pupil writes a short story of approximately five to ten sentences.
2 Stories are written only on the left-hand side of a page folded in half and each sentence is begun on a new line. (Pupils may benefit from writing the story first and then copying it out in this way.)
3 Each person's story is then passed to someone else in the group who chooses one of the sentences to paraphrase. The paraphrase is written on the right-hand side, next to the original.
4 The story is then passed on and another group member paraphrases another sentence.
5 When all sentences have been paraphrased, the stories are returned to their authors.
6 The original authors look at each pair of sentences in turn and decide which sentence contributes most to the story. The story can then be revised as necessary.
7 The final version of each story can be read to the class and points of interest discussed.

Extension: With younger pupils, stories with fewer sentences could be used. The task may be focused on particular genres.

Observational research and inspection evidence suggest that these kinds of guided writing tasks are not widely used in schools. The presentational and process approaches tend to be more common. Guided writing offers greater opportunities for young writers to make valuable connections between text, sentence and word level decisions and to be helped to shape texts with particular criteria in mind.

Conclusion

Recent years have seen a great deal of increase in interest in writing processes. This has led to much more attention being given to how children write, as well as to why and what they write. In building upon these developments in the new millennium, however, it is important to understand the importance of the early foundations on which these writing processes are built. This is the topic of the next chapter.

Early Writing

I Lac ratig Bcos I juts duw
(Rachel, aged five)

This chapter

- discusses children's early mark making
- explores how children learn about the writing system
- reviews influential research on early literacy development
- identifies some key influences on early writing progress.

Early Mark Making

There seems to be a natural desire in young children to make marks, to experience the visual pleasure of creating their own individual sign on a convenient surface. They may make early scribbles with paper and pencil, with paintbrush and easel, with finger on misted window and so on. The marks that they make may appear random and meaningless. However, studies of large numbers of children's scribbling have revealed how simple patterns and images soon begin to appear in their spontaneous explorations with writing implements and suitable surfaces. Rhoda Kellogg studied the scribbles of several hundred thousand children and detected a particular pattern of development.[1] She was concerned with what children could do, rather than what they had been taught. She reminds us that, although animals can scratch lines on a surface, none can make the range of scribbles found in small children. There appear to be three broad stages, involving 'basic scribbles', 'diagrams' and 'combinations'.

BASIC SCRIBBLES

There are up to 20 basic scribbles, some of which are developed into 'scribble streamers'

It is important to note that the list in Figure 4.1 does not imply any developmental sequence, although scribbles 6 to 9 may be easier for many children.

Children may begin scribbling at the age of two or occasionally even earlier. According to Kellogg, they typically place one scribble over another, making clear-cut examples difficult to find.

By the age of three or four, children are more likely to put a single kind of scribble on one piece of paper, forming what Kellogg refers to as 'placement patterns'.

Figure 4.1

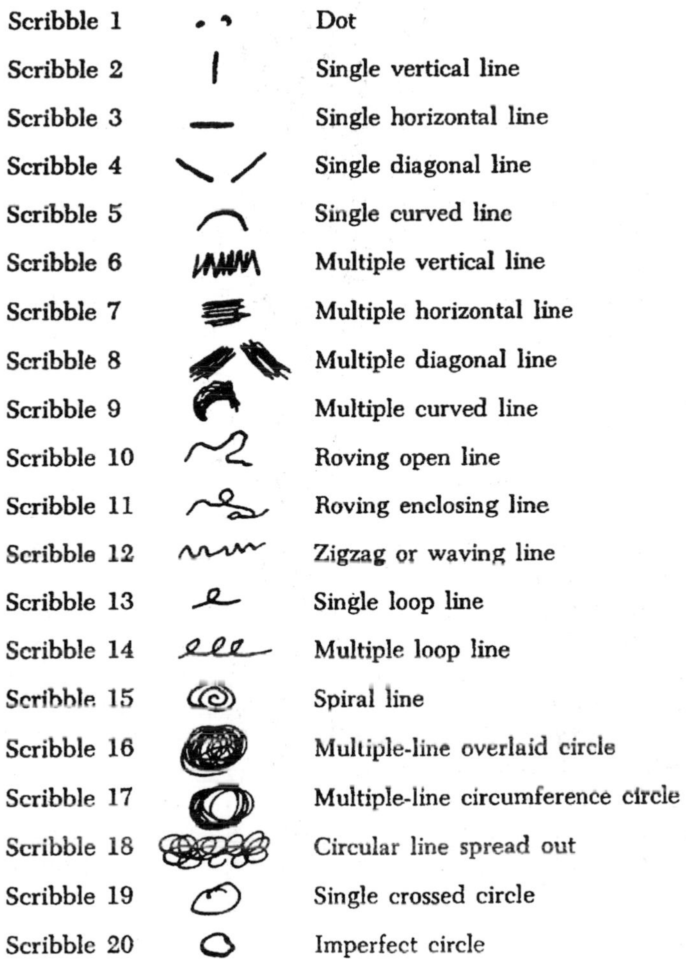

Scribble 1	• ◥	Dot
Scribble 2			Single vertical line
Scribble 3	—	Single horizontal line
Scribble 4	\ /	Single diagonal line
Scribble 5	⌒	Single curved line
Scribble 6	⩙⩙⩙	Multiple vertical line
Scribble 7	≋	Multiple horizontal line
Scribble 8	⫻	Multiple diagonal line
Scribble 9	⌒	Multiple curved line
Scribble 10	⌁	Roving open line
Scribble 11	⌁	Roving enclosing line
Scribble 12	⋀⋁⋀⋁	Zigzag or waving line
Scribble 13	ℓ	Single loop line
Scribble 14	ℓℓℓ	Multiple loop line
Scribble 15	◎	Spiral line
Scribble 16	●	Multiple-line overlaid circle
Scribble 17	⊘	Multiple-line circumference circle
Scribble 18	⬭⬭⬭	Circular line spread out
Scribble 19	⊘	Single crossed circle
Scribble 20	◯	Imperfect circle

Figure 4.2

Left: E1, multiple line crossings which could have been made without lifting the crayon (26 months)

Right: E2, multiple line crosses which could only have been made by lifting the crayon (25 months)

Left: E3, small crossings. Short lines cross other lines (27 months)

Right: E3, small crossings. Many small lines appear here (30 months)

PLACEMENT PATTERNS

Figure 4.3

The next stage involves 'placement patterns' which require more eye control in order to locate the scribble within the dimensions of the available space.

P1, over-all (32 months)

DIAGRAMS

By the age of three, children make diagrams with single lines, to form crosses and to outline circles, triangles and other shapes. Soon these are developed into at least six diagram shapes: rectangle; square; ovals; circles; Greek cross (+); diagonal cross (x). The scribbling of these shapes gives evidence of planning and deliberation, as a growing memory of shapes comes into play, adding forethought to exploration.

Figure 4.4

COMBINATIONS

A further stage is reached when these six diagrams are brought together in different ways, either in pairs, or in overlapping forms, or in ways that put one diagram inside another.

Figure 4.5

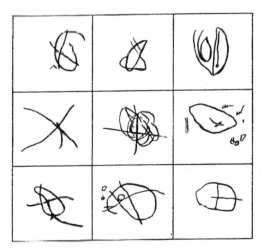

The exploration of these combinations will involve the use of greater control and memory. When all permutations of these six shapes are allowed for, over 60 basic combinations are possible. From here, all kinds of more contrived combinations can be put together from three or more diagrams. Further explorations can also extend to include the following:

Figure 4.6

a mandala   b sun   c radial lines

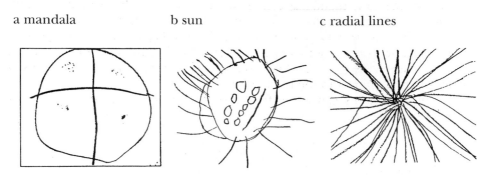

These may be part of a sequence that leads from abstract work to pictorial drawings, which often begin with the human form. Later pictorial development is likely to include animals, buildings, vegetation and various kinds of transport. Many features of earlier spontaneous art can be incorporated in these early representations.

Figure 4.7

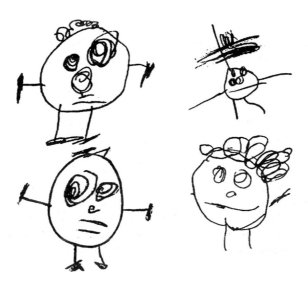

Kellogg argues that children's early pictures are normally not based on observations of objects or persons in the child's environment. She argues instead that such drawings are aesthetic compositions evolved out of earlier work. Even though the child may attribute meaning to the picture (mummy, boy, man etc.), the picture may nevertheless be more of an integration of circles, radials and mandalas etc. than the result of observation in itself. Kellogg is at great pains to point out that children's scribbles should not be dismissed because they are not realistic. Early 'people pictures' should be seen as an indication of an advanced stage of the child's growing mental capacity. This capacity enables the child to create complex, meaningful and organised forms of great interest to the human eye.

All kinds of gains can come from extensive experience of spontaneous exploratory scribbling:

- pleasure in leaving a physical trace of the hand movement;
- eye–hand coordination, including placement skills for arranging print on the page;
- the learning of many forms used in letter formation.

The kinds of scribbling outlined above can promote much of the hand–eye coordination needed for writing. The pleasure associated with scribbling may carry over into the more restricted movement of writing. In fact, Kellogg suggests that most letter forms can be produced incidentally by earlier spontaneous scribbles.

A	B, b	C, c	D, d	E, e	F, f	g	H, h	I, i	J	K	L, l
M, m	N, n	O, o	P, p	r		S, s	T	U	V, v	W, w	X, x y
Z, z											

Of the 43 basic letter shapes, the only ones that are not produced incidentally by spontaneous scribbles appear to be the following:

a   G   j   k   Q, q   R   t   u   Y

(Note that Kellogg refers to the letter forms produced by young children and not the precise forms of many printed typefaces, with their serifs and other typographic features.)

Kellogg argues that children who are able to scribble freely should learn the alphabet with relative ease because they may already have tacit knowledge of over 30 letter shapes. Children still have much to learn, of course, particularly the significance of these shapes in the writing system. They also have to learn how the shapes are normally placed on the page and the most efficient hand movements for forming alphabet letters (see later in this chapter).

Drawing and Writing: Making the Distinction

A significant point is reached when children begin to distinguish between drawing and writing. As Marie Clay notes, parents and teachers may find it difficult to explain the difference, but somehow many pre-school children do learn what it is.[2] Anne Dyson made a detailed study in Georgia of how children learned to make this distinction by working closely with kindergarten children over a three-month period.[3] These children were already communicating by using speech and drawings. Dyson investigated how they learned to communicate with the 'second-order' graphic symbols of writing that stand for speech. She studied how children combined pictorial symbols and letter-like symbols and also what they called them.

Dyson found that these children consistently used drawing and talk to support their early writing: 'writing houses and stuff'. They were also learning to distinguish writing from drawing by unconventional and partly overlapping use of the terms.

What the children *did* do:

- say they were writing when drawing to represent an object ('I'm gonna write him pants');
- say they were writing when producing a graphic object for another person ('I write my name and I write pictures for my grandma');
- say they were writing when representing a story (the child telling a story as he/she draws).

What the children *did not* do:

- say they were drawing when producing alphabet letters;
- say they were writing when producing non-letter-like symbols.

These findings are similar to those from a more experimental study of 48 children carried out in Burgundy by Jean Emile Gombert and Michel Fayol in order to study differentiation between writing and drawing. There were three groups of children (3–4 year olds; 4–5 year olds and 5–6 year olds), none of whom had yet been formally taught to read or write.[4] All were in nursery school, where their teachers regularly wrote the children's names on their drawings and encouraged the children to do the same. In the study, the children were asked to do several things including:

- trying to write *chat, chapeau, pain, lapin, cheval* and *chevaux*;
- to draw these things (*cat, hat, bread, rabbit, horse and horses*);
- to write their name.

A range of types of writing resulted including:

- scribbling
- wavy lines ('scribble streamers')
- circles
- pseudo-letters
- letters from the child's name
- other letters.

However, as in Anne Dyson's study, there was no reliable evidence of pictorial representation of writing being part of children's literacy development.

So, what are the indications that children are beginning to distinguish between drawing and writing? According to the studies of Emilia Ferreiro and

Ana Teborosky in Buenos Aires, a key insight occurs when children use the definite or indefinite article when referring to their drawing (e.g., 'the bus' or 'a bus'), but *not* when they are referring to their writing, ('bus'):[5]

Figure 4.8

a *'the bus' (or 'a bus')*   b *'bus'*

This subtle distinction suggests that they are beginning to realise that writing is not just lines or marks, but that it represents something beyond the objects themselves. This realisation is the beginning of their learning of what Lev Vygotsky, the Russian psychologist, called the 'transparency of language'.[6]

This realisation is also the key to learning the 'sign concept'. The sign concept involves the understanding that marks like letters and words are used in an arbitrary but consistent way to stand for something else and to communicate meaning.

Letter-like Forms

Children's understanding of the sign concept is further shown when letter-like forms (signs) are separated from their drawings (shapes). Tom Gorman and Greg Brooks observed examples such as the one in Figure 4.9 in their evaluation of the Family Literacy programme. This programme was established in four areas of England in 1993 by the Basic Skills Agency.[7]

Children may take a little time to learn the basic principles on which a particular writing system is based. As was discussed in Chapter 2, written English uses alphabetic letters to represent speech sounds (phonemes). Other writing systems use written characters to represent words, ideas, syllables or units of meaning (morphemes).

Ferreiro and Teborosky have reported how children may experiment with other systems before adopting the one used in their own culture. Ferreiro has noted the following in Spanish-speaking children:

Figure 4.9

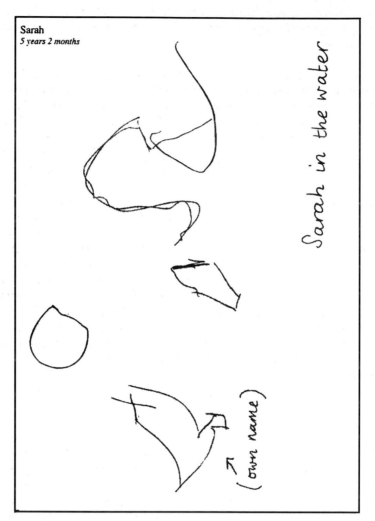

- They may assume a concrete link between writing and the size of the object or person who is represented. For instance, they may write their name and then write a parent's name 'with bigger letters because mummy is big'.
- They may assume that there should be different writing for different objects. For instance, they may repeat a string of letters for plurals, e.g.:
    PO PO PO for *patos* ('ducks') (*not* pronounced as 'duck, duck, duck').
- They may assume that each letter represents a word or syllable and may at first use syllables, rather than phonemes, in trying to write some words e.g.:
    PO for *pato* ('duck'): two syllables, two letters
    AIOA for *mariposa* ('butterfly'): four letters, four syllables.

- They may interpret a text with an accompanying picture (*los animales están, en al rio*: the animals are on the river) as a series of names (*mariposa, pescado, pájaro, plantas, flores, pato*: butterfly, fish, bird, plants, flowers, duck).

Ferreiro argues that such interpretations are not signs of 'confusion', but of the tentative hypotheses which children make. The oral symbol (the spoken word) is probably first conceived as a single entity without recognisable parts. When children realise that they need to make changes in their writing to show different meanings, they may first assume that these can be shown 'logically'. They may use more or fewer letters, larger or smaller letters and so on. Ferreiro suggests that children gradually learn about the alphabetic systems of Spanish, English and other languages by having to resolve tensions between what they write, observe and come to understand. This eventually leads on to them discovering the sound relationship between the writing on the object.[8]

Not everyone is completely sympathetic to these accounts. Pam Czerniewska, the former director of the UK National Writing Project, is not convinced of the experimental methods, which do not include unprompted writing.[9] Charles Temple and his colleagues in the USA suggest that the conclusions drawn from observations in the South American research are different from those of his own. He adds that some of the children's notions of writing reported by Ferreiro and Teberosky (such as the 'duck, duck, duck' example) appear to be rather 'exotic' and may not be representative of general trends.[10] There is, however, more agreement about the central importance of children writing their own name.

Children's Own Names

As children learn to write their own names, they are given direct evidence that some of their tentative hypotheses about writing may not be completely valid. Writing their name also forms a kind of 'repertory' from which other learning can grow. From this store of familiar and personally important alphabetic letters, learning can follow several directions. Marie Clay has shown how these directions reflect certain principles:[11]

Figure 4.10 Use of various kinds of 'recurring principle' for letter-like forms

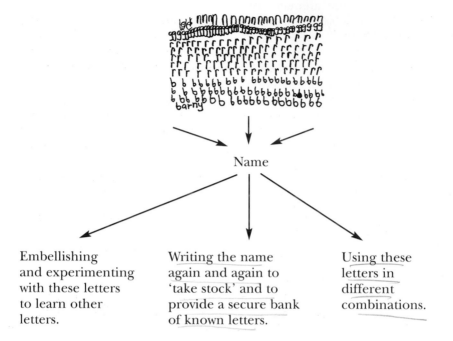

Name

Embellishing
and experimenting
with these letters
to learn other
letters.

Writing the name
again and again to
'take stock' and to
provide a secure bank
of known letters.

Using these
letters in
different
combinations.

Figure 4.11

a 'flexibility principle'

b 'inventory principle'

c 'generative principle'

Letter Formation

As Tom Gorman and Greg Brooks point out, learning to write letters correctly involves very careful observation, hand control and co-ordination. Moreover, children come across many different types and sizes of script. Learning to use the particular forms of script used by teachers may require a great deal of practice.

Surprisingly, many books on emergent or developmental writing give very little attention to letter formation. This is unfortunate because important research has been undertaken in recent years that provides insight into what children have to learn in order to establish efficient contact between pencil and paper. There is much which can go wrong.

One of the most authoritative handwriting researchers, Rosemary Sassoon, alerts us to a number of concepts that govern our writing system:[12]

1 **Direction**: written English is arranged from left to right and top to bottom down the page.
2 **Movement**: letters have correct movements, with definite starting and exit points.
3 **Height**: letters have specific height differences.
4 Several letters are **mirror images** of each other and may need extra care in teaching. Depending on various type faces these can include b-d; m-w; n-u; p-q.
5 **Capital and lower case** letters are used differently.
6 **Spaces** are used consistently between letters and words.

Sassoon's research has convinced her that few of these concepts come naturally to children. What is more, her investigations have warned her that, unless errors in relation to this learning are corrected early on, they may prove difficult to alter later.

Learning a Second Writing System

Rosemary Sassoon has also drawn up a comparison between the concepts underlying the English alphabet and the concepts underlying other writing systems.[13] Some of the principal differences are set out below, together with her advice for dealing with them when English is learned as an additional language.

Table 4.1

	English	Other writing systems	What to do
Direction	Normally set out left–right and top-bottom	Some writing systems are right–left (e.g. Arabic and Hebrew). Others can be written bottom–top (e.g. Japanese).	Place a strip of coloured paper at the point where the line should start. Perhaps add arrows to indicate direction.
Movement	Letters need to be formed in particular ways to assist fluency and subsequent joins.	Most writing systems have strict rules about order in which strokes should be written.	Avoid incorrect movements becoming automated. Use three modes of teaching: 1. visual (demonstration); 2. kinaesthetic (feeling the movement); 3. oral (explanation – e.g., for an e, 'start at the middle and go up and round').
Height and proportions	Clear height differentials between upper and most lower case letters.	Some writing systems have heights clearly defined within four lines, some between two, and some have none. Others have characters that are specifically arranged within a square frame (e.g. Chinese). In Arabic, the heights of letters vary according to their position in the word. Some Indian scripts hang from a top line.	Correct height differentials affect legibility. Letters can be taught as groups (e.g. **bdhkl** are the same height and need ascending strokes); **gjpqy** are the same height and need descending strokes). Guidelines can help, especially a baseline in English.
Capital and lower case	English has two sets of letters.	Some alphabets (e.g. Cyrillic) use mainly capital letters in print. Some traditionally did not have capital letters at all (e.g. Arabic and Hebrew). Others use bolder	In English, two forms of letters need to be learned, together with their different movements. The most troublesome pairs are **Dd**, **Ee**, **Ff**, **Mm** and **Nn**.

		characters where capitals would occur (e.g. Chinese and Japanese).	
Spaces	English separates words and characters, except when a joined hand is used. Then, only words are separated.	Writing systems have different rules for spacing. Hebrew had separate letters. Arabic is a joined hand.	When learning to write in English, pupils can be reminded as follows. The usual space between words should be that of a letter of the size that is being written.

It is sometimes argued that children can benefit from being freed from the burdens of skill acquisition and allowed to explore the richness and diversity of written language. An important related question is, however, how far this diversity can be authentically and explored satisfactorily (for both learner, teacher and parent) if children are allowed to persist with a random mix of capital and lower case letters, or writing from right to left, or beginning the formation of **g** or **p** at the tail, and so on. Such habits may reflect their own 'logic', but it is not clear how such errors can be put right if teachers and parents are not encouraged to assist systematically with them.

It is also sometimes assumed that environmental print can provide the necessary model. Research by Linnea Ehri and her colleagues in New York, however, has shown that children also need some awareness of the role of letters in words. This awareness helps them to transfer their learning from one context to another.[14]

Teachers and parents can provide environmental print of another kind, by scribing and modelling their dictated messages for them. Similarly, adults can provide a 'live commentary' on whatever features of the writing are of interest at that time. This can be an early form of the shared writing teaching approach that is now a central part of the National Literacy Strategy in England. Tom Gorman and Greg Brooks provide a number of interesting examples of children writing over, under and copying letters written by an adult.[15]

Figure 4.12

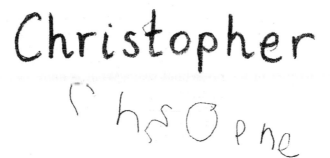

Cautions on Copying

There are, of course, a number of ways in which children can copy or trace which the adult did not intend, particularly if children are not carefully supervised. These include:

- writing from right to left;
- writing the letters in random order;
- forming the letters in inappropriate ways.

Charles Temple provides a helpful discussion on the advantages and limitations of copying in early writing development.[16] He distinguishes between three terms used by Marie Clay: tracing, copying and generating (independent writing without a model, and which may only approximate to conventional forms). Tracing is the easiest of the three and generating the most difficult. Temple reports how some children build up confidence by spontaneously tracing over an adult's writing before generating text on their own. Others prefer to copy first. Generally, though, children tend to stay at a task longer if they are generating writing. He concludes that a balance has to be struck: the balance between encouraging children to take valuable risks and providing also for children who are less mindful than they should be of the ultimately conservative nature of the writing system. Copying may be a useful way of helping children to form a small number of letters and words, but excessive copying can reduce motivation and opportunities for learning.

The Significance of Name Writing

According to several studies, children being able to write their own name correctly and accurately represents a significant point in their development. Children's handwriting skill (as measured by their ability to write their name without a model) has been found to be correlated with a number of aspects of writing at 7 years by Peter Blatchford at the London Institute of Education.[17] He compared the handwriting skills of 331 children on entry to school and their performance in writing narrative and descriptions at age 7. This association still held even four years later. Indeed, at that point, handwriting skill at 5 was a better predictor of reading at 11 than any other factor (letter identification, vocabulary, word matching or concepts about print).[18] Blatchford found that indicators of pre-school parental teaching and vocabulary at age 4 were also associated with writing performance at age 7. This association was greater than measures of knowledge of literacy and experience of books. The findings support the importance of parents helping and supporting writing in the pre-school years. What is more, according to Rosemary Sassoon, children being able to write their own name is a watershed. It is the time to teach letterforms, whatever children's previous inclinations to scribble or experiment with writing.

Name Writing: Time to Teach?

[handwritten: of importance of teachers]

Rosemary Sassoon gives clear advice. When children can write their names, it is time for teachers – and parents – to ensure that correct letter formation is established. The letters in children's names are those that they write most often. These are the letters that will become most quickly automated. If they are not corrected early on, they are likely to be the ones most difficult to alter.[19]

Even then, though, what is 'correct' is not always self-evident. The formation of some letters such as **f**, **k** and **t** can vary considerably. Parents of pre-school children are strongly advised to obtain a copy of the letterforms adopted by their local school before embarking on regular teaching at home. Nowadays, schools tend to use letterforms that encourage letter joins. The problem with a print script is that all the pressure is on the finishing point at the baseline, rather than on the flowing movement that helps the joins. Sassoon herself has designed a typeface with definite exit strokes, in which printed letters resemble written ones. As can be seen in Figure 4.13, the exit strokes also help to 'clump' the letters together in words.

Figure 4.13

Sassoon Primary was designed to look somewhat like handwriting. Exit strokes clump the words together to make them more easily readable. Line, word, and letter spacing can be varied to help problem readers.

'Sassoon Primary' is the typeface that provides a link between reading and writing. The exit strokes not only mean that the printed letters resemble written ones, but they have a function in clumping the words to accentuate the word shape. Different line, word and letter spacing is suggested for those with reading problems.

Handwriting requires systematic teaching but, as handwriting develops, so too does the need for flexibility. Sassoon argues that the emphasis should be on the hand movement and not so much on neatness. Correct hand movement lays the basis for handwriting to become automatic, legible and adaptable. This may involve: a slow, neat formality when the situation demands it; a faster, less neat, but still legible, style for note-taking and other speedy tasks. In today's world, increasing speed while retaining legibility takes priority over adherence to a specific model.

[handwritten: Importance on getting the early basics accurate]

The Three Ps of the Second R

There are also three alliterative and interdependent factors to consider as children settle into independent writing:

- **Posture**: Anyone sitting down to write should feel comfortable. A sloping surface encourages good posture, although such surfaces are rarely found in todays' schools.
- **Penhold**: The pencil or pen needs to be one that the writer is at home with, in size, shape and feel. The feel of a writing implement includes the point of the pen as well as the barrel and the softness of the lead of a pencil. Pens and pencils are normally held by a tripod of thumb and index and forefingers. Some alternatives may indicate an adjustment to new kinds of pen, which may work best at a different angle to the paper, compared with pencils and fountain pens, and suit some individuals better.
- **Paper position**: This in turn can affect posture. Right-handers are likely to benefit from placing the paper to their right but tilting to the left:

Left-handers are likely to benefit from placing the paper to their left but tilting it to the right:

The paper needs to be tilted so that the writing hand can move freely and the writer can see what is written. If a fountain pen is used, it should be fitted with a left-handed nib. In all these aspects of writing, comfort is the key word.

Looking after Left-Handers

There are whole books about the difficulties that left-handers face in a predominantly right-handed world.[20] The three Ps above apply particularly to them. Left-handers need to be able to sit comfortably in a classroom (not joggling elbows with a right-hander neighbour). They need to position the paper carefully (as mentioned above). They may need to hold the pencil or pen a little higher, in order to free up vision. The latter is especially important, as left-handers write towards their bodies and can easily become cramped up.

It is easy to overlook the importance of handwriting. It can influence an individual's self-concept and be a central link to an individual's educational performance. As will be seen again later in this chapter, swift, well-formed handwriting is closely related to success in spelling. Despite the advent of information and communication technology, handwriting remains the personal and immediate means of graphic communication. People present themselves to the world through their handwriting and are inevitably judged by it.

The Curious Case of Letter-Name Knowledge

As children begin to write, they are likely to show an interest in individual letters, letter names and the speech sounds that these letters most commonly represent. The significance of early letter knowledge in general literacy development involves something of a paradox. In two other papers, Peter Blatchford and his colleagues report a significant association between children's letter identification when they began school and the children's subsequent reading attainment. In a separate study of over 700 children, the naming and sounding of alphabet letters at the end of the Reception year (aged 5) were compared with the reading scores at the end of Year 1 (aged 6). Blatchford *et al.* found that there was an even higher association between letter-naming and later reading attainment than between letter-sounding and later reading attainment.[21] Blatchford is at pains to point out that these correlations do not imply a causal relationship, but they do draw attention to the significance of letter-name knowledge in early literacy development.

Jeni Riley, also at the London Institute, notes that similar findings about letter-name knowledge were reported as long ago as 1967 by Jeanne Chall. Riley's own research also produced similar findings as recently as 1996, from her study of 191 children. She points out, however, that the results on later attainment from the direct teaching of letter names have been largely inconclusive.[22] The explanation for this apparent paradox may be as follows:

- Letter knowledge is an indication of broader literacy experience and learning.
- Names provide an unambiguous way of referring to alphabetic letters as 'objects', particularly if children have been taught the alphabet at an early age.
- Knowing the alphabet provides 'pegs' on which to hang the visual recognition of individual letters as objects.[23]
- Learning to read and write, however, involves something more than just recognising objects and naming them. It involves treating letters as 'symbols' that represent sounds.
- Thus the early letter-name knowledge and recognition provide a concrete foundation on which the symbolic learning of letter-sound correspondences can be built.[24]

Early Writing: A Question of Stages?

Various attempts have been made to establish stages in writing development in the 3–13 age-range and several models are set out in **Chapter 9**. In relation to early writing, these attempts have sometimes focused on early reading and spelling and several examples are set out in Table 4.2. One of the few research studies to focus on early writing as a whole came from the Beginning Writing group at the University of East Anglia, led by John Nicholls. This group constructed the following model to outline writing development up to the age of 9 or so.[25]

Table 4.2   Early writing development: an introductory model

	Kind of writing produced:	A child is learning:	
		Composing aspect	Performing aspect
Orientation towards writing	Scribble text – with or without illustration	(i) How writing differs from drawing (ii) Concept of 'word'	(i) To pay attention to print (ii) To control a writing implement (iii) To write across the page from left to right (iv) To produce some letter-like shapes.
Early text-making	Writing which the child can read and which includes some conventional letters	(i) To choose own words to make a written message (ii) Concepts of 'letter' and 'word structure'	(i) To form and orient letters (ii) To control letter size (iii) To use letters to make words (iv) To leave spaces between words
Initial independent writing	Simple texts which can be read, at least in part, by others	(i) How to produce messages that others can read. (ii) Concepts of 'sentence' and 'total text'	(i) To organise words into sentences (ii) To distinguish between upper- and lower-case letters (iii) How to spell some familiar words (iv) To spell some words by sound
Associative writing	Fairly accurate and fluent texts in which ideas are set down without much difficulty	(i) How to write extended, coherent and fairly accurate texts (ii) Concepts of 'story', 'report' and 'spelling rules'	(i) To link sentences (ii) To use some punctuation (iii) To use conventional spelling patterns (iv) To monitor and alter text
Beyond Associative Writing	Texts using different genre schemes, e.g. personal narratives, reports, explanations etc.	(i) How to plan a text in terms of the reader's needs and the writer's intentions (ii) Concepts of 'audience' and 'point of view'	(i) To control tense sequence (ii) To produce complex sentences (iii) To maintain cohesion, both within and between sentences (iv) To revise text

As can be seen, the model makes a clear separation between composing and performing, similar to that outlined in **Chapter 3**. The model also makes interesting links between the kinds of writing undertaken in the pre-school years and the writing skills that are often outlined in various National Curriculum documents.

The Beginning Writing model has been criticised by Pam Czerniewska, director of the 1985–1988 National Writing Project in England and Wales. She points out that it is misleading to plot writing as involving linear development from 'word' to 'sentence' and 'story'. It may be more valid to see early writing as more recursive. Three year olds write what to them are stories and then learn to refine their story-writing abilities over time. Similarly, Czerniewska reminds us of the socio-cultural context in which writing is undertaken. What is written about and why is likely to reflect the values and priorities of the contexts which institutions create. Understanding early writing means taking account of these contexts and keeping them under critical review.[26]

Nevertheless, the Beginning Writing model is one of the few to identify some key markers towards independence, fluency and accuracy in writing a range of texts. These markers are taken up in the reference to baseline assessments later in this chapter. Other models of early writing development have been less wide-ranging and have focused more on specific skills, particularly spelling and the links with reading.

An exception to this trend was a study of young children's writing strategies undertaken by Robert Bates at the University of Leeds. The study focused on the planning strategies of Year 1 children (5–6 year olds).[27] In particular, it looked at the ways in which their non-chronological writing, related to a zoo visit, was supported by a variety of 'pre-text-forming' strategies. These strategies included drawing, talking, question-generation, note-making and the use of a matrix grid. The findings demonstrated considerable individual differences in children's favoured composing behaviours. The findings also supported the conclusions of earlier studies regarding children's use of writing plans.[28] Drawing, talking and some note-making formats (e.g. matrices) were rarely used spontaneously to structure written texts. Plans of different formats were used far more as sources of content information than as potential strategies for organising ideas. The study offered further confirmation that the relationships between experience, composing and writing are less straightforward than is sometimes assumed.

Early Independent Writing with Approximated Spelling

As children gain control of individual letter forms, they may begin to write independently, even though they may not fully realise how the letters represent speech sounds. A number of studies in recent years have suggested how early understanding of the spelling system seems to develop. One of the most influential studies was written by Glenda Bissex who reports the spelling development of her son, Paul, in her book *GNYS AT WRK*.[29]

The book begins with Paul's early 'invented spelling' at the age of 5. By this time, he could correctly form the letters of the alphabet. Paul had clearly grown up in an advantaged home. He had been read to almost nightly since he was aged one and he had his own collection of books, a set of wooden letters, magnetic letters and rubber letter stamps. His parents had frequently referred to letter names (probably singing the alphabet to the tune of *Twinkle, Twinkle Little Star*). He had watched *Sesame Street* on television since he was three and knew the sounds of some consonants. He would write his own name, enjoyed writing letters and had access to paper, pencil, crayons, magic markers and a typewriter. He was an only child, living in the country, and he had 'long stretches of solitude'. It is important to keep these background factors in mind, because Glenda Bissex's work has sometimes been used for generalisations that may not be necessarily appropriate for children from different kinds of backgrounds. Bissex reports that Paul had not been given instruction in letter formation by his family. However, it seems reasonable to suggest that Paul may have learned a good deal about this from specific parts of *Sesame Street*.

Development in Spelling

GNYS AT WRK has been used by Richard Gentry in North Carolina to outline a stage model of spelling development, which is further discussed in **Chapter 8**.[30] Its main stages are as follows:

1   'Pre-Communicative': Using symbols from the alphabet to represent words.
2   'Semi-phonetic': First attempts to use an alphabetic system.
3   'Phonetic': A complete mapping of sounds and letters.
4   'Transitional': Some phonetic and some conventional spelling.
5   'Conventional': The basis of a knowledge of English orthography is firmly established.

SPELLING IN CONTEXT

It is important to bear in mind several cautions about such stage models, which attempt to map out complex patterns of thinking and behaviour.

It is not always possible to place a child at a stage from a small sample of writing. Some researchers have expressed reservations about this.[31] Features of more than one stage may be found in a piece of writing as a child's spelling moves from one stage to the next. At the same time, Gentry's model does seem to provide a clear sense of direction. There is little evidence that spelling development substantially regresses once one stage of development is reached.

Another caution is that development is fostered by purposeful writing and sympathetic adult support. Glenda Bissex reports that even within one stage of development, the phonetic, Paul wrote signs, lists, notes, letters, labels and captions, stories, greeting cards, game boards, directions and statements.

It is also important to recognise that parents and teachers can have a great deal of influence on children's spelling. In fact, in an original study of nearly 1,000 9-10 year old children, another researcher, Margaret Peters, found that success in spelling was influenced more by what teachers did than by any other factor.[32]

We can sense the impact of parental support in *GNYS AT WRK*. Bissex reports that Paul's spelling only remained at the semi-phonetic stage for a few weeks. He seems to have benefited from encouragement to leave spaces between words, from being supplied with letter sound correspondences and from parental encouragement and interest.

A third caution is that spelling development should be related to reading development. As was discussed in **Chapter 2**, written English is an alphabetic system in which alphabet letters are used to represent speech sounds. However, as was indicated in **Chapter 3**, spelling is not the flip-side of reading. In fact, these two skills develop out of step with each other and learning to be literate involves a kind of 'cross-over' between these two skills:

- Children may try to begin to read by using a logographic approach, attending to and remembering whole words.
- Children may try to begin to spell by using an alphabetic approach, trying to represent the sounds in words.
- Children will develop as readers by using phonological knowledge which partly comes from alphabetic spelling to decode unfamiliar words.
- Children will develop as spellers by using the orthographic knowledge that comes from their reading, in particular from remembering the look of words and common strings of letters.

Uta Frith, who is responsible for one of the best-known stage models, has pointed out that reading and spelling act as 'pacemakers' for each other in the journey towards 'orthographic' (conventional) reading and writing.[33] The precise way in which these pacemakers interact is a matter of debate. Some researchers suggest that children go through a 'logographic' stage in both reading and spelling, where they treat words as wholes, although others suggest that this is much more evident in reading. Children seem intuitively to use their phonological knowledge much more in their early writing than they do in their early reading. The main point is, though, that children need to draw on their learning from the one in order to develop their learning in the other.

The Pace-Maker Links Between Reading and Spelling

Figure 4.14 attempts to indicate the nature of these links and the ways in which one skill may assist the other.

Figure 4.14

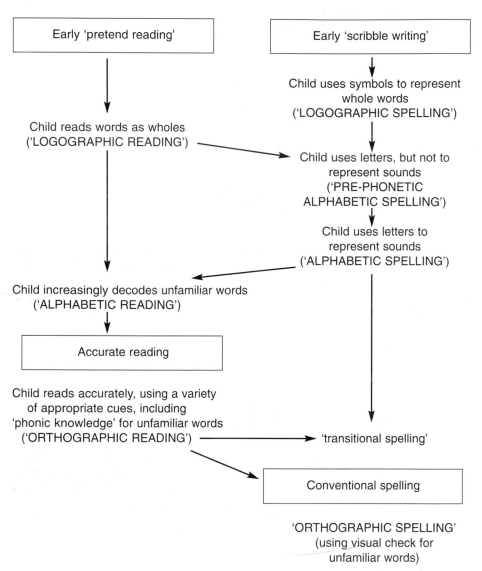

Peter Bryant and Lynette Bradley have suggested, on the basis of their work at the University of Oxford, the need for the use of these links. Sometimes children can read words that they cannot spell and can spell words that they cannot read.[34]

These links are further helped by other sources of knowledge and skill. Fluent reading skill comes from a suitable combination of several kinds of cue, what the National Literacy Strategy in England calls the 'searchlights' of reading. These comprise the recognition of familiar words and groups of letters ('graphic knowledge'), grammatical knowledge of word order and contextual understanding.[35]

These can be shown diagrammatically, as in Figure 4.15:

Figure 4.15

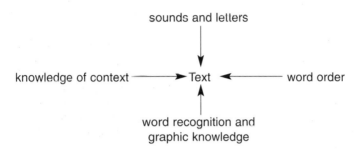

The key to reading unfamiliar words is phonological knowledge. Contextual and other cues may assist but, in themselves, they are not enough. Readers ultimately have to map the sounds in words onto the letters in words. This mapping helps young learners to read words they have never seen before, e.g.:[36]

Hackmatack

Hypermetropical

Accurate spelling skill, on the other hand, only partly comes from attending to the sounds that learners can hear in words. Successful spelling comes more from the look and the kinaesthetic 'feel' of words. This feel is the result of successive hand movements in writing common letter strings over and over again: *-ould, -ing, -ed, th-, bl-* and so on. Swift and well-formed handwriting provides good support for this facility. The key to writing unfamiliar words is orthographic knowledge, writing down attempts to see if they look right:

~~expadition~~ ~~expedition~~ expedition

Dealing with Difficulties in Reading and Spelling

Two teaching approaches have been developed in recent years that help to exploit those links between early reading and writing: making and breaking words and the use of word boxes. Both approaches are based on children's identified needs as they try to read connected text and involve synthetic and analytic approaches. Figure 4.16 below indicates the significance of the approaches by slotting them into the main features of Figure 4.14.

Figure 4.16

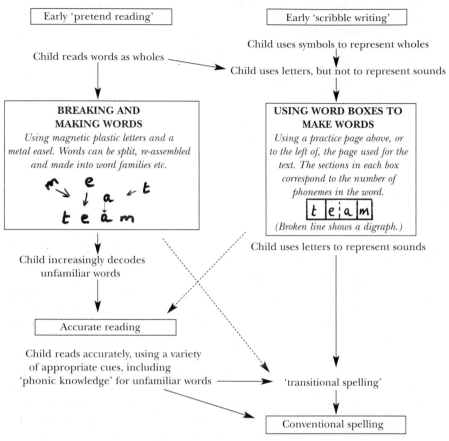

These practices are now well established as part of the Reading Recovery programme which was developed in New Zealand in the 1970s. The programme has been widely used in several other countries, including the United Kingdom.[37] Reading Recovery integrates six teaching approaches which exploit several important links, between reading and writing and between decoding and comprehension.

1 Child re-reads some books that have been read previously.
2 Child reads a book that was introduced in the previous session, while the teacher uses a running record to identify learning needs.
3 On the basis of the child's needs, the teacher helps the child to make and break words.
4 The child writes in response to the reading and attempts unfamiliar words on a practice page. The teacher draws word boxes for these words,

divided with one section for each sound (phoneme). Digraphs (two letters representing one sound) are indicated by dividing a section by a dotted line.

5   The teacher writes out what the child has written on a strip of card and cuts it up in individual words. These words can be re-assembled and banked for future use.

6   The teacher introduces a new book that has similar demands, or slightly more demands, than the book just read.

Reading Recovery has been discussed in many publications, but the wider implications of its teaching approaches for mainstream provision are not always appreciated.

'Invented Spelling': Useful but not Enough

Reading Recovery is perhaps the best-known example of links being made between reading and spelling while ensuring that children continue to tackle continuous text. Further support for the way spelling approximations can assist early literacy comes from Linda Clarke's research in Ottawa.[38] She investigated the effects of using invented and traditional spelling on the reading and spelling of one hundred 6 year olds over a four-month period. In the post-tests, children using invented spelling had significantly greater skill in spelling and in word analysis in reading, but not in flash card recognition, than children using traditional spelling. Most of the gains in spelling and reading were found in children whose pre-tests scores were low. These findings again suggest the importance of making links between reading and writing and of allowing children the opportunity of approximating words that they do not know. As Marilyn Jager Adams suggests, using spelling approximations may help low attaining children to develop phonemic awareness in order to confront holes in their knowledge.[39]

Phonemic awareness plays a key role in the learning of alphabetic writing systems like English. But in learning to spell it is not enough. If children are encouraged to invent spelling, they will also benefit from feedback from teachers on why some approximations are inappropriate. Well-informed teaching will also alert children to related spelling patterns to be found in shared, guided and independent reading. In this way children can continue to experience the multi-faceted nature of the English writing system with its subtle combinations of grammar, meaning and sound-symbol relationships. Understanding how this combination can work is crucial in the development from transitional to conventional spelling.

Transitional Spelling and Grammar

There have been several recent studies that have examined aspects of children's transitional spelling in greater detail. As the previous chapter indicated, there has been increasing interest in how conventional spelling is influenced by children's understanding of the grammatical function of words. The same sound is often spelled differently in different words for entirely grammatical reasons. The words 'kissed' and 'gist' have the same final phoneme but are spelled differently because the first uses 'ed' to show a past tense of a regular verb. Peter Bryant's studies have convinced him that there is a strong link between children's knowledge and awareness of grammar and their success in learning to spell and that this has important educational implications.[40] Bryant and his colleagues at Oxford University have studied children's spelling of words with apostrophes. The meanings of the sentences 'I saw the boys sail' and 'I saw the boy's sail' are very different. The difference is shown by the presence or absence of an apostrophe that has an entirely grammatical base. Curiously, the understanding of the apostrophe has until recently been largely overlooked in studies of children's reading and spelling.

Bryant's studies indicate that the apostrophe causes children in the 9–11 age-range a great deal of difficulty, even though they have spelling skills that are normal for their age. Before they are taught the apostrophe, they rarely use it and, when they do use it, they are as likely to put it in the wrong kind of word as in the right one.

Children of this age may not even know what an apostrophe is: one child suggested that it was a follower of Jesus ('apostle'). Bryant's research showed that, after only 30 minutes of group teaching, children were much more likely to use apostrophes correctly to show possession. However, it was much more difficult to provide teaching that discouraged them from continuing to include apostrophes incorrectly in the spelling of plurals. In another study, it was found that children seem to find it easier to learn the apostrophe for the contraction of two words ('it is' – 'it's') than to show possession.

The studies did show, though, that there is a relationship between children's explicit awareness of the relationship with words showing possession and their use of apostrophes in these words. Interestingly, a relationship was not found between children's explicit awareness of the relationship with genitive words and its use in contractions, once age and spelling skill had been taken into account.

Bryant's studies in this area suggest that children's progress through the transitional stage in spelling development may be broken down in the following way:

PHONETIC STAGE

Frequent phonetic spelling with little use of conventional spellings of morphemes, e.g.: *kist* for kissed, *slept* for slept, *soft* for soft

TRANSITIONAL STAGE

a) Children show some awareness that the 'ed' morpheme could be used instead of 't' in generalisations to verbs but use it in 'over-generalisations' to nouns as well, e.g.: *kissed* for kissed, *sleped* for slept, *sofed* for soft

b) Children realise that the '-ed' ending indicates the past tense in verbs, but generalise it to include irregular verbs as well, e.g.: *kissed* for kissed, *sleped* for slept, *soft* for soft

CONVENTIONAL SPELLING

Children use '-ed' spellings only with regular past tense verbs, e.g.: *kissed* for kissed, *slept* for slept, *soft* for soft

Convincing Contexts for Encouraging Writing

In pulling some of the central ideas of this chapter together, the following questions are worth asking whenever children are involved in writing:

- Are they helped to understand why we need to write?
- Are they encouraged to think about the purpose and audience?
- Are they assisted to take an interest in the different aspects of writing, such as spelling, word choice, word order, punctuation and layout?[41]

These suggestions receive support from a variety of studies that have tried to characterise the conditions in homes and schools that seem particularly to support early writing development.

Helpful Classroom Conditions

Brian Cambourne has spent a great deal of time observing children writing in Australian schools. He suggests that the following conditions are likely to promote literacy learning, particularly if they are used together:[42]

Immersion in meaningful print: being surrounded by print; having access to books, notices, posters, songs and poems; being read to.

Demonstration: adults writing in front of pupils and talking about what is involved in writing.

Expectations: teachers and parents providing strong messages that writing is important and that children's writing is valued.

Responsibility: pupils taking responsibility for deciding what to pay attention to.

Employment: regularly using writing in a variety of contexts for a variety of purposes.

Approximation: encouraging and accepting approximations that are part of 'having a go'.

Response: adults giving informative and non-threatening feedback to children's efforts to communicate.

Engagement: pupils actively participating in language events. This is the essential condition, on which the effectiveness of the other conditions is based.

Cambourne's suggestions have a certain intuitive appeal to them. Several of the conditions have been very evident in British classrooms for some years; others have been more recently provided because of the influence of the National Curriculum and National Literacy Strategy. Others, particularly approximation and response, are very much part of the ethos created by individual teachers and sustained on a day-to-day basis. Of all the conditions, engagement is perhaps the most difficult to engender, but it is more likely if the other conditions are in place.[43]

Helpful Home Conditions

The home conditions which support writing have been less extensively studied. One of the most systematic studies was carried out over two years in the industrial North East of the USA by a team from Harvard University. The findings are reported in two volumes written by Jeanne Chall and Catherine Snow and their respective colleagues.[44] The study was a longitudinal one of 30 families. Narrative and expository writing samples were collected from the 7, 9 and 11 year old children and again a year later.

It is important to note that this research was concentrated on low income families, who had limited resources and who often lived in crowded housing. The research identifies factors that help typify 'resilient' families, who created circumstances to help children become good learners, despite the difficulties that the family faced.

The index of writing quality was found to be significantly related to a range of practices in the home, including the family's ability:

- to set rules, e.g. how long and what television is watched;
- to get children to school on time;
- to keep appointments;
- to keep the house fairly neat and organised;
- to organise a variety of after-school activities for children.

This relationship between helpful home conditions and writing attainment was found to be of greatest statistical significance in the case of the 9–10 year old children. It is interesting to speculate on why these home factors appear to influence writing attainment. Catherine Snow and her colleagues suggest that the 'resilient home' may help give children greater confidence. It may give them experience of organising their time to meet goals. It may generally give them 'more to say' when they have the opportunity to write.

Baseline Assessment of Writing

Early writing has been more researched in recent years than many other aspects of writing. Many of the principal findings have confirmed that learning literacy involves different processes from learning to talk. The findings also highlight the key role that teachers can play in complementing and extending the support which many children receive from home.[45] A number of the principal findings have informed central government policy in England, especially in establishing early learning goals for the 'foundation' stage. This stage spans the 3–5 age range and leads on to 'baseline' assessment on entry to school.[46] In the assessment materials put forward by the Qualifications and Curriculum Authority in relation to writing, these goals were first focused on the following scale:

- distinguishing between print and picture in children's own work;
- writing letter type shapes;
- independently writing own name spelt correctly;
- writing words.

Such goals are inevitably debatable, as a recent paper by Cathy Nutbrown of Sheffield University shows.[47] However, the hierarchical relationships between these particular items have been confirmed in research led by Marian Sainsbury at the National Foundation for Educational Research. When the scales were used to assess 372 children in the 4.6–5.1 age-range, the first 'easier' skills provided reliable precursors for the later skills.[48] As Sheila Wolfendale and Geoff Lindsay point out, though, the production of a small number of baseline scores sits uneasily with the richer analysis of a child's learning which recent research and publications have reflected.[49]

This chapter has explored a variety of aspects of early writing development. The next chapter builds on this exploration. It considers the range of writing which children can undertake and how this range can be conceptualised.

Range in Writing

> *True ease in writing comes from art, not chance,*
> *As those move easiest who have learned to dance.*
> (Alexander Pope)[1]

This chapter

- outlines different ways of discussing range in writing
- reviews some teaching approaches for developing certain kinds of writing
- suggests ways of extending range in writing.

The need for well-roundedness in writing

In recent years, it has been increasingly recognised that children need to develop well-rounded writing abilities, so that they can tackle prose and poetry, stories and information, letters and reports, and so on. This is a far cry from the recurrent criticism of attitudes towards school writing in England that were summed up at the beginning of the twentieth century by Sir Philip Hartog.[2] He argued that much of what was done in school at that time did not go beyond writing something, about anything, for no-one in particular. Hartog issued something of a clarion call for the twentieth century: that schooling should be concerned with writing for a particular audience and with a particular object in view.[3] It was not really until the middle years of the century that the call began to be properly heeded.

There are many ways of distinguishing between the different kinds of writing that can make up a repertoire of well-roundedness.

- the WHAT (the forms of the writing)
- the HOW (how the writing is organised)
- the WHY (the aim or purpose)
- the WHO FOR (the audience)
- the WHAT ABOUT (the content)

This chapter will look at each of these in turn and then will show how they can be brought together in different ways. As will be seen, all provide helpful insights and all have some limitations. The chapter will end by trying to draw these different approaches together, to indicate some advantages of taking a broad-based approach to planning for range in writing.

The WHAT: the forms of writing

This approach to ensuring range in writing lays great stress on children being encouraged to write a variety of texts that vary from each other in their *final forms*. The visual features of different types of writing can be seen at work in real-life environments. The approach can gain in authenticity as the main features of a poem, letter, notice, list or recipe are carefully observed, noted and emulated. Curriculum coverage can be easily checked and recorded.

This approach to range is shown in the 2000 National Curriculum for England and Wales (although the National Curriculum also uses several other aspects of range):

Table 5.1

Key Stage 1 (5–7 year olds)	Key Stage 2 (7–11 year olds)
narratives	narrative
poems	poetry
notes	playscript
lists	report
captions	explanation
records	opinion
messages	instruction
instructions	review
	commentary

Key Stage 3 (11–14 year olds)	
stories	summaries
poems	brochures
playscripts	advertisements
autobiography	editorials
screenplays	articles and letters
diaries	conveying opinions
memos	campaign literature
minutes	polemical essays
accounts	reviews
information leaflets	commentaries
prospectuses	articles
plans	essays
records	reports

THE LIMITATIONS OF USING FINAL FORM AS A BASIS FOR 'RANGE'

There are also limitations of encouraging range by form. For instance, the main purpose of the writing may be over-looked. Conventional formats are relatively easy to imitate without appropriate immersion in a realistic communicative context. Children can write letters to the man on the moon. They can write a diary of the classroom hamster. They can write warning notices designed for sites of nuclear waste. The outcomes from such tasks may look effective and may provide useful practice in following conventions of layout. Nevertheless, without the use of an underlying rationale and some attention to other aspects of range, such writing may only have short-term value. Throughout the century, publications from British central government have consistently called for range in writing to be supported by a framework that goes beyond its final form.[4] Such calls have referred to such aspects as aim, audience, content and organisation. For many years it was the last of these that attracted most attention.

The HOW: organisation in writing

For the first half of the twentieth century, range in writing was often referred to in terms of the *mode of organisation.* Many text books for the teaching of English drew upon the work of the nineteenth-century Scottish grammarian, Alexander Bain. Bain identified four ways in which writing could be organised.[5] Frank D'Angelo, at the University of Texas, has summarised Bain's model in the following way:[6]

Table 5.2 Traditional ways of organising writing

mode	**description**	**exposition**	**narrative**	**argument**
focus on	objects of senses	ideas, generalisations	people and events	issues
organisation	space and time	logical analysis and classification	space and time	deduction and induction

Bain's analysis has been influential in the United Kingdom throughout much of the twentieth century. Back in 1931, for instance, the report of the Hadow Committee, *The Primary School,* suggested that older junior children's writing should range over several writing types, narrative, description and some exposition and argument.[7] The 1970s Schools Council report into the development of writing abilities in secondary schools also drew upon these modes. It then went on to concentrate on intentions in writing, particularly James Britton's framework of writing 'functions',[8] which is discussed later. The legacy of Bain's work is also very evident in recent research and publications in North America. James Kinneavy's work at the University of Texas, *The Aims of Discourse and Writing: Basic Modes of Organisation,* draws directly on Bain's earlier work.[9] So, too, do Marlene Scardamalia's investigations in Ottawa into the teaching of the discourse knowledge demanded by different genres.[10]

Such widespread take-up suggests that the modes of text organisation had some deep-seated advantages for helping children to develop range in writing. Bain provides some striking examples of celebrated writers using these modes in accomplished and inspiring ways. However, it is important to note that, in many texts, these modes are rarely used in isolation. Instead they are used selectively and eclectically, according to the task undertaken and the basic purpose for writing. For instance, a novel is likely to be dominated by the used of the narrative mode. It may also be likely to contain descriptions of settings, some expository background information and perhaps some features of argument in an author's commentary.

Katharine Perera, now Professor of Educational Linguistics at Manchester University, has suggested a more modest framework, based on two dimensions:[11]

- from time-related writing (chronological) to non-time-related writing (non-chronological).
- the relationship of the writer to the subject matter and the reader (from 'close' personal writing to 'distant' impersonal writing), indicated particularly by the number and kind of personal pronouns in the text.

The framework, devised with school writing in mind, is set out in Table 5.3.

Table 5.3

◄-------------- easier ---------------- more difficult ----------------►

Writer's relationship to the subject matter and to the reader

	Close personal (known to the writer)	Intermediate personal (unknown to writer)	Distant impersonal
Organisation of subject matter	making use of pronouns he, she, they, I, we, you	making use of pronouns he, she, they (I, we, you)	making use of pronouns it, they
Chronological	e.g. autobiographical account, story	biographical account	account of a process
Non-chronological	e.g. description of a friend	description of a type of person	description of a structure, evaluation of an idea

Perera suggests that it is easy to identify writing at the extremes of the dimensions used. Between the two extremes, there is a large rather indeterminate area of writing that is about people, but people who are not personally known to the writer. Such writing occurs frequently in history and religious education.

THE LIMITATIONS OF USING ORGANISATION AS A BASIS FOR 'RANGE'

Of the three approaches to organisation referred to in Table 5.3, in the last few years Katharine Perera's has probably been the most influential. The chronological–non-chronological distinction was very evident in the first version of the National Curriculum for England and Wales and is still evident in a less clear-cut way in the subsequent versions. However, this distinction has also been subjected to very careful scrutiny in a paper by Howard Gibson and Richard Andrews.[12] They raise a number of concerns:

- The distinction has been used in NC Programmes of Study for Writing in the 5–11 age-range but not for other age-ranges, nor for Reading or Speaking and Listening.

- The distinction has been used ambiguously: reports have been described as 'chronological', whereas news reports have been described as 'non-chronological'.
- The distinction is more of a continuum and, in many texts, a blend of different modes of organisation may be detected.

An emphasis on organisation can be extended to identifying the distinctive features of different texts. As will be seen later in this chapter, there have been several curriculum development projects on this aspect of writing. More generally, though, a focus on organisation needs to be balanced with attention to the purpose of the writing. It also needs to take account of how the final form of the writing relates to the audience for whom it is written. The 'why' and 'who for' are the subject of the next two sections.

The WHY: aims in writing

In the years after the Second World War, there was increasing awareness of the importance of establishing a purpose for the writing that is undertaken in schools. A handbook of suggestions from central government in 1954 warned against the fragmentation of English teaching. It encouraged teachers to help children develop the 'craft' of writing and to plan beyond a 'shapeless transcription of memories and impressions'.[13] Five years later another government report, *Primary Education* stressed the use of first-hand experience, reasons for writing, respect for the reader and a purposeful but not over-anxious approach to accuracy.[14]

The WHY of writing in the 5–11 age-range received an important boost in the 1960s from the 'creative writing' movement, with books like Alec Clegg's *The Excitement of Writing*, Barry Maybury's *Creative Writing for Juniors* and Sheila Lane's *Creative Writing in the Primary School*.[15] These books showed how children could be stimulated – even startled – into writing in entertaining ways about the world around them, particularly about such perennial topics as the weather and the seasons. This approach often results in writing of a distinctly poetic kind, as is shown in the examples below.

Figure 5.1

a

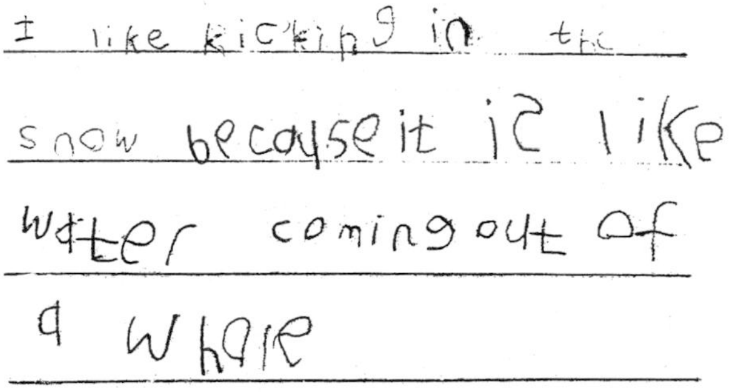

Seasonal weather can promote early creativity, as with the memorable simile written by Haresh (5).

b

Nobodys ——— Yet Mine

I am walking down the riverside,
Nobodys River, and yet ——— my river.
A strip of silver paper,
Stretches into the distance until you
Can only see a glimpse of silver.
Nobodys river or ——— my river,
Is beautiful it reminds me of Love,
I walk back through the twilight ———
——— heading for ——— HOME.

Music moved Karen (11) to write creatively and romantically.

c

Reading is ...

Reading is
words, and pictures, and grammar
on a page in a book.

Reading is
silence...chuckles...interaction with the text
a mouthful of many whispers.

Reading is
a delicate touch of silky, transformed wood
a rustling of turning pages.

Reading is
an everlasting banquet of learning
a meal to feed your imagination.

Reading is
a soothing massage for the brain
an adventure into unknown worlds

Reading is
a key to ultimate knowledge!
power for the mind!

Shared writing with a class of 11 year old children led to this celebration of words and metaphors.

By 1975, the Bullock Committee, set up by the British government to inquire into the teaching of English, reported a 'healthy scepticism' about the value of 'creative writing'. It was especially concerned about such writing being 'pumped up' by the teacher and divorced from real feeling.[16] The report acknowledged the need for a more wide-ranging framework to support the teaching of writing in schools. Such a framework needed to provide for genuine personal expression and growth through writing as well as the construction of the poetic forms beloved of the creative writing approach. It also needed to include the kinds of writing involved in conveying information and which sometimes allowed for pupils explicitly to argue a point of view. The report adopted the framework of three writing *functions*: poetic, expressive and transactional, developed by James Britton and his colleagues at London University.[17]

Britton's framework is one of the best-known British sources of its kind, although a surprisingly large number of writers have mistakenly referred to it as one that focuses on the 'modes'. For instance, Charles Temple's otherwise excellent *The Beginnings of Writing*, has made this error through three editions, over 15 years.[18]

By distinguishing between three main functions, Britton's framework stresses the importance of the writer's *intentions*. Britton suggests that these intentions can be tackled by using one or more modes of organisation, such as narrative, description, exposition or argument, which were discussed earlier in this chapter. The model can be sent out diagrammatically, as in Figure 5.2:

Figure 5.2

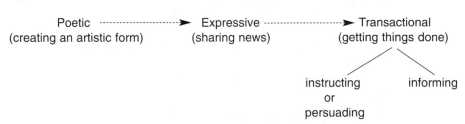

Writing can be placed along this continuum. The expressive category is the central one, describing writing that assumes a close relationship with the reader. Expressive writing may be relatively unstructured and can be seen in everyday 'news' and personal diaries. Britton's framework was particularly influential in giving this kind of writing additional status in schools. He suggested that expressive writing can act as a seedbed for subsequent writing development. It helps children to gain in confidence and fluency as they write about things that they may know more about than anyone. This individuality and authenticity may be sensed in the examples in Figure 5.3.

Figure 5.3

a

when I growup

When I growup I want
to be on televison I want
to be gymnastic I want
to jump very high and
very long .

*Children's ambitions often bring expression and elegance to their writing, as with
Jackie (7).*

b

A thought

I'd like to have a little
dog,
That is black all
over,
With beady eyes and a wagging
tail,
And I would call him
Snuff.
We would jump and play,
walk through the wood, go through
the fields play with a ball, run up
a hill, chase after cats, jump across
streams.
Theres so many things you can
do with a dog but I know I
wont be allowed to have one.

*Continuing opportunities for personal writing allowed Helen (9) to shape and share
her daydream.*

c

KERSPLOSH

One Thursday we were playing football in the afternoon. Somebody took a shot at the goal it missed and shot straight into the stream, I went to the bank to see where it was, then I got down onto some stones in the stream and held onto a branch of a tree that was growing on the bank. Suddenly it snapped and I fell wildly backwards into the cold water. Everybody on the bank laughed at me. I got out and went to go and tell Mr Beard, My boots went squelch, squelch, squelch, squelch, squelch.

Hugh (9) had a true story to tell and made the most of telling it.

d

When I come home from school,
I sit down by the fire
Slowy my eyes drowse
My head dizzy from watching the flames.

My eyes watching the flames
My head drooping.
The flames sound as though their calling me names.
Nearly falling asleep.

I tried to pull myself away
I couldn't keep myself from it
I seemed to be glued there.
And slowy but finally,
I fell asleep.

Fiona (9) infused her writing with a sense of the drowsiness that her writing described.

Poetic writing, similar to the notion of 'creative writing', can be admired for its artistic form, as in novels, poetry, plays and songs. Transactional writing uses the language of getting things done, as in record-keeping, factual reports, essays and letters of complaint.

There are additional sub-categories in the model. These include the kind of writing undertaken in 'dummy run' English exercises, that fail to take up the proper demands of the task to which they relate. 'Dual function' writing, such as a poem deliberately written to effect action, can be dealt with by additional bracketed items – for example, poetic (persuasive).

Other writers have analysed purposes at a deeper level and tried to establish some of the fundamental *aims* of writing. One of the best-known North American publications that deal with the WHY of writing is the framework of *aims* outlined by James Kinneavy at the University of Texas. Kinneavy has discussed and applied his framework in scholarly publications stretching over 25 years. In the preface of Kinneavy's seminal book *The Aims of Discourse*, the author makes it clear that his framework represents an attempt to present a coherent and unified view of the field of English.[19] Kinneavy takes as his basic structure the nature of the language process itself, as represented in the so-called communication triangle. The origins of this can be traced back to Aristotle's *The 'Art' of Rhetoric* over 2000 years ago. Applied to writing, the triangle can be constructed as follows:

Figure 5.4

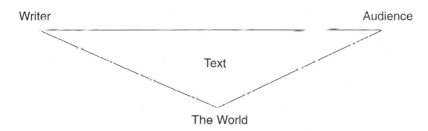

Kinneavy shows how abstractions from the triangle can be made to establish three basic areas of study in English: syntactics, semantics and pragmatics (the study of discourse). In applying the triangle to the latter, he highlights how four basic 'aims' of discourse can be related to the emphasis in the communication process. It can be on either the producer, the audience, the product or the 'reality of the world' to which it refers. These different aims are shown in Figure 5.5:

Figure 5.5

Expressive aims		***Persuasive aims***
('to share news')		***('to persuade')***
e.g. journals, diaries, protests		e.g. advertising, debates, arguments

Literary aims
('to entertain')
e.g. stories, songs, poetry, jokes

Referential aims
('to inform')
e.g. reports, catalogues, including
exploratory aims (questionnaires and interviews)
and **scientific** aims (based on evidence)

In *expressive* writing, the main focus of the communication is on the writer and how the personality of the writer influences what is written. The main feature of expressive writing is the writer's individual *style*.

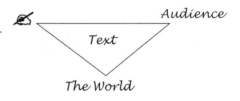

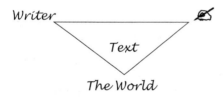

In *persuasive* writing, the main focus of the communication is on the audience and how the writing attempts to change their behaviour or beliefs. The main feature of persuasive writing is the use of *emotional appeals* and *pseudo-logic*.

In *referential* writing, the main focus of the communication is on the reality of the world. The main feature of true referential writing is that it designates or reproduces this reality. (Kinneavy prefers referential to 'expository', as the latter does not distinguish *what* is said from *why* it is said.)

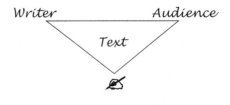

In *literary* writing, the main focus of the communication is on the text itself, as an object capable of being appreciated in its own right. The main feature of true literary writing is on the *structure, unity* and *fit* of the text.

These ideas are used again in the discussion of assessing writing in **Chapter 8**.

This framework underlines some of the distinguishing features of different kinds of writing, in terms of where the writer's aims give greatest emphasis. For instance, 'factual' writing in schools can easily become rather flat, unstructured and generalised. Kinneavy reminds us that such writing may often be best enhanced if its focus is on first-hand experiences, whose reality the writer faithfully tries to reproduce.

Figure 5.6

THE GROWING OF A HYACINTH

Just a little bulb like an onion. As it lies over water for a few weeks, thin white roots start edging themselves to the bottom of the jar with others joining. A sharp speck of green appears from the top of the bulb. The stem grows longer and leaves start sprouting. The roots at the bottom become a tangled mass. At the top of the stem a bud has formed and is gradually opening up. In the middle there is a blue blossom getting bigger and bigger as the bud opens out. As the blossom gets higher its colour deepens. When it is fully formed it only lasts for one short week.

Factual writing is often more convincing if it is underpinned by personal experience and close observation (Lindsey, 9).

THE LIMITATIONS OF USING FUNCTIONS AND AIMS AS A BASIS FOR 'RANGE'

One of the most insightful critiques of James Britton's framework on range has come from Katharine Perera.[20] She makes three main criticisms:

- there are no linguistic features to identify one type of writing from another;
- there is no psycholinguistic evidence of the development from expressive to transactional and poetic that the framework assumes;
- the framework does not reveal anything about the demands that different kinds of writing make on how the writing is organised.

There have also been criticisms of Kinneavy's model:

- the framework is based on written *products*, not language processes;[21]
- there are difficulties in categorising writing in this way, especially where aims are unclear or where pieces that are categorised similarly feel intuitively different;
- how 'pure' the aims of writing are: we write for many reasons.[22]

Nevertheless, theoretical frameworks like those of Britton and Kinneavy can be useful in making us aware of some of the basic purposes for which written language can be used. An awareness of these purposes can help ensure that curriculum provision promotes the kinds of well-roundedness in writing that were outlined at the beginning of this chapter. As Lee Odell warns, skill in fulfilling one kind of aim in writing does not necessarily imply skill in accomplishing another.[23]

Writing for a range of purposes is now well-established in the various British National Curriculum details, as is shown in Table 5.4.

Table 5.4

	England and Wales[24]	Northern Ireland[25]	Scotland[26]
Key Stage 1 (5–7 year olds)	• to communicate to others • to create imaginary worlds • to explore experience • to organise and explain information	• to write for their own amusement and enjoyment • to express their thoughts, feelings and imaginings • to inform and explain • to describe • to narrate • to report • to record findings	• to convey information • to express feelings • to order, clarify, record and reflect upon ideas, experiences and opinions • to give imaginative and aesthetic pleasure.
Additional purposes for Key Stage 2 (7–11 year olds)	• to imagine and explore feelings and ideas • to inform and explain • to persuade • to review and comment	• to persuade • to interpret data • to express a point of view • to give instructions	• successive uses of *personal writing* (to write personal narratives, diaries, journals, letters and free verse) • *functional writing* (to instruct, report, note, list, make diagrams and summarise); • *imaginative writing* (to write stories, poetry, plays, and radio/TV scripts)
Additional purposes for Key Stages 3/4 (11–16 year olds)	• to imagine, explore and entertain • to inform, describe and explain • to persuade, argue and advise • to analyse, review and comment	• to interpret and analyse data • to argue a case • communicate opinions and beliefs • to appreciate differences between spoken and written English	• as above

These lists of purposes clearly show how far British educational thinking has developed since Sir Philip Hartog expressed his concerns at the beginning of this century. Plenty of ideas are now available to ensure that school writing is no longer a vaguely defined something, about a loosely considered anything. There have been similar changes in relation to the third criticism – that writing was often for no-one in particular.

The WHO FOR: audience in writing

James Britton also outlined one of the best-known frameworks of *audience* categories:

Self

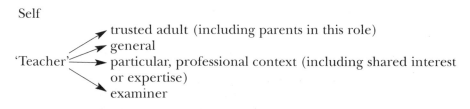

'Teacher' trusted adult (including parents in this role)
general
particular, professional context (including shared interest or expertise)
examiner

Wider known audience (e.g. peer group)

Unknown audience

Britton's work helped to illuminate some of the interpersonal assumptions that underpinned children's writing. His work raised awareness of how sensitively teachers sometimes had to respond.

Figure 5.7

Monday 9th February
         Temptation
I live just down the road from the new Tesco and   came to my house and we had tea at Tesco. When we came out we ran home, gave the change to my mum, and went up the street. After a while we saw   hund his brother and their stepbrother   They ran over to us with their pockets bulging. I asked them what they had in thire but they would not tell us. I was really curious and I begged them to tell me, so they did. They said "You had better not tell anyone or else your dead" Then they said 'we have stolen an pounds worth of Lynx spray from Tesco'. They started spraying it on them and in the air thinking that they were good, but I just felt sorry for them. The next day I went to Tesco and saw them doing it again. I said to them, 'You had better stop doing that because the cameras will catch you and then if the police come you will be dead.' They didn't listen. They said to follow them, so I stupidly did. They told me to nick some sweets. They said that no one was watching, I wanted to stick my hand out and put aload of sweets into my pocket but I couldnot do it, so I refused. They called me names, saying I was a wimp. I felt trapped and empty. I ended up running out. When I got home I told my mum and she told one of the security guards who court them in the act. They are now band from Tescos, but they don't know who told on them. I think stealing is a bad thing because once you start you cant stop, and you can get into serious trouble and get a criminal record.

Provision for personal writing allowed this 11 year old to write cathartically and to use the teacher as a 'trusted adult'.

The extent to which these ideas have become influential can be gauged from the details on audience that have been built into the different versions of the British National Curricula.

Table 5.5

	England and Wales[27]	Northern Ireland[28]	Scotland[29]
5–11 year olds	for: • themselves • teachers • other adults • other children • the class • the wider community • imagined readers	for: • themselves • teachers • parents • adults whom they know well • other pupils	Pupils will write functionally, personally and imaginatively, to convey meaning in language appropriate to audience and purpose.
11–14 year olds	• a large, unknown readership	• pupils in their and other schools • audiences from outside the school	as above

It is easy to overlook the central role of the value of children writing for themselves including, as the Northern Ireland National Curriculum notes, for their own amusement and enjoyment. There may be much to be gained from investigations of how particular formats help in supporting and consolidating learning. Examples might include lists, columns, spider diagrams, grids, bunches of ideas, algorithms and various kinds of brainstorm.[30] Each may help to make learning visible in subtly different ways.

This dimension of 'range' in writing has often been linked to aims and purposes and relatively little research has been done on how children's writing can be specifically varied according to its 'who for'. A concern with audience makes intuitive sense to many teachers. Nevertheless, there is still relatively little known about how children in the 3–13 age-range learn to adjust their writing in this way and about the textual features that are part of this adjustment.[31]

The WHAT ABOUT: the content of writing

Much of the decision-making in British schools about the range of *content* of writing has been reduced by the introduction of a National Curriculum. Yet any multi-subject curriculum brings with it new choices about the way in which writing is used to support learning. The opportunities for writing involving different purposes, audiences, organisation and final forms have to be carefully linked to the content that each subject area provides. Grids such as that in Figure 5.8, which link some basic writing aims to the National

Curriculum subjects for England and Wales, can appear deceptively simple, but they raise important questions.

Figure 5.8

	English	Mathematics	Science	History	Geography	MRE	Music	PE	Design and Technology	Art
to share news										
to entertain										
to inform										
to persuade										

all using appropriate organisation and form

Some questions which it may be useful to ask in connection with Figure 5.8 include:

- Does the writing of personal recounts (in 'to share news') have a place in subjects other than English?
- What might be gained from the writing of poems in Religious Education?
- Which kinds of writing might be enlivened by focusing on the subject matter of PE lessons?
- Which subject areas provide engaging material for the cut and thrust of persuasive writing?

In recent years, there has been an increasing number of publications that give guidance on the kinds of writing that can be promoted in different subject areas.[32] These publications provide a helpful reminder of the importance of the What About in developing range in writing.

REAL-WORLD WRITING AND IMAGINATIVE WRITING

Much of the writing in subjects across the curriculum is predominantly concerned with aspects of the real world. Even the celebrated tradition of creative writing, which was referred to earlier, has often been concerned with embellishing the words and images associated with sensory experiences. Research and publications on children's writing have tended to concentrate on real-world writing. The possibilities of imaginative writing have not been investigated so thoroughly and yet imaginative content provides an important aspect of the content of what is written about.

The importance of the imagination in education has been long recognised, especially in the field of literacy. Yet the definition of imagination is not straightforward. It is a term that dates back to ancient Greece and is used with a variety of applications and implications. In an MEd thesis at the University of Leeds, Michael Smit identified the work of Brian Sutton-Smith at the University of Pennsylvania[33] as providing a particularly helpful framework for studying children's imaginative writing.[34] Sutton-Smith does not apply a single or limited definition but accepts diversity, contradiction and variance. His ideas use six broad areas of definition:

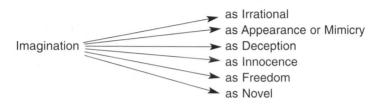

Imagination
- as Irrational
- as Appearance or Mimicry
- as Deception
- as Innocence
- as Freedom
- as Novel

Those who write about imaginative writing tend to draw on one or more of these areas. For instance, Richard Gregory has drawn attention to the internal world of mental experiments.[35] He explores the human quality of 'brain fictions'. Fiction has the immense biological significance of allowing behaviour to follow plans removed from, though sometimes related in subtle ways to, world events. We respond not merely to what happens, but also to what might happen. Indeed, Gregory suggests that at times we may live more by fiction than by fact.

Other writers have argued that imaginative reading, especially of myths, legends and fairy tales help to promote the imaginative mind. Ted Hughes showed how myths provide large-scale accounts of the struggles between the powers of the 'inner world' and the 'outer world'. The inner world contains potentially irrational beliefs and values. The outer world is made up of the stubborn conditions where ordinary people live. He suggested that the reading of the great myths can provide 'blue prints for the imagination'.[36]

Similarly, Bruno Bettelheim has drawn attention to the significance of fairy tales. He argues that the deep inner conflicts that can be traced in primitive drives and violent emotions are not always effectively dealt with in other genres of modern children's literature. Children can be helped to cope with jealousy, aggression and selfishness through the vicarious experiences of fairy tales, which deal directly with them. Fairy tales acknowledge and give vent to the darker side of human nature. They also provide encouragement to us all, by implying that struggles against severe difficulties are an intrinsic part of human existence.[37]

The value of children's imaginative writing has been explored by Helen Cowie.[38] She treads a careful path between two views. One view is that imagination is a deceptive flight from reality, a kind of escapist activity whose place in the curriculum is debatable. The other view is that the internal world of the imagination is a 'real' one, as it provides a means of liberation from and of working through anxieties and emotional conflicts. Cowie argues that it is constructive to focus on the inner experience of the child, but that the resolution of emotional conflicts is only part of the child's imaginative process. The imagination also contributes to social and intellectual development.

Cowie suggests how children's imaginative writing develops in the primary school years. Her analysis is similar to that of Andrew Wilkinson, whose study of affective development through writing in the 8–13 age-range is discussed in **Chapter 9**.[39]

7+	Chains of events; physical character traits; *what* happened rather than *why*.
9+	Empathy with characters; links between growing understanding of people and a wider knowledge of the world.
11+	Greater self-awareness; increasing responsiveness to the feelings of others; growing use of metaphorical language.

These suggestions remind us of the importance of content-based approaches to providing for range in writing. Different curriculum subjects provide specific experiences, ideas and issues that can be tackled in writing through various aims and through organising writing in particular ways. But, when the content of writing is considered, there are many gains from going beyond real-life contexts to the inner world of the imagination. Literature, in particular, feeds the imagination in subtle ways that are sometimes evident in the structure and themes of what children write.

Figure 5.9

a

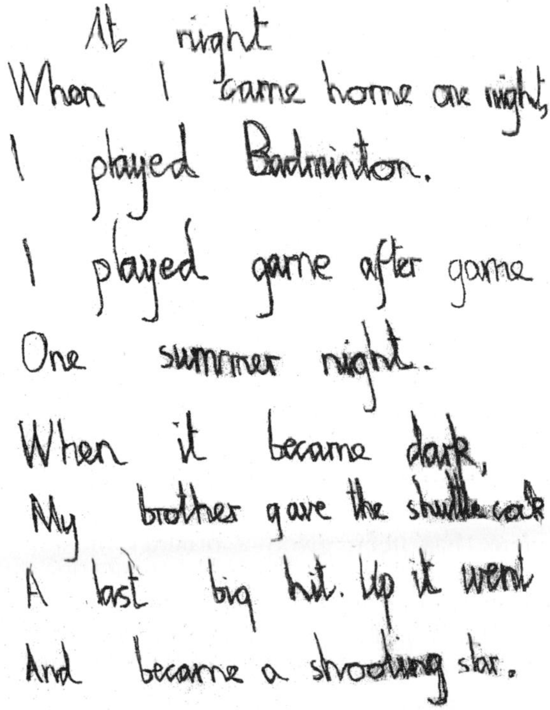

At night
When I came home one night,
I played Badminton.

I played game after game
One summer night.

When it became dark,
My brother gave the shuttlecock
A last big hit. Up it went
And became a shooting star.

Christopher (11) modelled his 'At Night' on David Sutton's poem 'Out On A Limb' b   *It began as quite an ordinary day ...*

It began as quite an ordinary day, the sun was shining and the birds were singing. So I decided to go for a walk.

The park was empty so I went to the pond in the middle, then I sat down beside it and looked up at the sky. Then suddenly the pond water started to drain away! "That's funny" I thought, so I got up and stepped into the empty space and there I saw a tiny little door. I tugged at it and it came open quite easily. Nobody was about so I crawled inside.

When I could stand on my feet again, I had the surprise of my life, it could'nt be true, for there, sitting round a little table were 12 little dwarfs, or elves, or how ever you like to put it.

For a moment I just stood there, with my mouth wide open, speechless. Then I realised what I must look like to them, but they didn't seem to understand my language. They gave me a bowl of .... well, something like oat-meal, so cautiously I took a spoon-full and it seemed quite nice so I carried on. They seemed quite friendly so I stayed for a while, then one of the dwarfs seemed to want me to go with him. "Perhaps there'll make me their queen", I thought. The dwarf led me up some steps and through a door, and to my disappointment I was back where I had started beside the pond. I turned to thank him but he had disappeared, and the pond was filling up with water.

That night when I lay in bed, I thought "how strange, just like Alice through the looking Glass!"

Clare (10) drew upon her leisure reading when writing about an extraordinary day

Recent approaches to range: genre theory

In the late 1980s and through the 1990s, a new set of ideas became influential that drew together several aspects of range in writing. These ideas can be grouped under the general label 'genre theory'. Anyone new to this field might well expect it to be primarily concerned with literary writing. Established dictionary definitions of genre tend to define it in terms of 'a literary or artistic type of style'.[40] However, in literacy education across the world, the term genre has been given a broader meaning. It has been increasingly used to distinguish between different kinds of writing in general.

The main feature of genre theory, though, is that it links writing to wider *social* processes in a way that other ideas about range in writing do not. Genre theory has been used to link what Peter Medway calls 'textual regularities' to what Carolyn Miller refers to as the 'typified rhetorical action', that is, the action which the text is used to accomplish.[41] Genre theory would not normally be used just to explain the features of a set of instructions, such as visual form, the syntax and vocabulary. Genre theory would also be used to show how the instructions were used to influence behaviour within a community and perhaps to highlight their links with sources of power and authority. Instructions for assembling a toy might be studied for how they reflect a significant difference in expertise between designer and user. (This is something I recall from my childhood days as a *Meccano* construction toy enthusiast.) Similarly, instructions on how to behave in a public examination can be studied to identify the ways in which they carry with them implied threats of disqualification and ostracism.

Thus genre theory represents an interesting way of linking text to context. Such theory can provide all kinds of insights for investigating how social processes impinge upon acts of written communication. More controversially, genre theory has been caught up in a number of debates, most notably between North American and Australian writers, which go to the heart of how range in writing can be effectively taught. The debates have centred on the value of explicitly teaching different genres. Such teaching has been seen as particularly necessary because the influential child-centred 'process writing' approaches do not necessarily provide for flexibility and range in children's writing development. At the same time, explicit teaching of certain genres can also be seen as problematic. Such teaching may reflect an acceptance of the status quo in ways that some writers feel uncomfortable about. It is also salutary to note that the effectiveness of this teaching is not easy to demonstrate.

RANGE IN FACTUAL GENRES

As was pointed out in **Chapter 3**, reviews of research by George Hillocks have identified three broad approaches to the teaching of writing. In the presentational approach, teachers set tasks and mark outcomes. In the process approach, teachers set up general procedures, for example encouraging pupils to write several drafts and to seek the comments of other pupils. In the guided approach, teachers develop materials and activities to engage pupils in task-specific processes. The presentational approach has been widely used in Britain, Australia and North America. Only in the last twenty years or so have the other approaches been used on a wider scale. In the USA, the process approach became very influential after intensive case studies by Donald Graves in New Hampshire.

Process writing also became extremely influential in Australia in the 1980s. Despite its altruistic intentions, it has been criticised for favouring already advantaged pupils. As Mary Kalantzis and Bill Cope point out, in process writing classrooms the pupils who are likely to make the most of the 'control' and 'ownership' of writing are pupils from 'print-immersed' homes.[42] They know what text does and they have an inkling how it works. Pupils from less advantaged homes may lack such intuitions. Process writing, with its largely self-selected topics, is likely to recycle pupils' limited genre knowledge. Genres where accomplishment is linked to social influence and power will be further denied them.

Australia has become an influential source of shared and guided teaching approaches that are based on genre theory. Jim Martin at the University of Sydney analysed different kinds of 'factual writing', so that the demands of school literacy could be better understood.[43] His analysis included reports, explanations, procedures, discussions, recounts and narratives.[44] Martin also identified the grammatical features that often distinguish one genre from another. In referring to 'factual' writing, Martin is concerned with writing that refers to 'how things are'. He compares this with other kinds of writing with which children may be more familiar, such as personal narratives or 'recounts'. In writing recounts, children write about things that 'actually happened' (including in their imaginations). They can draw upon the past tense story structures that are widely used in children's literature: 'I went to the shop and bought the beans. Then I brought them home.' In factual writing, children have to learn to use other structures and verb forms such as those set out in Table 5.6.

Table 5.6 – Some factual genres
(the text in these genres often refers to accompanying diagrams)

Genre	Features
Procedure: 'How something is done'	Writing sequenced in generalised ways by using timeless' verbs: • *Instructions*: Imperative clauses in chronological order, e.g. go to the shop, buy the beans, bring them home. • *Directions*: Declarative clauses in simple present tense and again in chronological order e.g. you go to the shop, you buy the beans, you bring them home.
Description: 'What some particular thing is like.' In many ways a description is an example of a report. (See below).	Specific statements often written in the present tense. Extensive use of the verbs 'to be' or 'to have'.
Report: 'What an entire class or group of things is like.'	General statements often written in the present tense. Extensive use of the verbs 'to be' or 'to have'.
Explanation: A reason why a judgement has been made or details of some kind of process.	Opening topic. Logical steps. Simple present tense. Temporal or casual connectives.
Exposition: 'Arguments for why a point of view has been proposed.'[45]	• Exhorting (e.g. editorial, memos, letters to the press). • Analysing (e.g. essays).

OTHER 'NON-FICTION' GENRES

Later Australian genre studies have set out the features of two other kinds of genre: 'discussion' and 'persuasion'. These have been described as 'non-fiction' rather than 'factual', because they go beyond a concern with 'how things are'. These two genres are more concerned with *alternative views* on how things are. The main features of these two genres are summarised in Table 5.7:

Table 5.7 Two discursive genres

Genre	Features
Discussion: 'Considering different viewpoints.'	An introduction to what is being discussed: arguments and evidence for and against. Conclusion and/or recommendation. Present simple tense ('I feel...', 'The local people believe...'). Causal connectives ('As a result...', 'So...' 'Therefore...' etc.)
Persuasion: 'The use of one point of view to change the view of others.'	An opening position statement or 'headline'. Arguments and evidence. A re-statement of the point of view. Present simple tense. Causal connectives. Emotional vocabulary choice and imagery.

This list differs slightly from that adapted by Maureen Lewis and David Wray in the EXEL project at Exeter in their work on 'non-fiction writing', which is discussed later in the chapter. They include recounts and omit exposition and description.[46]

SOME RESERVATIONS ABOUT TEACHING GENRES

This approach has not won universal approval. Even one of the founding fathers of genre theory, Gunther Kress, has expressed several reservations:

- Is it wise to try to categorise texts that do not actually share all the characteristics imposed upon them?
- What if a text is not quite a report, not quite a recount and not quite a procedure?
- How valid is it to encourage the teaching of a 'correct' way to write a report when the world is full of texts that do not seem to fit the generic descriptions put forward by the teacher?[47]

Ironically for someone whose work brought the notion of genre to an international audience, Kress has been concerned not to attach too great an importance to genre theory. Indeed, he has even suggested that he might just as easily have used the term 'mode' when first writing about textual features. Kress seems to use the term mode similarly to how it was used earlier in this chapter.[48] As Cope and Kalantzis acknowledge, Kress prefers to see genre as a device to account for stability and variation from text to text, rather than to classify or model them according to their formal features.[49]

DIFFERENCES BETWEEN AUSTRALIAN AND NORTH AMERICAN GENRE STUDIES

There are also differences between Australian and North American genre studies. One set of ideas has developed in Australia and another in North America and there are clear tensions between the two. The Australian approach to genre studies is very much associated with Michael Halliday's work at the University of Sydney after he became founding Professor of Linguistics in 1976. Ironically he did not actually seem to use the term genre himself in his publications at the time. Halliday developed a theory called 'systemic functional linguistics', a kind of 'linguistics for consumers'. This work sets out to link system and structure in language to its social purpose. It allows grammar teaching to be tied more to how language is used. The choice of words and sentence structure in a text or utterance can be related to the different aspects of its 'register' or style including:

- the *field*: 'what is going on';
- the *tenor* 'who is involved';
- the *mode* 'the role language is playing'. (It is important to note that in this case this use of 'mode' is different from that used earlier in the chapter.)

Australian genre theory grew out of this work, through the research of Jim Martin, Joan Rothery, Frances Christie and others.

North American writers, on the other hand, have tended to develop genre studies from earlier work in 'rhetoric', the scholarly study of discourse. As the work of James Kinneavy at the University of Texas shows, the study of rhetoric can be traced back to the political and legal processes of ancient Greece. In the second half of the twentieth century, North American scholars became increasingly interested in the ways in which the study of rhetoric could contribute to, and be developed through, literacy education. This interest was fostered by several kinds of theory. These include how knowledge is socially constructed and how the meaning of 'speech acts' can be defined by reference to the context and to the participants' understanding of it.

The differences between these two approaches to genre studies are clearly shown in the work of Aviva Freedman and Peter Medway in Ontario. In the introduction to their significantly titled *Genre and the New Rhetoric*, Freedman and Medway argue that the North American and 'Sydney School' approaches are strikingly different:[50]

Table 5.8 Different approaches to genre studies

	North American	Australian
Focus on:	complex relations between text and context	explication of textual features
Genre assumed to be:	evolving and dynamic	relatively static
Priority given to:	study	teaching
Underlying values:	status quo	social change

Frances Christie has provided a reply on behalf of the Australian approach.[51] She has argued that Australian genre studies are not as presumptive nor as concerned with 'static' language models as Freedman and Medway suggest. She also points out that North American genre studies tend to treat genres in too generalised a way and that they would benefit from providing more examples. More specifically, Christie argues that, without analysing texts by using functional grammar that is based on Michael Halliday's work, genre studies will remain little more than 'a running commentary on a text'.

Curiously, all three writers appear to overlook the fact that some practical teaching suggestions were published by North American genre studies in the 1980s. These suggestions, from Marlene Scardamalia and her colleagues in Ontario, are referred to later in the chapter.

INTEGRATING DIFFERENT APPROACHES TO RANGE IN WRITING

The above sections show that there are a great many sources of professional ideas now available to promote range in writing. However, many of these sources tend to concentrate on just one or two ways of considering this range in writing. Very few integrate the purpose and audience with the content, organisation and form of writing. Yet this kind of integration can add valuable breadth and balance to curriculum planning. Without such planning, it is easy to concentrate on one aspect of writing without taking account of its links with other aspects. It is easy to encourage children to write captions without sufficient thought about who might read them or descriptions without attention to why they are being written or stories without consideration of the available content in children's minds. The framework below sets out one possible framework for such planning. It brings together the WHY and WHO FOR with the WHAT and HOW of writing, for both real-life and imaginative content. Three long-established literary genres are included: fiction, poetry and drama.[52] Others could be added, according to the level of planning required.

It needs to be noted that frameworks like this will never capture the full range of considerations when planning to write or to teach writing. Writing is a complex process in which all kinds of subtle influences may be at work. Intuition can play a central role in some tasks. As Howard Gibson and Richard Andrews argue, defining the 'thematic unity' in a text can be difficult and quite subjective.[53] They suggest that it may be more helpful to see many texts as being made up as a series of 'episodes'. These episodes provide thematic unity, in terms of reference to identical participants, location, events or actions. These episodes inhabit a level between the sentences and the overall meaning.

Table 5.9 – Linking different kinds of range in writing

WHY / WHO FOR	WHAT	HOW (using modes *and/or* genres)	WHAT

to 'share news'
    oneself
    friends
    family
for teacher
    other known
    audiences
    unknown
    audiences
    etc.
		by narrating
		
		Non-fiction
		genres e.g.
		by describing recounts
		procedures
		instructions
		directions
		explanations
		discussion
		persuasion
			stories
			poems
			notes
			lists
			captions
			labels
			records
			messages
			instructions
			playscripts
			posters
			commentaries
			letters
			diaries
			memos
			notices
			essays
			newspapers
			magazines
			booklets
			charts
			etc.

to entertain
    oneself
    friends
    family
for teacher
    other known
    audiences
    unknown
    audiences
    etc.
	real life		

to inform
    oneself
    friends
    family
for teacher
    other known
    audiences
    unknown
    audiences
    etc.
	imaginative	by using
		exposition
		
		Literary genres
		e.g.
		poetry
		fiction
		drama	

to persuade
    oneself
    friends
    family
for teacher
    other known
    audiences
    unknown
    audiences
    etc.
		by arguing	

However, the inspection evidence summarised in **Chapter 1** suggests that children and young people do sometimes have too narrow a range of writing experience and that greater variety is needed on several dimensions. The above framework may help indicate where such variety can be developed and the way in which it further promotes well-roundedness in writing. The final sections of this chapter will deal with how this well-roundedness can also be extended in different ways.

EXTENDING RANGE IN NON-FICTION GENRES BY USING 'FRAMES'

The teaching of genres in the United Kingdom has been investigated by David Wray and Maureen Lewis at the University of Exeter. After working extensively with primary teachers, Lewis and Wray suggest that children and teachers can benefit from using specific writing 'frames' to help support them in non-fiction writing.[54] 'Frames' here are taken to mean skeleton outlines of texts. The use of the term is similar to that of Martin Minsky in his 'schema theory' of reading comprehension. Minsky uses the term frames to refer to 'cognitive structures', which help comprehension and recall.[55] Frames in writing are used more to structure communication and include sentence starters, connectives and sentence modifiers. These frames can support children in building early non-fiction writing around the outline structures which frames provide.

Lewis and Wray provide numerous examples of frames, such as the following 'explanation frame':

I want to explain why

There are several reasons for this. The chief reason is

Another reason is

A further reason is

So now you can see why

CAUTIONS ABOUT USING WRITING FRAMES

Lewis and Wray are quick to point out that writing frames are not intended to be used as skills exercises. Instead, they are intended to be used as a kind of prompt, eventually to be dispensed with, as children begin to adopt the features of a genre for themselves. Frames do not have any set form, but can be provided by the teacher as a form of 'scaffolding', drafted by the pupil or negotiated between the two, according to circumstances and needs.

This approach is relatively new and will benefit from further investigation. There may be risks of children being channelled into rather stereotyped writing or of children not effectively transferring learning to new tasks and contexts. Especially in more discursive and persuasive tasks, the organisation of sentence structure of a text may not be so easy to generalise about and to fit into a frame as those concerned with genres that deal with 'how things are'.

Discussion and persuasion have to address two or more viewpoints. These genres have either to reconcile these viewpoints or to shape the text to take account of, and perhaps try to circumvent, competing views of how things are or should be. As with all the suggestions being discussed here, writing frames have to be sensitively linked to the context in which they are felt to be useful.

EXTENDING RANGE IN LITERARY GENRES BY USING POETIC FEATURES

The National Literacy Strategy in England also uses structural features of texts for encouraging range in poetic writing. Most of these poetic features are different from writing frames, however, in that they are defining elements of the literary genre itself.

Table 5.10 summarises the origins and features of these poetic genres and provides some well-known examples.

Table 5.10

	Origins	Features	Some well-known examples
Acrostic	A sixteenth-century term, from French *acrostiche*, (Greek *akrostikhis*), meaning 'point or end of line'	A poem or puzzle in which the first letters of each line spell a word, phrase or sentence. Double acrostics use beginning and end of lines. Triple acrostics use the middle letters in words.	**A** boat, beneath a sunny sky **L**ingering onward dreamily **I**n an evening in July – **C**hildren three that nestle near, **E**ager eye and willing ear..... **L**ovingly shall nestle near. **I**n a Wonderland they lie, **D**reaming as the days go by, **D**reaming as the summers die: **E**ver drifting down the stream – **L**ingering in the golden gleam – **L**ife, what is it but a dream? (Lewis Carroll in *Alice through the Looking Glass*)
| Calligram | from Greek *kallos* ('beauty'); *graphein* ('to write'). | A poem in which the style of calligraphy or typing indicates the subject. | ```
          r
        a a  p
       g      u n
The eveni n      ctual gem
 s h i                  m
      n                  e
       e                  d
        l                a i
         i              d
          i            h 's
          k a r a j a h
          e
``` |
| Cinquain | Invented by the American Adelaide Crapsey (1878–1914). | A five-line poem with 22 syllables (2, 4, 6. 8, 2) | Dreamer,
What do you see
In that pot of dreams you
Hold? I see nothing you can't see
But you. |
| Clerihew | Invented by Edward Clerihew Bentley (UK) c.1890 while at school, apparently during a boring chemistry lesson. | A four-line irregular poem, rhyming **aabb**, normally naming someone in the first line and then adding more lines about them. | Sir Humphrey Davey
Abominated gravy.
He lived in the odium
Of having discovered sodium.
(Said to be the original) |
```

Haiku	Japanese (mid sixteenth-century)	A three-line poem of 17 syllables (5,7,5).	The west wind whispered And touched the eyelids of Spring Her eyes Primroses.
Kenning	Old English and Old Norse poetry.	Figurative descriptions, often in compound nouns.	'the swan-road' (the sea) 'the twilight-spoiler' (the dragon) 'the peace-bringer among nations' (the queen) (*Beowulf*)
Limerick	Invented in the town of Limerick in Ireland in the 1800s.	Five lines of light verse, rhyming **aabba**.	There was a young lady named Bright Who could travel much faster than light She started one day In a relative way And came back the previous night. (*Anon.*)
Renga	Japanese	A series of haiku, with some links between successive haiku and a final haiku which draws the links together.	
Shape poem		A poem whose layout indicates some aspect of the topic	*A Caucus-Race and a Long Tale* 35 "You promised to tell me your history, you know," said Alice, "and why it is you hate C and D," she added in a whisper, half afraid that it would be offended again. "Mine is a long and a sad tale" said the Mouse, turning to Alice, and sighing. "It *is* a long tail, certainly," said Alice, looking down with wonder at the Mouse's tail; "but why do you call it sad?" And she kept on puzzling about it while the Mouse was speaking, so that her idea of the tale was something like this:——"Fury said to a mouse, That he met in the house, 'Let us both go to law: I will prose- cute you.— Come, I'll take no de- nial; We must have the trial; For really this morn- ing I've nothing to do.' Said the mouse to the cur, 'Such a trial, dear sir, With no jury or judge, would be wast- ing our breath.' 'I'll be judge, I'll be jury,' said cun- ning old Fury: 'I'll try the whole cause, and con- demn you to death'."
			('The mouse's tale' [sic] in Lewis Carroll's *Alice's Adventures in Wonderland*)
Sonnet	From the Italian *sonnetto* ('a little sound') in the sixteenth-century.	A lyric poem of 14 lines, with a particular rhythm and rhyme pattern, e.g. iambic pentameters and **ababcdcdefefgg**.	Shakespeare's sonnets (see Sandy Brownjohn's *To Rhyme or Not to Rhyme* pp.181–3 for examples of related work with children).
Tanka	Japanese (fifteenth-century)	A five-line poem of 31 syllables (5, 7, 5, 7, 7).	

EXTENDING RANGE IN PROSE-BASED GENRES BY MANIPULATING SYNTAX
AND ORGANISATION

Specific techniques for improving writing in several genres have been
developed in Ontario by a team led by Marlene Scardamalia. The emphasis is
on composing processes and on interactive teaching, with the teacher
encouraging pupils to tackle writing and share their writing strategies in a
spirit of problem-solving, review and reflection. Table 5.11 below summarises
a few of the 60 activities that the original study developed.[56]

Table 5.11

---

a) Genre knowledge tasks

What's the purpose? (10+)

1. Pairs of pupils are given a topic and two different purposes (e.g. (1) inform the reader (2) entertain the reader).
2. Each partner writes a paragraph for a different one of the two purposes.
3. Each paragraph is read by the partner who has the right to remove any 'giveaway' features and to suggest improvements.
4. Paragraphs are read aloud to the class.
5. Other pupils have to decide what the purposes were and how they could tell.
6. The writers are deemed to be successful if the other children can decide what the purposes were.
Extension: other purposes (to share news, persuade) or types of text (narrative, exposition, description, argument etc.)

List the features (9+)

1. Pupils work in pairs to decide on two types of text (e.g. directions, news report, prayer, letter of complaint etc.)
2. Each pupil writes a brief example of a different one of the two types of text, making sure that all agreed features are included.
3. The texts are read aloud to the class.
4. The class has to suggest what kind of text each is and the features they think were deliberately used.
5. The writers succeed if the class can recognise the type of text and list the features.
Extension: Pupils can also be encouraged to use specific technical terms e.g. in science and geography.

b) Improving Narrative Technique

Comic strips (8+)

1. Pupils bring a comic strip of about four panels (not shown to anyone).
2. They write the story that the comic shows.
3. They also imagine an extra panel and include that part of the story as well.
4. The writing is read aloud.
5. Other pupils have to describe what they think the original comic strip showed and which part of the story has been added

Other viewpoints (9+)

1. Pupils are given a well-known story with several characters in it (e.g. a traditional fairy tale, such as *Cinderella* or *Three Little Pigs*.
2. They choose a character other than the main one and retell the story from this character's point of view.
3. The rewritten story is read aloud.
4. The class discusses how well the writer has

Whose story? (10+)

1. Pupils work in groups of three.
2. They talk about interesting personal experiences (most frightening, embarrassing etc.).
3. They choose one person's experience and discuss it in detail.
4. Each pupil goes off to write about it as if it happened to him or her (no real names included).
5. Each member of the group reads his or her story to

Extension: including dialogue or description, using pictures of famous art works.

succeeded in writing from the new viewpoint.
Extension: play scripts; variation in style; using different settings.

the rest of the class.

6. The class have to guess which story was written by the person whose experience it really was and to give reasons for their guesses.
Extension: family studies (experiences with siblings); fact and fiction in history; 'real-life' accounts of historical events.

c) Improving descriptive technique

Similar pictures (8+)

1. Pupils are shown a set of similar pictures that are individually numbered.
2. Each pupil picks a number.
3. They then write a description of picture that corresponds to their number.
4. Descriptions are read aloud.
5. The class guess which picture is being described.
Extension: similar microscopic organisms in science; similar maps in maps in geography, pictures of similar paintings in art.

Forbidden words (9+)

1. Pupils sit in groups of five or six.
2. The teacher asks the class to suggest some occupations and to list some words that are commonly used in talking about them (e.g. teacher; pupils; classroom; lessons; blackboard; school).
3. Each pupil is given a card that lists an occupation and five words often used when talking about it.
4. Pupils have to write a description of the occupation without using any of the words on the card.
5. Each pupil reads his or her description aloud.
6. The rest of the class try to guess (i) the occupation (ii) the forbidden words.
Extension: historical figures, geographical features, scientific phenomena etc.

d) Improving technique in writing instructions

Direct a robot (9+)

1. The class decides on vocabulary suitable for directing movement of a robot (e.g. 'stand up', 'sit down', 'go', 'stop', 'forward', 'back', 'turn', 'right', 'left', 'steps' etc. and numbers one to twenty).
2. Pupils work in pairs. One decides on something for his/her partner to do and writes instructions, using *only* the words in the agreed vocabulary.
3. Partner follows these instructions exactly (stopping if the instructions are clearly impossible).
4. Pairs and class discuss adequacy of each set of instructions and need for accuracy and revision etc.
Extension: map reading; second language learning; drama.

Draw it this way (9+)

1. Pupils work in pairs.
2. One draws a picture (building, person, flowers, scenery etc.) which their partner does not see.
3. They then write instructions so that their partner could reproduce the drawing accurately.
4. The completed drawings are returned so that they can be checked against the original.
5. If necessary, each writer revises the instructions to include the missing information.
6. The partner then adjusts the drawing accordingly.
Extension: geometric shapes; use of second language vocabulary; mapwork

e) Improving technique in writing argument

Pet peeves (9+)

1. Each pupil lists up to three 'pet peeves' and lists at least three reasons (not personal tastes) for each (e.g. 'I don't like skateboarding because it is dangerous').
2. Lists are swapped and the partner picks a peeve and writes something to persuade the partner to take a more positive view (e.g. 'You can protect yourself by using safety equipment').
3. The class can discuss whether the replies deal effectively with all the original reasons.
   Extension: opinions on current or historical events;
   Extension: current events; opinions on historical events

Pick a strategy (11+)

1. The teacher asks pupils to suggest how arguments are based on various strategies e.g.:
   • appeal to authority: 'Exercise is good for you because doctors say so'.
   • by example: 'Exercise is good for you because fit people are healthy people'.
   • by consequence: 'Exercise is good for you because you become unhealthy otherwise'.
   • appeal to common beliefs: 'Exercise is good for you because we all know it is'.
2. Each group selects a strategy.
3. The teacher provides a proposition.
4. Each group decides whether to support or oppose it and writes the most convincing argument using the strategy they have chosen.
5. Each group's writing can be read aloud and discussed in turn.
   Extension: examining and practising these strategies in advertising copy or newspaper editorials; controversial topics in history, geography, current events etc.

Again it is important not to treat these suggestions as skills exercises. They need to be sensitively linked to a convincing and authentic context. They may be of particular value as guided writing is increasingly used in the wake of the influence of the National Literacy Strategy in England.

Scardamalia stresses that the value of this kind of teaching may come after pupils have had several attempts at similar tasks. They will benefit from trying to achieve the desired results, finding out how well they succeed and then having a chance to try again. This revisiting of the features of the text and the challenges of the task is more likely to develop the mental processes that lead to good writing.

LINKING READING AND WRITING TO EXTEND RANGE

Recent work in Australia has used reading–writing links to develop writing performance in different genres. As was noted earlier, Australian genre studies are clearly more committed to teaching approaches than their North American counter-parts. One of the best known is the wheel model that was used in the *Literacy and Education Research Network* (*LERN*) in New South Wales in the late 1980s.

Figure 5.10

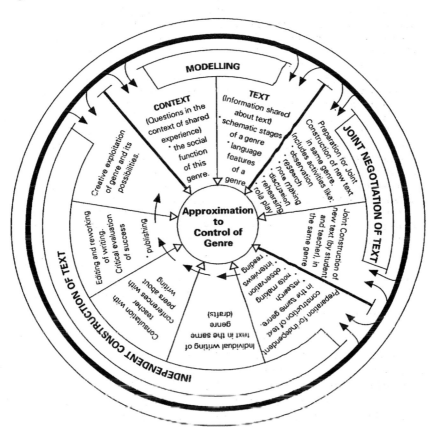

There are three phases in this teaching approach:

A: Modelling

1 Decide which genre(s) children need to develop.
2 Choose several texts that represent genre.
3 Provide for shared experience of the genre (reading, being read to).
4 Discuss: what the text is for (purpose);
   how the text is organised (text level structure);
   the way the text 'speaks' (sentences and words).

B: Joint Negotiation of the class text

1 Researching and planning a new text in the same genre.
2 Joint construction of the new text; children contribute; teacher acts as scribe and guides them towards appropriate structure, sentences and words.

C: Independent Construction of Text

1 Preparation of independent construction of text.
2 Individual drafting.
3 Consultation with teacher and peers.
4 Editing and publishing.
5 Evaluation and future planning.

Conclusion

Range in writing is a complex area of literacy education. Providing for the development of range can be endlessly rewarding, as different genres are used to produce the forms of text to achieve various purposes. Provision for range also requires sensitivity to achieve a helpful balance in what children write, how they write it, why they write it, whom they write for and what the writing is about. There may be much to be gained from maintaining opportunities for children to choose what they write and to encourage them to tackle the writing in their own way. They will thus continue to experience the satisfaction of writing for themselves (and sometimes to support their own learning).

They are also likely to benefit from being helped to attend to how texts can be organised and from opportunities to wrestle with the distinctive features of different modes and genres. Their writing is likely to be more effectively shaped if it is undertaken with a clear sense of purpose. Similarly it will gain from an identifiable readership, a sense of what a particular audience will judge to be important.

Writing will undoubtedly benefit if there is something to write about which is accessible and which implicitly justifies the time and energy expended. On such a breadth of balanced experience, young writers are more likely to learn to read with a writer's alertness to technique. They are also more likely to appreciate what can be gained from looking closely at the structure of language itself and the grammatical rules that govern it. These rules are the focus of the next chapter.

Writing and Grammar

Grammar... the central, organising principle of language.
(David Crystal)[1]

This chapter

- explores some different meanings attached to the term 'grammar'
- illustrates some aspects of modern descriptive grammar
- examines the basic elements of sentences
- discusses how variety in writing can be created by different kinds of sentences and by sentence cohesion.

Introduction

Most dictionaries define grammar as the study of the way language is organised, especially the study of the rules between words (syntax) and within words (morphology) (see Figure 2.3 on p.24).

Surprisingly, many books on children's writing make little or no reference to grammar, even though it is the central organising system of spoken and written language. This omission reflects a major change in the English-speaking world over the past 30 years. Pupils and students have not been explicitly taught about grammar as they once were. It has been assumed that the benefits from directly teaching grammar are not worth the efforts expounded; children's writing, for instance, will be unlikely to improve as a consequence.

Nevertheless, there has been a growing feeling that grammar teaching has an unfulfilled potential, particularly if it reflects contemporary English, rather than a Latin-based model of language. Grammar may also have an unfulfilled potential if it is authentically related to the purposes for which language and literacy are used. This feeling has been supported by a number of recent publications that are discussed later in this chapter and in the following one. For many years the main questions about grammar teaching in the 3–13 age-range tended to be concerned with whether it was worth tackling at all. Recently, the main questions about this teaching have increasingly become more concerned with the 'what' and the ' how'.

This chapter will review some of the main issues underlying the teaching of grammar by exploring some of the rules and relationships that affect word order in English. As in Chapter 2, key technical terms appear in **bold**. The chapter also needs a general word of warning, as well. Grammar is a difficult topic to discuss because it requires a variety of cautious qualifications. These cautions may be particularly helpful for anyone brought up on a diet of traditional grammar, whose educational values went unquestioned for many years. The main cautions are as follows:

- *Grammar means different things to different people.* To some people, grammar may mean little more than recognising the 'parts of speech' (verbs, adjectives etc.); to other people, grammar may mean prescribing rules for speaking or writing 'correctly'; to linguists it is likely to mean describing the rule system by which words and parts of words can be ordered. And there are many ways of describing these rules.[2]
- *Grammar can be known, talked about and referred to.* Adults and school-age children intuitively know a great deal of grammar. The uncertainty for teachers is how far to make this knowledge explicit and then which technical terms to use when referring to its different aspects.
- *Grammar may not be what it used to be.* Traditional grammar (which was mostly based on Latin) has now been largely replaced by grammatical descriptions that can deal more accurately with contemporary English.
- *Grammar operates through different levels.* The rules of grammar run through sentences (and to some extent how different sentences are linked together). Rules also run through the **elements** that are found within sentences: the subject, verb, object, complement and adverbial elements. While sentences can include a number of elements, the only *essential* element in a sentence is a **verb**, which refers to actions, sensations or states of being.

  The term 'element' is used because each element can be made up of single words or groups of words. Specific patterns of elements that include a verb are known as **clauses**. (As will be shown later in this chapter, there are surprisingly few of these patterns.)

  The elements are expressed by **phrases**. Many phrases are made up of **groups of words**. However, modern descriptive grammar also refers to **individual words** as phrases if that word acts alone as a particular clause element. Thus, in 'she opened the door quietly', 'opened' is the verb phrase, even though it is a single word.

  Words themselves are made up of one or more **morphemes** (see **Chapter 2**), such as prefixes, suffixes and word stems, whose patterns are also governed by rules. In the word 'opened' there are two morphemes, 'open' and 'ed'. All these levels of language, sentence to morpheme, can be seen at work in Table 6.1.

Table 6.1

one sentence	She opened the door quietly.
one clause	She opened the door quietly.
four elements	She (*subject*) opened (*verb*) the door (*object*) quietly (*adverb*).
four phrases	She (*noun phrase*) opened (*verb phrase*) the door (*noun phrase*) quietly (*adverbial phrase*).[3]
five words	She opened the door quietly.
seven morphemes	She open ed the door quiet ly.

- *New understanding requires new terms of reference.* New technical terms have replaced, or been added to, those used in traditional grammar. For example, 'parts of speech' have been replaced by 'word classes' to help avoid unreliable labelling. Take the word 'table', for instance:

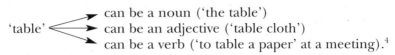

'table'
- can be a noun ('the table')
- can be an adjective ('table cloth')
- can be a verb ('to table a paper' at a meeting).[4]

- *Grammar teaching may not improve writing.* This caution is perhaps the most debatable one. Research reviews have consistently failed to provide evidence that grammar teaching makes any difference to the quality of pupils' writing. A succession of eminent writers have expressed surprise at this[5] and the research methods have been questioned but, in this respect, the case for grammar teaching still remains largely unproven.

- *More grammar teaching may still be needed.* Since the late 1960s, there has been a rapid decline in grammar teaching in schools.[6] The resulting 'vacuum' has meant that many higher education students have only a tenuous grasp even of basic word classes (parts of speech). Some basic grammatical content was introduced into the British initial teacher training requirements in 1998 and this may herald greater coverage of grammar in schools in the new millennium.[7] Further signs of a possible sea-change in thinking were the publications, in 1998 and 1999, by the English and Welsh Curriculum Authorities, of *The Grammar Papers* and a follow-up publication, *Not whether but how*.[8] These booklets seemed to signal a determination to re-examine the nature and interpretation of previously published evidence that grammar teaching did not directly influence pupil performance in writing. One paper in particular, written by David Tomlinson, has attracted a great deal of attention.[9] It is discussed in **Chapter 8**.

However, if there is an increase in the amount of grammar teaching in the United Kingdom, it will make very specific demands on the professional knowledge of many teachers. Recent studies suggest that many British teachers of the 3–13 age-range have a limited knowledge of grammatical terminology.[10] Where they do have a framework for analysing grammatical structure, it may be disproportionately influenced by a 'naming of parts' approach. Such an approach focuses on individual words and the parts of speech that were a feature of traditional grammar teaching.

In the light of this state of affairs, it may be helpful to look first at the parts of speech approach itself and how it has been superseded by a concern with word classes. In order to avoid the potentially misleading labelling of words like 'table', the word class approach identifies the **function** that the word performs in relation to other words.

From 'Parts of Speech' to 'Word Classes'

The different emphasis in modern descriptive grammar can be shown in Table 6.2. In it, the traditional parts of speech are described in a Victorian rhyme.[11] Beside each entry is a more up-to-date description of the word class referred to. This description is based on the function that each word class performs.

Table 6.2

One day, I am told, and as it was cold,
I suppose it occurr'd in cold weather,
The NINE PARTS OF SPEECH, having
no one to teach,
Resolv'd on a picnic together. [...]

The Articles

An A and a THE, two
ARTICLES small,
Had on their best clothes, to attend
at THE Ball,
Like two little lackeys, they stood
at the door,
That, when the nouns came, they
might run in before [...]

The **articles** are now seen as examples of **determiners** that express the 'definiteness' of nouns and noun phrases. The definite article (*the*) and the indefinite article (*a* or *an*) are **central determiners**. Other examples are *this* and *that*, *each* and *every* *some* and *any*, when these words are used before a noun. (Sometimes, these words can act as pronouns, of course.) Other kinds of determiner include words like *both* (the teams) or *what* (a surprise) which are **predeterminers**, coming *before* the central determiner. This class also includes words like numerals or ordinals (the *three* eldest children or the *last* one to arrive), which are **postdeterminers**, coming *after* the central determiner.

The Nouns or Substantives

The tribe of great NOUNS, whom
we SUBSTANTIVES call,
Although it was numerous, came
one and all.
There were MR and MRS, MISS
KITTY and SUE,
With ANNA-MATILDA, MARIA
and PRUE.[...]
These were all the FAMILY
proper; but then
There came such a NUMBER OF
BOYS, MAIDS and MEN.
And such common PEOPLE, who
brought in the FARE!
What a LOT of PLUMS, APPLES
and SWEETMEATS was there!

The idea that a noun is a naming word is helpful, but it does not quite do justice to the grammatical function of nouns. Nouns are now seen as fulfilling the following:
- Nouns can act as subject, object or complement.
- The meaning of nouns is often decided by a **determiner** (see above).
- Nouns change their form to show singular, plural or possession e.g. *cat*; *cats*; the *cat's tail*; the *cats' faces*.

Common Nouns

Some borne upon TRAYS, some in
PLATES, some in DISHES;
With all kinds of POULTRY, of
GAME, and of FISHES; [...]

In truth, every THING in the
EARTH, SEA and AIR
Belongs to the NOUN, though the
whole was not there.

- Nouns can be classified into a hierarchy, beginning with the distinction between **proper nouns** and **common nouns**.
- Proper (or 'substantive') nouns refer to a unique person, place or thing and often begin with a capital letter (*George*, *Guernsey* etc.).
- Common nouns can then be divided into **count nouns** and **noncount nouns**. Count nouns do not usually stand alone in the singular without a determiner (e.g. *a cat*; *this cat*). Noncount (or 'mass') nouns can stand alone, but cannot normally be turned into a plural (e.g. *health* and *happiness*). Some nouns can be either (e.g. *light* and *sound*). Count and noncount nouns can be either concrete or abstract.

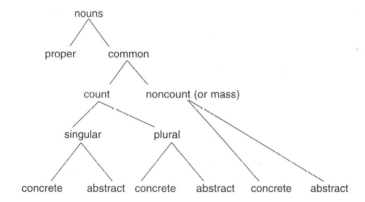

The Adjectives

Next the ADJECTIVES came,
with grave solemn faces,
And wigs like the judges: they
soon took their places. [...]
Some were GOOD, some were
BAD, some PRETTY, some
MILD,
Some were MODEST,
some IMPUDENT, WICKED and
WILD. [...]

Adjectives express various 'qualities' of nouns. To qualify as an adjective, a word has to fulfil one or more functions:

- It can 'pre-modify' a noun (e.g. *old, stone* house). Any number of adjectives can be inserted between determiner and noun, but the number rarely exceeds three.
- Adjectives themselves can be pre-modified by words like *very* or *every* which act as **intensifiers**.
- Adjectives (e.g. *large*) can be used in comparative (*larger*) or superlative ways (*largest*).
- Adjectives can be used alone as **complements** (e.g. the pond was *muddy*).
- There are specific suffixes that are typically used in adjectives (e.g. *-able, -ed, -ful, -ish, -ive, -ous* and *-y*).

The Pronouns

At this moment a bustle was heard
at the door
From a party of PRONOUNS, who
came by the score. [...]
And THEIR boldness was such, as
I live IT is true,
One declar'd HE was I, and ONE
call'd HIMSELF YOU. [...]

Pronouns are used to replace nouns or one or more noun phrases. However there are some important grammatical differences between nouns and pronouns:

- Pronouns perform similar functions to nouns, but in a less specific way. This partly accounts for the fact that there are thousands of nouns in English, but only about 60 pronouns. In fact, sometimes pronouns refer to a very wide range of possibilities: ' "Is there *anybody* there?", said the traveller'.
- In some ways, though, pronouns are more adaptable than nouns. For instance, some have different forms for subject and object (*I* and *me*; *he* and *him*; *she* and *her*) or for personal and nonpersonal gender (*he/she* c.f. *it*; *who* c.f. *which*).
- In other ways, pronouns are less adaptable in that they do not normally allow modification. (e.g. *A little flower* cannot be expressed as **A little it*).[12]

The Verbs

Some actors of eminence made
their appearance,
And the Servants, Nouns common,
with speed made a clearance [...]
And these actors the VERBS,
when they'd room to DISPLAY,
Both WRESTLED, and
TUMBLED, and GAMBOL'D away,
They PLAYED and they RAN,
They JUMPED and they DANCED
FRISKED, AMBLED AND KICKED,
LAUGHED, CHATTERED and PRANCED.

Verbs are far more than 'doing words'. They do indeed express actions, but they also express states of being or processes where there is little action (e.g. *sensing*, *remembering* or just *being*.) As was discussed earlier in this chapter, the verb element is the only essential element of clauses. Verbs can be grouped according to the job they do:

- There is an indefinite number of **main** (or **lexical**) verbs that can stand alone in full (major) sentences (e.g. *work, rest and play*). Main verbs are 'marked' to show tense and number:
  He walks (*present*). He walked (*past*).
  He walks (*singular*). They walk (*plural*).
- There are about a dozen **modal auxiliary** verbs which 'qualify' main verbs in different ways (e.g. *can, could, may, might, should, would*). Up to three (or very occasionally four) modal auxiliaries can occur together. (e.g. He *could have been* shopping).
- There are three **primary auxiliary** verbs that can act as main or auxiliary verbs: *be, have* and *do*.

The Adverbs

And these had attendants, called
ADVERBS by name:
To teach the Verbs proper
behaviour they came.
They told them how they might
more GRACEFULLY dance.
More QUICKLY might run, or
more MERRILY prance. [...]

Adverbs are the most versatile of all the word classes. They certainly provide more information about a verb, as the traditional definition suggests, but they can also do much more:

• Adverbs can also add prior information about other classes of word in a process called **premodification**.

e.g. He was *extremely* happy (premodifying an adjective).
She sang *extremely* beautifully (premodifying an adverb).
It was *quite* a mess (premodifying a noun phrase).
I saw *almost* everybody (premodifying a pronoun).

• Adverbs can also provide further information about other word classes in a process called **postmodification**.

e.g. A year *later* (postmodifying a noun).
Something *else* (postmodifying a pronoun).
Bring it *here* (postmodifying a preposition).

• Adverbs can appear in a variety of forms. Many are made by adding *-ly* to an adjective (e.g. *beautiful* → *beautifully*). Others are made by adding suffixes like *-wards* (e.g. *upwards*) *-ways* (e.g. *sideways*) or *-wise* (e.g. *otherwise*). Common adverbs also include single words (e.g. *here*, *later*) and compound words (e.g. *clockwise, therefore*).

The Prepositions

PREPOSITIONS were busy:
they ran in between,
And with Substantives, Pronouns
and Verbs they were seen.
Holding one IN each hand, thus
together TO bind,
AT, BY, FOR, EXCEPT, SINCE,
AFTER, BEHIND. [...]

Prepositions express links between parts of a sentence (e.g. He jumped *over* the wall. School starts *at* nine o'clock.)

• Prepositions are good examples of **closed system words** (sometimes referred to as grammatical or 'function' words). There are only about 150 closed system words (which also include determiners, pronouns, primary auxiliary verbs and conjunctions). Unlike **open system words** (nouns, adjectives, verbs and adverbs), it is very difficult to add new members.

• Structurally, prepositions do not occur on their own; they are always part of a phrase.

• Sometimes prepositions have an adjective or adverb as a complement (e.g. *at last*; *in haste*; *on time*). Sometimes prepositions themselves contain two or three words (e.g. *except for* or *in spite of*). These are called **complex prepositions**.

The Conjunctions

The useful CONJUNCTIONS now
came at a call,
To superintend the concerns of the Ball,
AND these soon began to join
Nouns with each other,
THOUGH 'tis not the fashion to
dance with a brother.
The sentences, too, they united together,
With an AND and an OR, - BUT I
ought to say rather
The latter disjoined them, by
coming between;
For them back to back were the
sentences seen. [...]

Conjunctions link clauses together. Sometimes they **coordinate** clauses (e.g. He walked down the road *and* caught the bus). At other times they **subordinate** a clause (e.g. *After* walking down the road, he caught the bus). These last examples show how coordinating conjunctions such as *and* can convey a range of meanings, including sequence (e.g. The next thing he did was to catch a bus). Such conjunctions can also convey result (e.g. He stood beside the bus stop and the bus stopped beside him). Other examples of coordinating conjunctions include *but* and *or*.

- Subordinating conjunctions tend to provide clearer links between structure and meaning e.g.:
  After, until, when (*time*)
  So, so that (*result*)
  Because, for since, *(reason)*
  If, in case, unless *(condition)*
  Although, even if, *(concession)*
  even though, despite

The Interjection [...]

But such litter was scattered about
in the room
That, when INTERJECTION came
up with her broom,
Her surprise was so great that she
nothing could say,
But O! AH! ALAS! GOOD
LACK! WELL-A-DAY!

Interjections are now seen as 'minor sentences'. They use unusual word orders and their grammatical structures cannot be easily analysed. They include 'formulae' for archetypal situations (e.g. *cheerio*); proverbs (e.g. *No names, no pack drill.*); abbreviated forms (e.g. *See you.*); or short exclamations, questions or commands (e.g. *Nice one, Cyril!*). Minor sentences are especially influenced by fashions, cults and social change.

Beyond Parts of Speech and Word Classes

Whatever approach is used to support an increase in the teaching of grammar in the new millennium, it needs to go beyond a limited preoccupation with parts of speech or word classes. Such teaching is likely to be more effective if it is based on an understanding, however rudimentary, of how English grammar can be described in relation to words, sentences and, to some extent, texts. As mentioned earlier, there are different ways of tackling this description. The following sections are based on the work of Randolph Quirk and his colleagues at London University. Quirk's major work *A Comprehensive Grammar of the English Language*, a mammoth volume of 1779 pages, has in turn influenced many other important writers on the subject, including David Crystal and Katharine Perera. Perera's *Children's Writing and Reading* is an exceptionally lucid and scholarly book that is unfortunately now out of print. Much of the later part of this chapter draws heavily on her analysis and discussion, which deserve continuing dissemination.

Quirk reminds us that the aim of a grammar is to describe how the sentences in a language are constructed. He also acknowledges that the term 'sentence' itself is not easy to define. Traditional grammar might have suggested that a sentence was a group of words expressing a complete thought. But some sentences contain several thoughts: 'In that part of the garden, I am going to plant daffodils, tulips and crocuses'. Furthermore, complete thoughts can be expressed in words that seem not to be sentences: 'Phew!'

As mentioned earlier, this last example can be described as a **minor sentence**. The great majority of English sentences contain specific patterns of words and are called **major sentences**. Major sentences are made up of particular **patterns of elements** (and, as was mentioned earlier, the elements themselves are made up of phrases). These patterns of elements are called **clauses**. A sentence that is made up of one **independent** or 'main' clause is called a **simple sentence**. Sentences made up of two or more clauses are called **multiple sentences**. Multiple sentences that link two or more independent clauses by using conjunctions like 'and' or 'but' are called **compound** sentences. Multiple sentences that link an independent (or main) clause to **dependent** or subordinate clauses are called **complex** sentences. As was shown earlier in the chapter, simple sentences are made up by combinations of the following five clause elements:

subject
verb
object
complement
adverbial element

These elements are often abbreviated to their initial letter: S, V, O, C and A. Each element will now be discussed in turn.

1 THE VERB ELEMENT

Verbs express actions, sensations and states of being. The **verb** element is the only essential element in a clause. No independent clause is complete without a **finite verb**. Finite verbs are 'marked' by endings etc., to show tense, number, mood, and aspect.[13]

Figure 6.1

The blackbirds *were singing*.[14 15]

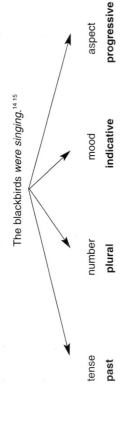

tense
past

number
plural

mood
indicative

aspect
progressive

Tense refers to the time when the 'action' of the verbs is effected: in the **present**, **past** or **future**. The tense is indicated by different forms of the verb, e.g. 'sing' or 'sings' (present); 'sang' or 'were singing' (past). Strictly speaking, there is no future tense form as such in English. Instead, 'will' or 'shall' is added: 'They will sing…'.

Number refers to the way many verbs are marked to show whether the subject is **singular** or **plural**: 'a blackbird sings'; 'blackbirds sing'.

Mood refers here to the kind of meaning that the verb conveys. A factual meaning is conveyed by the **indicative** mood ('they are singing)'. A non-factual meaning is conveyed by the **subjunctive** mood ('I wish they were singing'). A directive meaning is conveyed by the **imperative** mood ('Listen to their singing.').

Aspect refers to how the time of the 'action' of verbs can be marked to show whether this action is complete, whether it is in progress or whether the action has 'duration'. The present and past tenses that are not marked in this way are referred to as **simple** tenses ('they sing'; 'they sang'). The two main ways of showing aspect in English are the **progressive** ('they are singing'); and the **perfective** ('they had sung'). The different forms of the progressive and perfective aspects can indicate events ('they had sung'); states ('they were singing') or habitual ('they had been singing').

Major sentences can be made by the use of just one verb, when the sentence is a directive: 'Listen!'

2 THE SUBJECT ELEMENT

The **subject** element expresses the theme or topic, e.g.:

> *The horses* were neighing.
>   S   V

The subject and verb need to agree (be 'in concord') in tense and number (e.g. present or past; singular or plural).

3 THE OBJECT ELEMENT

The **object** element can be of two kinds:

- The **direct object** element refers to who or what is affected by the action of the verb, e.g.:

  I opened *the bag.*
  S V   Od

- The **indirect object** refers to something or someone that is the recipient of the action involving the verb and the direct object, e.g.:

  I gave *the horses* some hay.
  S V   Oi   Od

4 THE COMPLEMENT ELEMENT

The **complement** element expresses further information about another clause element (the subject or the object).[16] The complement needs to agree with this other clause element in number (singular or plural), e.g.:

> The horses were *hungry.*
>   S   V   C

5 THE ADVERBIAL ELEMENT

The **adverbial element** provides further information about the time, manner, space etc. of the actions, sensation or states of being expressed by the verb. This information can be provided at several different places in the clause. Each version of the resulting sentence is subtly different. This flexible use of the adverbial element is discussed again in **Chapter 8**, e.g.:

> The horses ate the hay *noisily.*
>   S   V   Od   A

> *Noisily* the horses ate the hay.
>   A   S   V   Od

> The horses *noisily* ate the hay.
>   S   A   V   Od

Seven Types of Clause

The five clause elements can be used to create seven clause structures:

1	S V	The cat slept.
2	S V Od	The cat caught the mouse.
3	S V C	The cat was tired.
4	S V A	The cat slept quietly.
5	S V Oi Od	The cat brought me the mouse.
6	S V Od C	The cat found the box comfortable.
7	S V Od A	The cat caught the mouse quickly.

If the subject is indefinite and if the clause contains the verb 'to be', any of these structures can be **transformed** by being begun with 'there', e.g.:

An engineer was repairing the washing machine. (S V O)
There was a engineer repairing the washing machine.

Nobody was helping. (S V C)
There was nobody helping.

The basic clause structure of English is summed up in Table 6.3:

Table 6.3 The seven clause types using the five clause elements

Subject, Verb, Object, Complement, Adverbial (n = there may be several)

1	**Subject element**	**Verb element**
	(In 90% of clauses, the subject precedes the verb.)	(The only obligatory/compulsory element.)
	theme	actions
	topic	sensations
		states of being
	NOUN PHRASE (incl. single noun(s)) PRONOUNS SOME SUBORDINATE CLAUSES	VERB VERB PHRASE (more than one verb may be used) including auxiliaries (*may, could* etc.)
		May be 'marked' for
		tense (past, present or future)
		number (singular or plural)
		mood (indicative, subjunctive or imperative)
		aspect (the way the action is viewed in time)

	S	V	
2	S	V	**Object (direct) element** affected by action of verb NOUN PHRASE (incl. single noun(s)) PRONOUNS SOME SUBORDINATE CLAUSES
3	S	V	**Complement (subject) element** further information about another clause element (subject or object) with which it agrees in number (singular or plural) NOUN PHRASES (incl. single nouns) ADJECTIVE PHRASES (incl. single adjectives) PRONOUNS SOME SUBORDINATE CLAUSES
4	S	V	**Adverbial element (n)** further information (in several possible places in the clause) about time, manner, space etc. of situations ADVERBIAL PHRASE(S) (incl. single adverb(s)) PREPOSITIONAL PHRASES SOME NOUN PHRASES (incl. single nouns) SOME SUBORDINATE CLAUSES

For row 3, between V column and the complement description:

Often 'be'<--------------------> (*was*, *is*, etc.) Sometimes a copula verb (*became*, *sounds* etc.)

	S	V		
5	S	V	O (indirect)	O (direct)
6	S	V	O (direct)	C (object)
7	S	V	O (direct)	A (n)

Notes:
(a) A **vocative**[17] relates to the whole sentence and is not an element of clause structure in the way subjects and verbs are.
(b) **Primary** verbs (*be*, *have*, *do*) can act as full (lexical) verbs or auxiliaries
(c) Concord (Agreement) is necessary between
   S – V
   <---->
   S – V – C (Nouns)
   <-------->
   S – V – O – C (Nouns)
   <--->

It may seem odd to reduce a rich and varied language like written English to such a stark summary. However, the variety can be created in several different ways around these basic structures:

1. by using different kinds of sentences;
2. by varying the words and phrases in the different clause elements;
3. by linking simple sentences together to make compound or complex sentences (i.e. multiple sentences);
4. by creating cohesion between sentences.

These four will now be discussed in turn.

1. Different Kinds of Sentences

The great majority of English sentences are **statements**. There are, however, three other kinds of sentence: **questions**, **exclamations** and **directives**. Directives include commands, invitations, warnings and other kinds of advice. The four basic kinds of sentences are illustrated below:

The cows are in the field.	(statement)
Where are the cows?	(question)
There are the cows.	(exclamation)
Look at the cows.	(directive)

In the first three of these types of sentence, it is possible to use the same form of words and to indicate the different functions of the sentence by punctuation and, where spoken, tone of voice:

The cows are in the garden!	(exclamation)
The cows are in the garden?	(question)
The cows are in the garden.	(statement)

In fact, the seven clause structures can be converted from statements to questions or commands by making relatively small changes to the original word order. Take for instance the simple sentence:

The engineer repaired the washing machine.

CHANGING STATEMENTS TO QUESTIONS

All seven of the basic clause structures and their 'there transformations' can be used to ask questions:

- by changing word order: 'Did the engineer repair the washing machine?'
- by using a *wh-* word: 'Who repaired the washing machine?'
- by adding a 'tag': 'The engineer repaired the washing machine, did he?'

- by using the original wording and adding a question mark: 'The engineer repaired the washing machine?'

CHANGING STATEMENTS TO COMMANDS

All seven of the structures can be used to make commands:

- by leaving out the subject and using the 'stem' of the verb: 'Repair the washing machine.'
- by adding 'Do': 'Do repair the washing machine.'

CHANGING ACTIVE TO PASSIVE

Most of these structures can also be changed from an 'active voice' to a 'passive voice':

The engineer repaired the washing machine. (S V O)
The washing machine was repaired by the engineer.

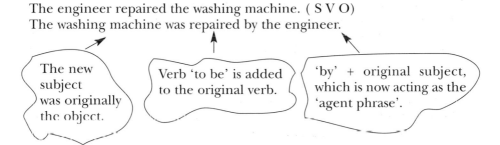

The new subject was originally the object.

Verb 'to be' is added to the original verb.

'by' + original subject, which is now acting as the 'agent phrase'.

The SVC structure cannot be changed from the active to the passive voice.

2. *Varying the Words and Phrases in each Clause Element*

Each clause element can be increased or decreased by varying the numbers of words that it contains. Take for instance the simple sentence:

The cows were in the field.

S The cows ⟶ Nearly a hundred Fresian cows
V were ⟶ were quietly grazing
A in the field. ⟶ in the ten acre field, near the river

Words are grouped in phrases. At the phrase level,[18] additional systems of rules operate. The main relationships between the clauses and phrases in grammatical description are summarised in Table 6.4:

Table 6.4

Clause Elements	Phrase Types	Using	
		500,000+ 'open-class' words (lexical or 'content' words)	150+ 'closed-system' words (grammatical or 'function' words)
Subjects			
Objects	(A) Noun phrases	nouns adjectives	pronouns intensifiers conjunctions determiners prepositions
Complements			
Verbs	(B) Verb phrases	lexical verbs	main auxiliary verbs (*be, have, do*) modal auxiliary verbs
Adverbials	(C) Adverbial phrases	adverbs	pronouns intensifiers etc.
Complements	(D) Adjective phrases	adjectives	pronouns intensifiers etc.

(a) NOUN PHRASES

The noun phrase regularly expresses the clause elements subject, object or complement. The noun phrase can be:

- a noun e.g. 'sky';
- a pronoun e.g. 'it';
- a group of words with a noun as its **head** (its most important member) e.g. 'the clear, blue sky'.

Linguists often use the abbreviation NP when a noun phrase is represented by a group of words. (Linguists also use VP, AP, AdjP when a verb phrase, an adverbial phrase or an adjectival phrase are respectively represented by groups of words.)

As was mentioned earlier, nouns can be proper or common, mass or count, singular or plural. The same is true of the NP. The most common NP is *the + a common noun* but there are many ways in which the NP can be expanded to add interest and detail e.g:

Pre-modification to a head-noun

- adding **determiners**
  the
  or *some, any* } mushrooms
  or *these, those*
  etc.

• adding **pre-determiner(s)**	*all of*	the mushrooms
• adding **post-determiner(s)**	all of the *large*	mushrooms
• adding **adjectives**	all of the large *white*	mushrooms
(normally no more than three)		
• adding **intensifier(s)**	all of the *very*	large white mushrooms.

POST-MODIFICATION TO A HEAD-NOUN

- adding a **prepositional phrase** all of the very large white mushrooms *in the shop.*
  If, as here, the prepositional phrase contains a preposition and a noun phrase, then this noun phrase can also be post-modified in the same way ad infinitum: *in the shop beside the bridge, near the town centre etc.*

Figure 6.2 shows how this expansion of the noun phrase can be analysed when it is part of a simple sentence, in this case, the object.

Figure 6.2

He bought mushrooms
S   V   O

He bought all of the very large white mushrooms in the shop.
S   V   ___ __ __ __ __ _____   _____
          pre-d d int adj adj   n   prep phrase
                                            __ __ __
                                            prep d n

Writing can be given further variety by coordinating noun phrases, e.g. '...all of the very large white mushrooms in the shop and a few of the small button mushrooms'.

As will be shown in later chapters, the expansion of noun phrases is an important part of writing development in the 3–13 age-range.

(b) VERB PHRASES

Note: There is a closer relationship between the clause element verb and the word class verb than there is between any other elements and word classes. The clause element verb has to be expressed by a member of the verb word class. In contrast, the subject, object and adverbial clause elements can each be expressed by a range of items. In the opposite direction, finite verbs can only express the element verb. Nouns, on the other hand, can function as subjects, objects and complements, e.g.:

> *The cat* ran up the curtain.
> The children fed *the cat.*
> The culprit was *the cat.*

Finite Lexical Verbs belong to **open class systems**. There are many thousands of members, as was glimpsed in the earlier Victorian rhyme in Table 6.2:

> They PLAYED and they RAN,
> They JUMPED and they DANCED,
> FRISKED, AMBLED AND KICKED,
> LAUGHED, CHATTERED and PRANCED.

Such verbs can be of three broad kinds:

(i) **transitives**, which take an object (SVO, SVOO, SVOC, SVOA) e.g. *hit, want, make*

(ii) **copula** verbs, which take a complement (SVC) e.g. *be, become, seem*

(iii) **intransitives**, which do not require either an object or a complement (SV) e.g. *exist, shout, fall*

Some verbs can be more than one of the above, e.g. *ran* or *ran a good race.*

Some lexical verbs can be 'chained' with other lexical verbs in combinations of their **infinitive stem** or **stem + *ing*** form. Within limits, this chaining can add a little entertainment to accounts of convoluted circumstances, e.g. 'Susie *hoped to try to remember to promise to help to wash up* the dishes.'

A few verb phrases are made up (*sic*) of verbs that are followed by a **particle.** Some of these are **prepositional verbs** (e.g. 'look *for*', 'made *up of*') which accept a pronoun without change of order. Others are **phrasal verbs** (e.g. '*wash up*') which accept a pronoun only if the particle and the pronoun change position (e.g. '*wash* it *up*').

AUXILIARY VERB PHRASES

Auxiliary verbs belong to **closed systems**. As the comments on the Victorian poem pointed out, auxiliary verbs fall into two main groups. They also share several functions.

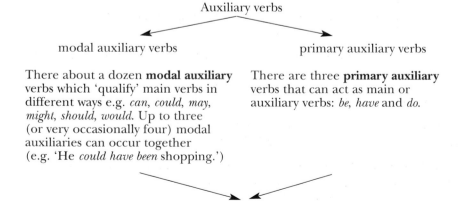

Auxiliary verbs

modal auxiliary verbs   primary auxiliary verbs

There about a dozen **modal auxiliary** verbs which 'qualify' main verbs in different ways e.g. *can, could, may, might, should, would.* Up to three (or very occasionally four) modal auxiliaries can occur together (e.g. 'He *could have been* shopping.')

There are three **primary auxiliary** verbs that can act as main or auxiliary verbs: *be, have* and *do.*

- In full sentences, these auxiliaries always occur with a lexical verb: 'He *might* go', although they can occur alone in elliptical clauses: 'Mum is going, but I *cannot*.'
- Auxiliaries are needed for 'yes or no' questions: '*Did* you mend the washing machine?'
- Auxiliaries are needed for many negatives, which can have *n't* added. This is something that cannot normally be done to lexical verbs, except *be* and *have*. *'I thoughtn't.'
- Auxiliaries can also stand for another verb element to help prevent repetition, e.g. 'Who can mend a puncture?' 'I *can*.'. This use of an auxiliary verb is known as a verbal **pro-form**.
- 'Be' and 'have' can be used as auxiliary verbs in order to form sentences in the passive voice from sentences where there is a transitive verb. The passive may add variety to the sentence structure of continuous text. It may also lose the original subject and add a discreet or impersonal tone to what is said or written, e.g.

    'The boy next door broke our fence yesterday.'
    '*Our fence was broken yesterday.*'
- The main modal auxiliaries (*can, could, may, might, must, ought to, shall, should, will, would*) are often used to make a judgement on the likelihood of an event or state, e.g. 'He *may* cooperate.' 'There *must* be an answer to this question.'
- Auxiliaries can express senses of obligation, permission, ability and willingness, e.g. 'She *should* do this.' 'I *will* help you out.'

(c) ADVERBIAL PHRASES

There are four main kinds of adverbial phrase:

(i)   a single-word adverb } closed system (e.g. *now, then, yesterday* etc.)
                            } open system (made from **adjective(s) + ly**)
(ii) the adverb adverbial phrase (e.g. adverb + intensifier: *very happily*)
(iii) the nominal adverbial phrase (e.g. *every day*)
(iv) the prepositional adverbial phrase (preposition + noun phrase or adverb, e.g. *at* the window; *up* here).

The adverbial, nominal and prepositional noun phrases can all be coordinated.

(d) ADJECTIVE PHRASES

The adjective phrase can be used to express the complement clause element. The SVC structure can involve the following:

- subject + copula verb (*be* or *become* etc.) + noun phrase or adjective phrase
  e.g. 'He was *the very model of a modern major general.*'
- subject + copula verb + adjective phrase only
  e.g. 'The food was *wonderful.*'

There are three main kinds of adjective phrase:

- a single verb adjective (e.g. *pleased*[19])
- an intensifier + adjective (e.g. *very pleased*)
- an adjective + prepositional phrase (e.g. *very pleased at the results*).

Again, any of these phrases can be coordinated.

3. Linking Simple Sentences Together to Make Multiple (Compound or Complex) Sentences

(a) THE STRUCTURE OF COMPOUND SENTENCES

A compound sentence is made by joining two or more clauses (or simple sentences) together. There are several ways of joining two simple sentences, including by using conjunctions, commas, substitution or ellipsis.

(i) Joining by **conjunctions** (such as *and, or, but*): e.g. 'The confusion got worse every moment *and* Alice was very glad to get out of the wood into an open place...'. (There does, of course, need to be a meaningful link between the clauses to make the use of a conjunction justified.)

(ii) Joining by **commas**, e.g. 'The teacher shouted, the children stopped and everyone listened.

(iii) Joining by **substitution** if the two clauses contain common elements, e.g. '*Alice* was not a bit hurt and *she* jumped up on to her feet in a moment.' (As this last sentence shows, nouns and noun phrases, acting as subject, object or complement, can be replaced by **pronouns**.)

Adverbial phrases can be replaced by **pro-forms**. Pro-forms are auxiliary verbs used in the way referred to earlier, e.g. 'Susan loves going to the theatre and Janet *does* too.'

Verbs and all the other clause elements that come after (i.e. VO, VC, VOO, VOC, VAs, VOA) are, together, sometimes known as the **predicate**. Any of the elements in the **predicate** can also be replaced by auxiliary verbs, e.g. 'John *played very skilfully* and so *did* Peter.'

(iv) Joining by **ellipsis**: common elements in conjoined sentences are omitted without the reader having to guess what has been left out, e.g. 'The car turned the corner and [ ] came to a standstill.'

Ellipsis can be used with just auxiliary verbs, e.g. 'The secretary *has* written the minutes and the treasurer [ ] checked their accuracy.'

Ellipsis can be used with a whole verb phrase, if it occurs in both clauses, e.g. 'Lucy *quickly picked up* the food and Robert [ ] the luggage.'

If the subject or verb is ellipted, the omission is always in the second clause (as above). If the direct object or complement is ellipted, the omission can be in the first clause, e.g. 'Daniel has always been [ ], and Joseph has just become, *a supporter.*'

(B) THE STRUCTURE OF COMPLEX SENTENCES

Complex sentences are made when there is an unequal relationship between two clauses. **Subordinate clauses** can either follow or precede the main clause, e.g:

When Thomas heard the news, he did not believe it.

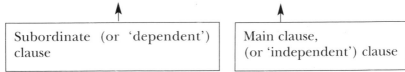

| Subordinate (or 'dependent') clause | Main clause, (or 'independent') clause |

There are three main kinds of subordinate clause: **finite**, **non-finite** and **verbless**.

(i) **Finite subordinate clauses**:
  - are 'complete' clauses (e.g. SVO, SVA, SVC);
  - have a finite verb;
  - are introduced by a **marker** word of some kind, a *wh-* word or *because, if, unless,* etc. e.g. 'When the van came along the road ...', 'Because the van came along the road, ...'

(ii) **Non-finite subordinate clauses** are not complete (they may lack a subject and the verb is non-finite (stem + *ing*; stem + *en*), e.g. 'Thomas watched *the news being broadcast*'; or '*Feeling rather tired,* Thomas sat down to watch television.'

(iii) **Verbless subordinate clauses** (the verb understood from the context). Often the verb is a form of *to be* or another auxiliary, because it is already linked to the main clause by some form of substitution or ellipsis (see above) to avoid repetition. Omitting this auxiliary can add to the economy or dramatic style of writing, e.g. 'The detective knew far more than anyone [*did*].'

The main kinds of function of subordinate clauses are to act as:

- clause elements i.e. nominal clauses + adverbial clauses (including finite, nonfinite or verbless (see above));
- parts of a phrase.

SUBORDINATE CLAUSES FUNCTIONING AS CLAUSE ELEMENTS

(i) **Nominal clauses: finite** (S or Od or Oi or Co or Cs)

Subject nominal clauses are more formal and are found more in writing than in speech, e.g: *Wh-* words: '*Why he did this*, no-one knows.'; *That* constructions: '*That he will resign* is very likely.'

This SVC structure is often transformed by moving the subject to the end of the sentence, e.g.: 'It is very likely *that he will resign*.'

Object nominal clauses are more common, for instance in direct and indirect speech. e.g: 'The manager said "*I am going to resign.*"' 'The manager said *(that) he was going to resign.*' (The **marker** *that* is optional).

This structure is also possible with other verbs and markers, e.g. believe *that*, realise *what*, learn *why*.
Less often, nominal clauses act in other ways:

- as an **indirect object**, e.g. 'The mayor gave *whoever finished the race* a packet of sweets.'
- as a **subject complement**, e.g. 'The most surprising thing was *that he attended at all.*'
- as an **object complement**, e.g. 'The manager will choose as captain *whoever can do the job best.*'

(ii) **Nominal clauses: non-finite**
These contain a non-finite verb: either *to* + stem or stem + *ing*.

These can occur as: subjects e.g. '*Working too hard* is not good for you.'
objects e.g.   'I didn't know *where to go.*'
complements e.g. 'The decision is *to re-interview.*'

(iii) **Adverbial clauses: finite**
The adverbial clause element is very often expressed by a clause, rather than by a single adverb. The use of an adverbial clause provides a writer with the opportunity to provide a whole range of additional information. Such extra details may be about the time, reason, result, place and manner of the information provided by the verb, e.g.:

The kitten was hungry
} *when we got home.* (time)
because no one had fed it. (reason)
so we gave it some food. (result)
in the cattery. (place)
as it was every morning. (manner)

The adverbial clause can also provide 'qualifying' information relating to conditions or concessions, e.g.:

If we don't buy some cat food, the kitten will be hungry. (condition)
Although the kitten was hungry, Peter still did not feed it. (concession)

Finite adverbial clauses are always marked by a **subordinator** (*when, because, so, as* etc.). **Adverbial clauses of time** have the largest number of subordinators, including *after, before, until, when, as soon as, while* etc.

(iv) **Adverbial clauses: non-finite**
Non-finite adverbial clauses can contain any of the three non-finite

verb forms: *to* + stem; stem + *ing*; stem + *en*. They tend to be used more with clauses of time, reason, purpose and concession, e.g.:

Being very hungry, the kitten ate all the food. (reason)
Having eaten some cat food, the kitten went to sleep. (time)
To avoid this happening again, we stocked up on cat food. (purpose)
Although spending all our money, we felt we had done the best thing. (concession)

(v) **Adverbial clauses: verbless**
e.g. 'When hungry, the kitten will eat anything.'

Subordinate clauses functioning as part of a phrase

(i) The clause in the noun phrase
There are two kinds of clause that can post-modify the 'head' noun in a noun clause. Both can begin with *that*, but the underlying structure is different.
- a **relative clause**, e.g. 'The news *that I wrote* was pinned on the board.' ('which')
- an **appositive clause**, e.g. 'The news *that I was better* was pinned on the board.' ('that is')

(ii) The finite relative clause
A relative clause provides additional information about the main noun in a noun phrase (often called the **antecedent**). Finite relative clauses are introduced by **relative pronouns** (*who* or *that* if antecedent is human; *which* or *that* if antecedent is non-human). These pronouns can act as either the subject or the object of the relative clause (in which case, *who* formally becomes *whom*).

The relative pronouns *whom* and *which* also occur less frequently with prepositions. When they are used, the syntax becomes very formal, e.g. 'This is the kind of thing *up with which* I will not put'; '*To whom* am I speaking?'

There are occasions when the relative pronoun can be omitted, e.g. 'The man (*that*) I met was very helpful.'

The relative pronoun *whose* acts as a determiner in a noun phrase, e.g. 'This is the puppy *whose lead* was broken.'

(iii) The non-finite relative clause
Non-finite relative clauses are made in several ways:
- stem + *ing*
e.g. 'Children *wishing to go on the outing* should sign up on the board.'
- stem + *en*
e.g. 'The team *beaten in the final* will still have medals.'
- *to* + stem
e.g. 'The last parents *to arrive* had to stand at the back of the hall.'
Relative clauses can be either 'restrictive' or 'non-restrictive' in their relationship to their antecedents. **Restrictive clauses** help to place the

main noun apart from others in the same group, e.g. *The Tiger Who Came To Tea.* **Non-restrictive clauses** provide a kind of 'aside', in commas, (sic) and are begun with *which* or *who*, e.g. 'Johnny, *who is keen on football,* said he would like to go to the match as well.'

(iv) The clause in the adverbial phrase

The adverbial element can be expressed by a prepositional phrase (comprising a preposition followed by a noun phrase), e.g. 'Joseph kicked the ball *over the fence that his dad had built.*'

The adverbial phrase may contain a **comparative** clause and this can also be elliptical, e.g. 'Amanda works *more consistently than her sister* (*does*).'

(v) The clause in the adjective phrase

Some adjectives can be followed by a relative clause beginning with *that*, although the marker can be omitted, e.g. 'I was sure (*that*) *I had lost.*'

Comparative clauses can also be added to adjectives, e.g. 'The pitch is greener *than it used to be.*'

Adjectives are often post-modified by a non-finite clause made up by an infinitive plus complementation, e.g. 'Granny was happy *to pick up all the toys.*'

(vi) Other types of subordinate clause

There are three (relatively rare) types of subordinate clause that can be found in complex sentences and yet which cannot be easily analysed.

- **Discontinuous clauses** linked to a noun phrase, e.g. 'More children bring packed lunches now *than used to bring them a few years ago.*'
- **Relative clauses** which have whole clauses or sentences as their antecedent, e.g. 'Anne said she was leaving the school, *which took us all by surprise.*'
- **Divided (or 'cleft') clauses** involve transforming a clause by 'cleaving' it into two. A word from the first clause can be emphasised by placing it at the end of the first clause in the transformed version and then adding 'it' and a form of the verb *to be*, e.g. '*Clive* scored the first goal' can be cleft into '*It was Clive who* scored the first goal.'

4. Creating Cohesion between Sentences

The most important links between sentences are **semantic**[20] rather than grammatical. Cohesion in the text is established by repeating key words or by replacing them by words related in meaning. In speech, links between sentences or clauses are also signalled by **intonation**.[21] In addition there are **grammatical connectives**, such as reference or substitution, in both speech and writing. The following section will deal firstly with the semantic links and then with grammatical devices that are used in creating text cohesion. The section will draw heavily on the pioneering work of Michael Halliday and Ruqaiya Hasan.[22] The chapter will not only adopt most of their analytical framework, but it will also continue their approach of taking examples from Lewis Carroll's *Alice* stories.

Halliday and Hasan outline the following ways in which cohesion is established by exploiting the meaningful connections between words. They call this **lexical** cohesion.

TYPES OF LEXICAL COHESION

REITERATION

i) same word (repetition)
ii) synonym
iii) superordinate
iv) general word

Some examples of **reiteration** in *Alice*:

i) **Same word:**
'There was a large *mushroom* growing near her, about the same height as herself; and, when she looked under it, it occurred to her that she might as well look and see what was on the top of it.
She stretched herself up on tiptoe, and peeped over the edge of the *mushroom*'.

ii) **Synonym** (or near-synonym, within the text):
'The Queen put on her spectacles, and began staring hard at *the Hatter*, who turned pale and fidgeted.
"Give your evidence", said the King; "and don't be nervous, or I'll have you executed on the spot."
This did not seem to encourage *the witness* at all...'

iii) **Superordinate:**
'In the very middle of the court was a table, with a large dish of *tarts* upon it: they looked so good that it made Alice quite hungry to look at them – "I wish they'd get the trial done" she thought, "and hand round *the refreshments!*"'

iv) **General word:**
'*The Mouse* gave a sudden leap out of the water and seemed to quiver all over with fright. "Oh, I beg your pardon!" cried Alice hastily, afraid that she had hurt the poor *animal's* feelings.'

COLLOCATION

An example of **collocation** (word associations) from *Alice*:

'Hardly knowing what she did, she picked up a little bit of stick, and held it out to *the puppy*; whereupon the puppy jumped into the air off all its feet at once, with a yelp of delight, and *rushed* at the stick ,,, *barking hoarsely* all the while, till at last it sat down a good way off, *panting*, with its *tongue hanging out* of its mouth'.

TYPES OF GRAMMATICAL CONNECTIVES

 i)   reference: personal, demonstratives, comparatives
 ii) substitution: of nouns, verbs and clauses
 iii) ellipsis ('substitution by zero')
 iv) connectives[23] (called 'conjunction' by Halliday and Hasan)

Some examples of **grammatical cohesion** in *Alice*

 i)   **Personal reference** (personal and possessive pronouns and possessive determiners):
      '"Aren't you sometimes frightened, at being planted out here, with nobody to take care of you?"
      "There's *the tree* in the middle," said the Rose. "What else is *it* good for?"
      "But what could *it* do, if danger came?" Alice asked.
      "*It* could bark," said the Rose.
      "*It* says 'Bough-wough!" cried a Daisy: "that's why *its* branches are called boughs!"'

      Demonstrative reference (this, that, these, those etc.):
      '"I couldn't afford to learn it" said the Mock Turtle with a sigh.
      "I only took the *regular course.*"
      "What was *that?*" inquired Alice.'

      Comparatives (general identity, similarity, difference or particular number or quality):
      '"*I see nobody on the road*" said Alice.
      "I only wish I had *such* eyes," the King remarked, "to be able to see nobody – and at that distance too."'

 ii) **Substitution of nouns/pronouns** (using *one, ones, some* etc.):
      '"I vote the young lady tells us a *story*." "I'm afraid I don't know *one,*" said Alice.'

      Substitution of verbs (using *do* etc.):
      '"They *lived on treacle*," said the Dormouse, after thinking a minute or two. "They couldn't have *done that*, you know," Alice gently remarked: "they'd have been ill."'

      Substitution of clauses (using *so, not* etc.):
      '"How am I to get in?" asked Alice again, in a wonder tone.
      "*Are* [original italics] you to get in at all?" said the Footman. "*That's the first question*, you know."
      It was, no doubt: only Alice did not like to be told *so.*'

 iii) **Ellipsis**
      Ellipsis is very similar to the process of substitution and is really 'substitution by zero'. Like substitution, cohesive links can be made by noun, verb and clause ellipsis:
      '"And how many hours a day did you do lessons?" said Alice in a hurry to change the subject.
      "Ten hours the first day," said the Mock Turtle: nine the next *[ ]* and so on."'

 iv) **Connectives** ('conjunction', according to Halliday and Hasan)
      The full range of conjunctive relations is summarised in Table 6.5.

Figure 6.5 Summary of conjunctive relations

	External/internal		Internal (unless otherwise specified)					
	type	**realization**	**type**	**realization**	**type**	**realization**	**type**	**realization**
Addition	Additive, simple: / Complex, emphatic: Additive Negative Alternative	and, and also nor, and ... not or, or else	Apposition: Additive Alternative Complex, de-emphatic: After-thought	furthermore, in addition, besides alternatively, incidentally, by the way	Comparison: Expository Exemplificatory	that is, I mean, in other words thus for instance	Similar Dissimilar	likewise, similarly, in the same way on the other hand, by contrast
Opposition	Adversative 'proper': Simple Containing 'and' Emphatic	yet, though, only but however, nevertheless, despite this	Contrastive: Avowal Contrastive (external): Simple Emphatic	in fact, actually, as a matter of fact but, and however, on the other hand, at the same time	Correction: Of meaning Of wording	instead, rather, on the contrary at least, rather, I mean	Dismissal: Closed Open-ended	in any case, in either case, whichever way it is in any case, anyhow, at any rate, however it is
Cause	Causal, general: Simple Emphatic Causal, specific: Reason Result Purpose	so, then, hence, therefore consequently, because of this for this reason, on account of this as a result, in consequence for this purpose, with this in mind	Conditional (also external): Simple Generalized Reason Result Purpose	for, because under the it follows, on this basis arising out of this to this end	Respective: Simple Emphatic Reversed Reversed polarity	then, in that case, in such an event, that being so otherwise, in circumstances otherwise, under other circumstances	Direct polarity	in this respect, in this regard, with reference to this other respects, aside from this
Time	Temporal, simple (external only): Sequential Simultaneous Preceding Conclusive: Simple Correlative forms: Sequential Conclusive	then, next, after that just then, at the same time previously, before that finally, at last first ... then at first ... in the end	Complex (external only): Immediate Interrupted Repetitive Specific Durative Terminal Punctiliar	at once, thereupon soon, after a time next time, on another occasion next day, an hour later meanwhile until then at this moment	Internal temporal: Sequential Conclusive Correlative forms: Sequential Conclusive	then, next, secondly finally, in conclusion first ... next ... finally	'Here and now': Past Present Future Summary: Summarizing Resumptive	up to now, hitherto at this point, here from now on, henceforward to sum up, in short, briefly to resume, to return to the point

Again it is not difficult to find examples in *Alice*:

Addition:

'"I was very nearly opening the window, and putting you out in the snow! *And* you'd have deserved it you little mischievous darling!"'

Opposition ('contrary to expectation'):

'"I like the Walrus best," said Alice: "because, you see, he was a *little* [original italics] sorry for the poor oysters".

"He ate more then the Carpenter, *though*", said Tweedledee.'

Cause ('a, therefore b'; or 'possibly a; if so, then b'):

'"Have some wine," the March Hare said in an encouraging tone.

Alice looked all round the table, but there was nothing on it but tea. "I don't see any wine", she remarked.

"There isn't any," said the March Hare.

"*Then* it wasn't very civil of you to offer it," said Alice angrily.'

Time:

'She heard a little shriek and a fall, and a crash of broken glass, from which she concluded that it was just possible it had fallen into a cucumber frame, or something of the sort. *Next* came an angry voice – the Rabbit's – "Pat! Pat! Where are you?" *And then* a voice she had never heard before ...'

Halliday and Hasan remind us that, if we hear or read a passage of English that is more than a sentence in length, we can normally sense whether it forms a unified whole or whether the passage is made up by a number of unrelated sentences. What makes the difference is whether the text has *cohesion*, created by links between meanings and grammatical features in succeeding sentences. This chapter has given some indications of some of the many ways in which these links can be made. If the basic framework of these links is understood, then it can provide a valuable resource for teaching, as the next two chapters will show.

Grammar and Teaching

Conscious manipulation of syntax deepens engagement and releases invention.
(Ted Hughes)[1]

This chapter

- discusses how teachers' grammatical knowledge can help in developing pupils' writing;
- suggests some effective teaching practices, based on research in the field.

There are many books that can help teachers to develop their own knowledge of English grammar. The number of these books is likely to grow in the light of the renewed interest in grammar that marked the final years of the twentieth century. Yet there are far fewer books to help teachers in applying this knowledge to the teaching of writing. Indeed, for analysing children's writing, there is really no equivalent to the LARSP procedure that was developed by David Crystal and his colleagues for analysing children's uses of spoken language.[2] LARSP (Language Assessment, Remediation and Screening Procedure) deals solely with grammar (syntax and morphology) in the early stages of language development. It provides a profile of the stages that were briefly referred to in **Chapter 2**. The profile has been widely used by speech therapists.

Suggestions for applying grammatical knowledge to the teaching of writing tend to focus on the following approaches:

1. Identifying non-standard dialect in writing;
2. Creating interest in grammatical rules (at word and sentence levels);
3. Improving general style;
4. Linking grammatical reference to 'language awareness';
5. Promoting specific grammatical structures in writing.

This chapter deals with the first four of these approaches. Promoting specific grammatical structures in writing is dealt with as part of the discussion of writing development in **Chapter 8**.

To reflect some of the growing interest in this aspect of writing, each section ends with an example from recent research that shows how grammatical knowledge can be used in teaching and assessment.

1 Identifying Non-standard Dialect in Writing

As was outlined in **Chapter 2**, a **dialect** is a variation of the same language in a particular region or social group. It includes variation in vocabulary, grammar and, if spoken, accent. The predominant dialect in Great Britain is **standard English**, which is the dialect normally used in published writing materials. This can be spoken in a variety of accents. Non-standard dialect features are found in the various geographical regions of the country.

Table 7.1 shows some non-standard features used by 11–15 year old pupils in a questionnaire survey undertaken by Viv Edwards and Jenny Cheshire at the Universities of Reading and London.[3]

Table 7.1

(a) Present tenses of verbs
   e.g. I *sees*...
        We *likes*...
        You *has* to do it.
	(b) Past tenses of verbs
	   e.g. He *done* it.
	        I *give* her a birthday present
	        yesterday.

(c) Present and past forms of the verb 'to be'
   e.g. He *be* the one.
        You *was* right.
	(d) Negatives
	   e.g. *shouldna*, *ain't*, *in't*, won't
	        do *nothing*

(e) Combined verbs
   e.g. I *d'* eat (I *do* eat)...
        do be
        done bought
	(f) Verb linkers
	   e.g He's *after going* away, but
	        he'll be back soon.

(g) Plurals
   e.g. twenty *mile*
        three *pound*
	(h) Pronoun forms
	   e.g. I saw *she* recently.
	        Give it to *he*.

(i) Possessives
   e.g. This is *me* coat.
        Eat up *thee* food.
	(j) Demonstratives
	   e.g. See *them* trees.
	        Look at *trees*.

(k) Determiners
   e.g. *a* old coat
        Look at *time*.
	(l) Relative clauses
	   e.g. the sweets *what* I like
	        the film *as* was on

(m) Determiners
   e.g. *more* better
        worser
	(n) Adverbs and prepositions
	   e.g. *real quick*
	        off of

It seems likely that some of these features will sometimes be carried over into the writing of continuous prose. Whether these kinds of features are seen as weaknesses or not will depend upon the kind of writing being undertaken and the values that are used in responding to it. In some kinds of literary and personal recount writing, the inclusion of non-standard features may be seen as a strength. Their inclusion can add a sense of authenticity to the writing, especially in dialogue.

However, if some pupils habitually use several of the above features in their writing, then more fundamental questions have to asked. The learning of standard English is likely to improve life-chances and, in the words of the Kingman Report, can be seen as the *right* of all children.[4] Examination success and occupational opportunity may well depend on this learning. The study of dialect differences provide revealing insights into the relationships between language and power.

There have been recurrent debates about the feasibility and desirability of teaching standard English grammar to children who habitually use a range of non-standard dialect features. The comparison of standard and non-standard dialects needs to be undertaken with care, as it may be misguided to treat them as 'alternatives'. As well as the asymmetry of life-chances mentioned above, there is also an interesting asymmetry in relation to ideas of 'correctness'. John Honey has written at length on this issue. He argues that standard and non-standard English are not just 'different', as some writers have suggested. Honey points out that standard English has standards of correctness that are simply not available in non-standard dialects. Standard English is codified in writing in the way that non-standard dialects are not.[5]

The National Curriculum for England and Wales has details in its Programmes of Study of the features of grammar and vocabulary of written standard English which children should be encouraged to understand and use at different ages. Since its first version in 1989, it has consolidated its references to these aspects of language development. In 1995 it added a separate strand on 'Standard English and Language Study'. In 2000, this was changed to 'Standard English and Language Structure'.[6]

The challenge that this presents for teachers should not be underestimated. Edwards and Cheshire report that the majority of British children are speakers of a non-standard dialect of English.[7] Survey evidence from 350 11 and 15 year olds in four English regions by Richard Hudson and Jasper Holmes suggests that young people's use of non-standard English (NSE) forms in their speech may tend to increase in the teenage years as a mark of group identity.[8] The majority of about a dozen forms were used in all four regions. This may reflect the existence of **sociolects**. These are speech patterns that are encouraged and sustained through cultural and media influences. The six most widely used non-standard forms were as follows:

Table 7.2

NSE form	Comparison with SSE (Standard Spoken English)	% speakers who used the NSE form[9]
'there is' (plural)	*is > are* NSE uses *is* after *there* and a following plural e.g., '*there is jobs* to do'.[10]	87%
'this guy'	*this > a* 'This' or 'these' is used with a noun to refer to a person or thing not mentioned before.	46%
'she come'	*come > came* The NSE form of the past tense is the same as the SSE past participle.	42%
'out the window'	*omitting the preposition 'of'* NSE omits this preposition especially before *window, door, room* or *house*.	62%

'have fell'	*fell* > *fallen* The NSE form of the past participle after the verb *have* is the SSE past tense.[11]	35%
'them books' or (in SW England) 'they books'	*them* or *they* > *those* The NSE form of the demonstrative pronoun or adjective uses either: (i) the SSE plural pronoun when it is the object of a sentence ('I saw *them*'); (ii) the SSE plural pronoun when it is the subject of a sentence ('*They* saw me').	42%

Annual reviews of writing performance at 7, 11 and 14 suggest that these non-standard features may be used more in speech than in writing. In the reviews of SATs performance in the late 1990s, very few non-standard features have been identified as occurring regularly in young people's writing.[12] John Williamson and Frank Hardman at the University of Newcastle have examined the writing performance of 11 and 15 year old pupils in four regions of England.[13] Like Hudson and Holmes (referred to above), they made use of data from earlier work by the Assessment of Performance Unit. Analysing 326 scripts, Williamson and Hardman found that the use of non-standard dialect was a relatively rare phenomenon. Of the 127 children who used non-standard dialect in their writing, 70 per cent did so on only one occasion. Only 7 per cent used more than two different dialect features. By far the highest incidence of non-standard use was in the writing of 11 year olds when they were writing a personal anecdote (recalling their earliest memory). Non-standard features could have added authenticity to this writing. Overall, the use of non-standard features declined with age. This was the reverse of the findings of Hudson and Holmes in their studies of speech.

As they grow older, then, pupils may increase their use of non-standard dialect in informal speech as a mark of group identity. At the same time, they may reduce their use of non-standard features in their writing in school as part of their adjustment to the demands and expectations of the context of the school. Overall, Williamson and Hardman conclude that the use of non-standard dialect is a relatively rare phenomenon in the writing of 10 and 15 year olds. They add that it shrinks into insignificance when compared, for example, with errors of spelling or punctuation.

In contrast, a number of non-standard dialect features have been identified in St. Lucian children's writing by Christopher Winch and John Gingell.[14]

A RESEARCH STUDY

Identifying non-standard dialect in writing

Christopher Winch and John Gingell, at University College, Northampton, studied the working performance of 155 9, 10 and 11 year olds in St. Lucia, in the Southern Caribbean. They were particularly interested in how far the local Creole (a 'strong' form of non-standard English) might interfere with children's written expression when writing letters of complaint and when finishing narratives begun by the teacher. The situation in St. Lucia is complicated by the fact that the majority of the population have some additional competence in French Creole. Winch and Gingell also collected similar data from a small sample of English children, using them as a 'control' group. As well as looking for signs of Creole interference, Winch and Gingell checked the scripts for several other kinds of error. These errors included those which could be attributed to weaknesses in dealing with the genre conventions of letters and personal narratives. The errors also related to using the conventions of speech in writing.

The highest occurrences of errors were the following (% of scripts containing errors in each category):

1. inappropriate shift of tenses in a sentence, e.g. 'Amos wen in the house   22.6%
   Boris went and meet him there.'
2. incorrect use of preposition   8.8%
3. use of imperfect (past continuous) tense for perfect (simple past)   5.5%
4. incorrect inflection of irregular past verb stems   5.1%
5. lack of agreement between subject and verb   4.5%
6. lack of plural markers (including count nouns)   4.2%

The commonest type of error, the inappropriate shift of tenses in a sentence (ISTIS), was found across the marking range. The ISTIS errors were found as much in scripts that were impressionistically marked higher as those which were marked lower. However, the authors caution that this kind of error is more related to children's development of the differentiated writing style than it is to Creole interference. By differentiated style, they mean adopting the grammar features of written language that distinguish it from spoken language. In particular, this style is a feature of attempts to construct compound and complex sentences.

The same kind of caution could apply to the incorrect use of preposition (IUP). This error was found across the marking range of the St. Lucian scripts and in 12.5 per cent of the sample of English children, mostly at the lower end of the marking range.

The only evidence of Creole interference in the three most common types of error was related to the use of the imperfect tense for the perfect (IFP), for instance 'I bought a bottle of juice and it was not tasting good' instead of 'I bought a bottle of juice and it did not taste good.'

This may be related to the fact that French uses the imperfect form of the past tense in this kind of construction. It may also be significant that this kind of error was not found at all in the sample of English scripts. However, it is possible that English pupils might have had more experience of tackling this kind of 'letter of complaint' task.

There is much more of interest in the original paper. It serves as a helpful reminder of how grammatical analysis can take us beyond impressions of writing performance.

Grammatical analysis provides greater insight into the fabric of a text. Grammatical terminology offers a helpful shorthand for referring to specific features. Winch and Gingell show how useful grammatical knowledge can be in diagnosing weaknesses in writing and in unravelling the complex relationship between dialect interference and other, broader aspects of writing development.

2 Creating an Interest in Grammatical Rules

It is widely agreed that we all know more grammar than we realise. By learning to speak fluently, we intuitively learn and apply many complex relations between parts of words and between words themselves. As Michael Halliday and Ruqaiya Hasan remind us, description involves discussing things that native speakers know already, but without knowing that they know them.[15] Such grammatical knowledge is only made explicit when we try to comment upon why words or word orders sound or look 'right' or 'wrong'. This explicit stage is, in some ways, an interim one between taken-for-grantedness and conscious use of various grammatical terms to refer to specific grammatical features or rules. The kinds of suggestions that follow in this chapter may help to provide the basis for well-informed use of grammatical terminology, related to a sense of proportion in the possibilities and uncertainties of grammatical description.

As was shown in **Chapter 2**, there are two branches of grammar: morphology (within-word rules) and syntax (between word rules). In fact, English makes relatively little use of word structure compared with word order.[16] Most of English grammar is concerned with the orders in which words can be combined. Nevertheless, interest in grammar can be enhanced by looking at how bits of words can be combined into meaningful wholes and how this meaning can often be indicated by particular prefixes or suffixes.

CREATING INTEREST IN GRAMMATICAL RULES: WORD LEVEL

The following suggestions can exploit children's interest in exploring links between words and word-families. The suggestions are likely to be of particular relevance in the increased word-level direct teaching promoted by the National Literacy Strategy. The success of these ideas is likely to be greater if the concentration on words is supported by shared reading and writing. Such text-level teaching will help to illustrate the way in which words can be effectively used in continuous text.

(a) Turning simple words (root words) into **compound words**

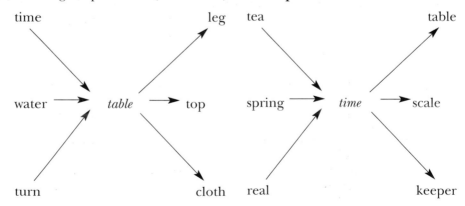

Other words could include: *boat, house, play, wind, fish, flower, solid, paper* etc.

(b) Turning simple words into **complex words** (using **free** and **bound morphemes**)

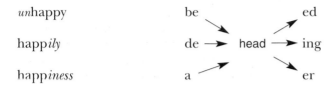

*un*happy   be   ed

happ*ily*   de ⟶ head ⟶ ing

happ*iness*   a   er

Other simple words could include: *believe, cover, grace, help, port*, etc.

(c) Using **prefixes** and **suffixes**

un-		-ing
dis-		-ed
mis-	root word	-er
	(a free morpheme)	
im-		-ly
ir-		-s
de-		-ible
		-est
		-ful
		-is
		-y

Several root words can be selected in order to work out which one can be used to make the largest number of complex words.

A variety of text types can be selected and a tally chart can be made of the simple compound and complex words in it, so that the texts can be compared and discussed.

(d) Grouping suffixes by type[17]

Suffixes making **grammatical inflections**		Suffixes making **abstract nouns**	
-s	plural	*-age* e.g.	mileage
-'s	possession	*-dom*	stardom
-ed	past tense	*-ery*	slavery
-n't	negative	*-ful*	spoonful
-ing	present participle	*-hood*	childhood
-er	comparison	*-ing*	playing
-est	comparison	*-ship*	friendship

Suffixes making **concrete nouns**		Suffixes making **adverbs**	
-eer e.g.	engineer	*-ly*	quickly
-er	cooker	*-wards*	upwards
-ess	waitress	*wise*	clockwise
-let	booklet		
-ling	duckling		
-ster	gangster		

Suffixes making **verbs**

-ate	navigate
-en	deafen
-ify	certify
-ise	advertise

Suffixes making **nouns from verbs**

-age	wastage
-al	refusal
-ant	applicant
-ation	education
-er	driver
-ing	clothing
-or	actor

Suffixes making **nouns from adjectives**

-ity	oddity
-ness	happiness

Suffixes making **adjectives from nouns**

-ed	pointed
-ful	useful
-ish	foolish
-ly	friendly
-ous	ambitious
-y	sandy

Suffixes making **adjectives from verbs**

-able	washable
-ive	attractive

(e) Grouping **prefixes** by type[18]

negatives

a-	atheist
dis-	dislike
in-	incomplete
non-	non-smoker
un-	unhelpful

reversals

de-	defrost
dis-	disobey
un-	unnecessary

imperfect

mal-	malfunction
mis-	mistreat

size or degree

co-	co-pilot
hyper-	hyper-market
mega-	mega-bomb
mini-	mini-bus
out-	out-class
over-	over-flow
sub-	sub-conscious
under-	under-charge
vice-	vice-president

orientation

anti-	anti-clockwise
contra-	contraflow
counter-	counteract

place and distance

extra-	extra-terrestrial
fore-	foreshore
inter-	inter-school
super-	superstructure
tele-	telephone
trans-	trans-atlantic

time and order

ex-	ex-president
post-	post-war
pre-	pre-school
re-	re-cycle

number

bi-	bicycle
di-	digraph
mono-	monoplane
multi-	multiracial
semi-	semicircle
tri-	trimaran
uni-	unicycle[19]

prefixes making **adjectives from verbs**

a-	aboard
a-	astride

prefixes making **verbs from nouns**

be-	befriend
en-	endanger

CREATING INTEREST IN GRAMMATICAL RULES: SENTENCE LEVEL

One of the biggest weaknesses of the 'naming of parts' approach is that it does not provide insights into the underlying rules of grammar. The limitations of just 'looking and labelling' can be seen by comparing it with an approach that reveals the grammatical function of words. This second approach involves applying little tests in which words are substituted, omitted or changed in parallel sentences.

See how the two approaches provide different kinds of insight and information about how the word 'table' can be used.

Looking and labelling	**The substitution test**
What part of speech or word class does the word *table* belong to?	The *table* was made of wood. The *chair* was made of wood. The *box* was made of wood. (Here *table* belongs to the same word class as *chair* and *box*.)
	We had to wash the *table* cloth. We had to wash the *blue* cloth. We had to wash the *chequered* cloth. (Here *table* belongs to the same word class as *blue* and *chequered*.)
	He had to *table* the report at the meeting. He had to *present* the report at the meeting. He had to *submit* the report at the meeting. (Here *table* belongs to the same word class as *present* and *submit*.)
	She decided to walk *quickly*. She decided to walk *quietly*. She decided to walk *table*. (Here *table* cannot belong to the same word class as *quietly* or *quickly*.)

These may appear to be relatively trivial examples, providing further information on a matter that is already obvious. However, the following examples may show how the substitution and other grammatical tests can help to provide subtle insights into the rules governing word order.

This test is designed to check whether different-sized groups of words have the same grammatical function.

A fallen conifer tree
A conifer tree ⟶ was blocking our path.
A tree

but not **A fallen was blocking our path.*

THE OMISSION TEST

This test indicates whether an element is essential or optional in a particular grammatical structure.

The dog ran around the garden. ⎫
The dog ran around   ⎬ *the garden* is optional

The dog was in the garden. ⎫
The dog was in   ⎬ *the garden* is essential

Omitting *the garden* from the two sentences shows how it is optional in the first, but essential in the second.

THE TRANSPOSITION TEST

This test shows whether sentences that appear similar are in fact structurally different.

Dad put *up* the shelf ⎫
Dad put the shelf *up*. ⎬ *up* acts as an adverb

Dad went *up* the road ⎫
*Dad went the road *up*. ⎬ *up* acts as a preposition

The word *up* performs different grammatical functions in the two sentences, both of which contain 'multi-word' verbs. In the first sentence, the word *up* is part of a 'phrasal verb' e.g. 'give in' or 'blow up'. In phrasal verbs, 'particles' like *up* can come before or after the object and act as an **adverb**. In the second sentence the word *up* is part of a 'prepositional verb', like 'looking after' 'calling for' or 'leading to'. Here, *up* can only come before the object and acts as a **preposition**. These subtle differences are only made clear when the transposition test is used.

THE EXPANSION TEST

This test is another way of showing that words belong to different word classes.

The dogs were *excited.*
The dogs were *Alsatians.*

The dogs were *very excited.*
*The dogs were *very Alsatians.*

The dogs were *pedigree Alsatians.*
*The dogs were *pedigree excited.*

The sentences containing words from the *excited* class (adjectives) can be expanded by *very.* The sentence containing the *Alsatians* class (nouns) cannot. Similarly, the noun constructions can be expanded by *pedigree,* but the adjective construction (acting a subject complement) cannot.

THE TRANSFORMATION TESTS

These tests are larger-scale ones and can include making negatives, questions and passives. As before, using such transformations can reveal structural differences between sentences that at first appear similar.

Making negatives
Mum *is* working. ────────────▶ Mum *is not* working.
Mum *enjoys* working. ────────────▶ Mum *does not enjoy* working.

Here the difference between the structures is shown by the need for *does* to be added in order to make a negative from the second sentence but not the first. Also, the word *not* can be placed after the main verb in the first sentence, but has to come before the main verb in the second.

Making questions
Mum *enjoys* working. ────────────▶ **Enjoys* Mum working?
Mum *is* working. ────────────▶ *Is* Mum working?

The difference between the structures is shown by the different results from changing the order of the first two words to create a question: one is grammatical; the other is not.

Making passives
Mum *felt* safe. ────────────▶ **Safe *was felt* by Mum.
Mum *felt* the material. ────────────▶ The material *was felt* by Mum.

The passive can only be applied to one construction, even though at first the two sentences look similar.

Little grammatical tests like this can show differences and similarities between sentences more reliably than 'looking and labelling' approaches. They provide interesting and challenging discussion points for teachers and pupils without making it necessary for anyone to use technical terminology. Instead, grammatical tests provide a context into which technical terms can be introduced in order to sum up specific features in a convenient shorthand. More importantly, though, grammatical tests provide a means of encouraging teachers and pupils to look 'between the words' at the rules that enable words to be assembled in some ways and that prohibit others.

CREATING INTEREST IN GRAMMATICAL RULES: SENTENCE-COMBINING

There are no equivalent tests for exploring the ways in which sentences can be combined into multiple sentences. Instead there are promising possibilities for creating interest in grammatical rules by using sentence-combining. Research into the effects of this technique suggests that it can assist the development of writing competence as well as providing insights into grammatical structure.[20]

In each case the first sentence is the form of the sentence-combining problem for the pupil and the last sentence is an acceptable answer. It should be noted that the examples below represent a range of possibilities. To be likely to assist writing performance, they may need to be targeted on certain grammatical features. These features may be best taught in a sustained way. Such teaching will benefit if alternatives are carefully discussed.

1. Turning statements into questions
   The school team won yesterday. ➜ Did the school team win yesterday?
2. Turning statements into negatives
   The school team played well yesterday. ➜ The school team didn't play well yesterday.
3. Adding details of 'how' and 'where'
   The jackdaw hopped (WHERE), picked up the ring (WHERE) and (HOW) flew off. ➜ The jackdaw quickly hopped in through the window, picked up the ring in its beak and immediately flew off.
4. Active to passive
   Jonathan should have closed the gate. ➜ The gate should have been closed by Jonathan.
5. Turning statements into 'there' constructions
   A tunnel is under the village. ➜ There is a tunnel under the village.
6. Turning statements into 'what' questions
   The policeman was writing something on the board. ➜ What was the policeman writing on the board?
7. Turning statements into 'who' questions
   Someone has taken my pen. ➜ Who has taken my pen?
8. Combining sentences using 'why'
   All the people wondered (SOMETHING). The music had stopped for some reason. (WHY) ➜ All the people wondered why the music had stopped.
9. Combining sentences using 'what'
   Something worried the explorers. The strange noise meant something. (WHAT) ➜ What the strange noise meant worried the explorers.
10. Combining sentences using 'how'
    Most teachers have learned (SOMETHING). Children compare homework somehow. (HOW) ➜ Most teachers have learned how children compare homework.
11. Combining sentences using 'when'
    Cathy wondered (SOMETHING). The bus would arrive in London sometime. (WHEN) ➜ Cathy wondered when the bus would arrive in London.

12. Combining sentences using 'if'
I don't get there by 6pm. (IF) Phone me. I shall have forgotten. ➔ If I don't get there by 6 pm, phone me as I shall have forgotten.

13. Combining sentences using 'once'
You overcome your fear of water. Learning to swim just takes a lot of practice. ➔ Once you overcome your fear of water, learning to swim just takes a lot of practice.

14. Combining sentences by changing a verb to its '-ing' form
Jo burst through the defence. (ING) Jo forced the goalkeeper to make
a   fine save. ➔ Bursting through the defence, Jo forced the goalkeeper to make a fine save.

15. Combining sentences using 'with' as a connector
Jo's leg was badly cut. (WITH) Jo just managed to play on. ➔ With her leg badly cut, Jo just managed to play on.

A RESEARCH STUDY

Creating an interest in grammatical rules

Many of the above examples come from an influential study of sentence-combining undertaken by Frank O'Hare of Florida State University using two experimental and two control classes of 12–13 year olds. The experimental group were given sentence-combining practice and a reduced form of the regular curriculum, whereas the control group were given a 'regular' curriculum. Central to the assessments used in this study was the T-unit, a main clause and any subordinate clauses that belong to it. Pre-test and post-test assessments were made of the pupils' words and clauses per T-unit; words per clause; and noun clauses, adverb clauses and adjective (relative) clauses per 100 T-units.

Single qualitative judgements were also made of the pupils' writing, taking account of ideas, organisation, style, vocabulary and sentence structure. The judgements were applied to pairs of compositions, one experimental and one control. The compositions had been matched according to the subjects' sex and IQ The compositions included personal and imaginative narratives, descriptive and discursive tasks that all reflected the pupils' experiences and interests.

The results of the study were that the experimental group experienced highly significant gains on all six factors. The experimental group wrote well beyond the syntactic maturity typical of 13 year olds. This encouraging outcome was not related to the influence of any particular teacher. Students who scored lower on tests of general ability achieved highly significant gains. Those with higher general ability scores improved even more. Both the narrative and descriptive groups were better than their control groups.[21]

There is currently a great deal of interest in pupils' writing performance and the relative underachievement of boys. Research and inspection evidence suggests that main teaching approaches in the United Kingdom tend to be focused on the presentational or process approaches. The kinds of guided writing represented by sentence-combining seems not to be widely used. Sentence-combining could have a valuable role to play in the guided writing that supports the shared and independent writing in the British government's National Literacy Strategy.

3 Grammatical Features of General Style

The next section is not so much related to specific grammatical constructions. Instead, it is more concerned with general features of **style**. There are some features of expression that are more characteristic of written rather than spoken language. It is important to bear these features in mind when fostering children's writing development in the primary and middle years. Many of these features are likely to be assimilated unconsciously through wide-ranging reading. However, if teachers are aware of their significance, then they can explicitly draw children's attention to them. Teachers can do this in the shared reading parts of a Literacy Hour teaching approach and also in making suggestions to children on how they might add maturity to their writing style.

Among these features are the following:

- thematic continuity, by use of 'fronting' or the passive;
- thematic variety;
- end-focus, by 'fronting', the use of the passive, or 'clefting';
- impersonal style;
- overall coherence.

Each of these points is considered in turn below.[22]

THEMATIC CONTINUITY

This aspect is related to a specific definition of the term 'theme'. Here, it refers to the first element in a clause, as opposed to definitions of the 'overall idea'. The first element in a clause normally expresses information that has already been mentioned (as in the sentence I am now writing); new information normally appears in the later part of a sentence (again, as in the sentence I am now completing). If new information is consistently introduced at the beginning of sentences, then the overall style of writing becomes disjointed, jarring the reader's attempts to follow what the writer is trying to say. Instead, the reader is likely to be assisted if the theme is expressed by the subject of the new sentence or perhaps by 'fronting' an adverbial element. If continuity is maintained in this way, then the reader is able to concentrate on the new information in a sentence. This new information is often most effective if it comes at what is sometimes called the 'end-focus' of the sentence. The example below shows how these stylistic features can operate:

> 'From there I went up a flimsy ladder. There was a hole in the wall and a cold draught was coming through it. *At the top of the ladder* was a very big wheel attached to a bell.'[23]

(adverbial element 'fronted' as the theme) (new information given 'end focus')

Thematic continuity can also be maintained by careful use of the passive. The passive allows the subject of the previous sentence to be used in expressing the theme at a point in the text where a different subject could act as a distraction.

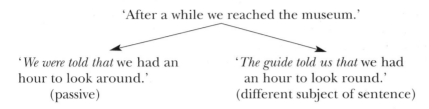

'After a while we reached the museum.'

'*We were told that* we had an hour to look around.'
(passive)

'*The guide told us that* we had an hour to look round.'
(different subject of sentence)

The effectiveness of the passive will depend on whether reference to the guide is felt to be necessary in the context of the writer's purposes. If the purpose is a personal recount, then the fronting of 'we' in 'we were told' helps to support the end-focus on the reference to the time limit. The avoidance of reference to 'the guide' also helps in this way.

THEMATIC VARIETY

At the same time, excessive repetition of the same subject (noun, multi-word noun phrase or pronoun) can create a rather tedious style (e.g. *I... I... I...*). This can be avoided if the object or complement of a previous sentence is sometimes used as the subject of the next. Lewis Carroll uses this device in *Alice's Adventures in Wonderland* when writing about the gardeners:

'Five and Seven said nothing, but looked at *Two*. *Two* began, in a low voice, "Why, the fact is, you see, Miss, this here ought to have been a *red* [original italics] rose-tree, and we put a white one in by mistake...."'

END-FOCUS

As was mentioned above, a more mature writing style can be fostered by choosing a word order that gives emphasis to the new information in a sentence. This may need to be placed at the end of a clause. The end focus will then coincide with the part of the clause that is emphasised when the sentence is spoken or read aloud. Such a coincidence of end-focus with the emphasis in pronunciation is a particular feature of English.

As was seen earlier, end-focus can be achieved by the use of fronting and the use of the passive. It can also be achieved by **clefting**. As was discussed earlier, **clefting** involves making two clauses out of one and putting the word to be emphasised at the end of the first clause, e.g.:

'Bilbo spoke first.' ——————→ 'It was Bilbo who spoke first'.

In the cleft sentence, the subject is *it*, the verb is a form of *be* and the emphasised part comes next. The rest of the sentence is usually introduced by *that* or *who*. A related, but less common, structure is what Sidney Greenbaum calls a 'pseudo-cleft' sentence, in which the emphasised part comes at the end,[24] e.g. 'What we want is justice.'

IMPERSONAL STYLE

General writing style needs to take on a variety of impersonal aspects to help the young writer to deal with the writing demands in and beyond school. An impersonal style of writing may include a variety of features, including the passive form, referred to earlier. In addition, it may contain writing that *avoids* a number of features which children readily include in personal writing:

- personal pronouns (*I, we, you*);
- direct or reported speech;
- the writer's own feelings;
- reference to anything that is not strictly relevant to the purpose of the writing.

The style of such esoteric writing is not only very different from that of personal writing, but also different from the structures and content of everyday speech. This contrast underlines the fact that young writers have limited resources to draw upon when they tackle impersonal writing. The most helpful resource is likely to be the impersonal style of the texts which young writers read, have read to them and whose distinctive features are pointed out to them. However, it is also important for teachers to strike a balance between the challenges of an impersonal writing style and the demands of new subject knowledge. Trying to develop an impersonal style when writing about conceptually difficult ideas will provide an excessive burden for many pupils. Instead, their attempts to use specific features in their writing – and to avoid others – are likely to be more productive if the subject material is familiar to them and if the purposes of the writing are clearly understood.

OVERALL COHERENCE

Finally, the style of the text needs to have overall coherence to help it to fulfil the writer's original intentions. This coherence can be created by a number of internal grammatical features.

Noun phrases need be referred to in a way that makes sense to the reader as well as the writer. For instance, when something is first mentioned in a text, it may be more helpful to refer to '*a* ___' or '*some* ___', rather than '*the* ___', unless the definite reference is widely understood ('the sun' or 'the moon'). As was mentioned earlier in the chapter, Richard Hudson and Jasper Holmes found that the use of *this* or *these* to refer to a person or thing not previously mentioned was a common non-standard feature of young people's speech.[25]

Pronouns need to be used so that whatever they refer to is clear and unambiguous. 'I picked *it* up' needs to be preceded by reference to what *it* was. The same applies to **pro-forms** (see p.139), items which stand for another part of a sentence to avoid repetition, e.g. 'I went *there*' needs to be preceded by reference to where *there* was. Such features may appear obvious to the literate adult, but they are very much part of the development of young writers (especially up to the age of nine or so). These features reflect how far they are learning to build into their writing the explicitness and coherence that give a text its 'self-sufficiency'. All these features can help a text in fulfilling its potential for unambiguous communication across space and time.

Genre consistency needs to be maintained and the principal features of a genre need to be included. Young, inexperienced writers may sometimes switch from an impersonal factual style to a personal anecdotal style in mid-text. Others may omit central genre features: because they do not yet appreciate that stories normally have a setting as well as main characters and some kind of plot. Others again may not have realised that a report will deal with several elements arranged in a logical order, with each 'signposted' in some way. They may need to be reminded that, if the text is first summarised with some kind of advance organiser, it may help to prepare the reader for what is to follow. Other genre-specific features were discussed in **Chapter 5**.

A RESEARCH STUDY

Grammatical features of general style

Mina Shaughnessy's book *Errors and Expectations* is based on 15 years experience of teaching basic writing. It provides enduring insights at every level of education. She classified syntactical problems identified in essays written by 4,000 students ranked as being in the bottom quarter of their classes. Central to Shaughnessy's analysis is a recognition that syntactical difficulties are signs of unfamiliarity with certain features of formal written English.

Shaughnessy's analysis identified four main kinds of syntactical errors:

1. **Accidental errors**: when the inclusion of one erroneous form sets up a different syntactic pattern from the one that the writer is following, e.g. *"Life is really hard today so you can imagine what it will in the coming future and for us generation'. Shaughnessy suggests that 'accidental' errors may be largely cured by more careful proof-reading. Other kinds of errors may need more substantial explanation and exploration.
2. **Blurred patterns**: when features from several patterns are incorrectly combined, e.g. 'at least I can say is that I will have ...'
3. **Consolidation errors**: when using the subordinate and conjoined structures which are more common in writing than in speech e.g:
   'Although some people don't realise the pressures that are put upon a person when he is at school, then comes out... and cannot get a better job'; or 'People are interested in better things in just listen to poetry or reading poetry'.
4. **Inversions**: Another kind of error is created when the writer inadvertently changes the direction of the sentence, for example by repeating a direct object,
   e.g. 'I believe that *what you do* you should be praised for *it*'; or by not following through a 'not only but also' structure, e.g. '... people are *not only* helping themselves *but it* will help everyone else.' Shaughnessy notes that the word *it* is often involved in these kinds of unintended inversions. The word *it* may be used too loosely or sometimes unnecessarily, causing 'knock-on' of confusion in the sentence structure.

Ways of dealing with grammatical errors

Shaughnessy reminds us that many of these errors are from attempts to manage more academic and impersonal writing. This kind of writing may require the kinds of formal complex sentences that are less rarely used in speech. She provides several ideas to help students to avoid 'mismanaging complexity'. In particular, she argues that pupils should be helped:

- to behave as writers, using all aspects of the process (composing, drafting, proof-reading etc.);
- to build confidence by providing for them supportive and sympathetic contexts for writing;
- to develop a knowledge of key grammatical concepts, e.g. subject, verb, object, indirect object and modifier etc.

Shaughnessy stresses that such knowledge is almost indispensable if teachers intend to talk with students about their sentences.

Finally, Shaughnessy recommends sentence-combining activities of the kind referred to in the previous section of this chapter. She especially recommends activities that involve the following transformations:

- changing simple sentences to complex sentences
- changing complex sentences to simple sentences
- changing simple sentences to compound sentences
- changing independent clauses to dependent clauses
- changing dependent clauses to independent clauses

Shaughnessy argues that sentence-combining may offer the closest thing to piano finger exercises for the inexperienced writer. Sentence-combining will provide a helpful focus for increasing pupils' interest in the grammatical rules that underpin all that we say and write.

The increase in direct teaching in the United Kingdom through the Literacy Hour approach will provide opportunities for this kind of conscious attention to grammatical rules. This may be particularly helpful if 'text level' teaching provides a framework for 'sentence level' teaching, in both reading and writing. Grammar can thus be related to genuinely communicative purposes.

4 Linking Grammatical Reference to 'Language Awareness'

A major influence in the 'language awareness' approach has been Eric Hawkins of the University of York, whose publications have been aimed at the 10–14 age range.[26] The teaching of language awareness aims to use ideas and themes from linguistics to help make pupils curious about and interested in language. It aims to inform pupils about the uses and abuses of language, not only in their school years but throughout their lives.[27]

One of Hawkins' main intentions was to help children in learning about language itself. He regrets that, at the time he wrote *Awareness of Language*, 'grammar had become a 'bogey word'.[28] Hawkins argues that teachers of writing should not apologise for teaching the structure of language any more than science teachers need to apologise for teaching the structure of matter or the laws of physics. He also recognises that the task of teaching the structure of language is not to be over-simplified. Yet, he argues, it is surely worthwhile taking the trouble to set up expectations in pupils' minds that grammar can be fun and interesting.

Much of the content of **Chapters 6** and **7** have included suggestions and examples that could be used in this way. This application is likely to be especially effective if these suggestions can be linked to teaching methods that are part of the National Literacy Strategy, shared and guided reading and writing. These methods should help to ensure that a balance is maintained between learning to use and learning to understand language.

If children have regular opportunities to use written language for a range of purposes, they are more likely to be able to reflect upon its structures and patterns. In turn, this reflection is eventually likely to form a secure basis for grammatical reference, the use of specific terminology. Grammatical reference can add valuable precision to the broader language awareness approach and enhance educational discourse in general.

It is important to bear in mind, of course, that there are many grammars on which 'language awareness' can be built. Each grammar has its own technical terms. A recent discussion paper from the Qualification and Curriculum Authority (QCA) shows the relationships in the historical development of grammar studies in Figure 7.1.[29]

This book has drawn upon the descriptive grammar of Randolph Quirk and those who follow this tradition. For professionals who work with children and young people, descriptive grammar is particularly useful. It assists the identification of growth in the use of language structures. It can indicate how these structures may be adapted to make them more appropriate for certain kinds of writing. It can provide insights into how these structures can be modified to add elegance to what is written. Such informed judgements rest on an understanding of modern descriptive grammar and of the limitations of traditional grammar. The new millennium has seen renewed interest in the use of grammar in teaching and in teacher education. If this interest can productively link grammar to language awareness, then grammar can be made fun and interesting in the way Eric Hawkins envisaged. As was mentioned earlier, the renewed interest has been partly sparked by David Tomlinson's paper that is summarised below.

A RESEARCH STUDY

Encouraging language awareness and grammatical reference

The final research study is connected to one of the cautions set out at the beginning of the previous chapter: 'Grammar teaching may not improve writing.' This assumption has been the legacy of a highly influential book published by Andrew Wilkinson, then at Birmingham University, in 1971.[30] Wilkinson drew upon a range of studies to conclude that the claims (for grammar teaching) are nearly all completely without foundation.[31] Only in the past few years has this conclusion been systematically challenged.

A quarter of a century on from Wilkinson's book, there was a re-awakening of interest in the teaching of grammar, sparked in particular by David Tomlinson, of Kumamoto University in

Japan. In 1994 Tomlinson published a paper that drew attention to the weaknesses in one of the most recent studies which Wilkinson considered. This was an unpublished MEd thesis by Nora Robinson in Manchester in 1959. Robinson gave tests of grammatical knowledge to all Y8 and Y10 pupils in four selective schools (29 classes altogether) and asked them to write three 30-minute compositions. Comparisons were then made between grammatical knowledge and composition performance in 129 pupils (five from each class). However, the compositions were only marked by impression and not analytically in ways that might reveal specific benefits from grammar teaching (e.g. sentence structure and cohesion). Also, the tests of grammatical knowledge focused on the naming of parts approach, rather than on sentence analysis. As Tomlinson points out, the Robinson study tested little that could carry over into pupils' writing anyway.

Tomlinson goes on to discuss another study referred to by Wilkinson. This was a 1962 PhD thesis by R.J. Harris, one-time deputy headteacher at Woodberry Down School in North London. Pairs of Y7 classes (11–12 year olds) were studied for two years in five schools. In each school, one class was taught 'formal grammar' from a 1939 textbook that, for instance, covered four classes of adjective, while the other spent the equivalent time writing. Harris's conclusions were that, at the end of the study, the writing of the first group was no better than that of the other group. However, as Tomlinson points out, it is clear that the second group was also being taught grammar. The teacher (often the same teacher that taught the first group) was drawing attention to the pupils' paragraph and sentence structure. He was also helping them to deal with errors. The teacher may well have tried to avoid using technical terms like subject and object pronoun. Yet it may be misleading to refer to these classes as 'non-grammar' ones, as they were in essence non-formal grammar text book classes. Again, Tomlinson agues, the possible advantages of sentence analysis of pupils' own writing are hardly examined.

Tomlinson reaches a firm conclusion. The studies reviewed by Wilkinson did not support any conclusion that the teaching of grammar had no value in schools. At best, such a conclusion is a *non sequitur* and possibly specious nonsense.

The general state of grammar teaching at the beginning of a new millennium is at an interesting point. The QCA's *The Grammar Papers* sums up some of the main dilemmas. In particular, it asks how grammar teaching can be systematic and progressive if it is only taught in the context of pupil's own work. The conclusions of *The Grammar Papers* include the following:

- discrete teaching of parts of speech and parsing in de-contextualised exercise form is not particularly effective;
- there is evidence that experience of the syntactic demands of different types of tasks is a key factor in pupils' writing performance and development;
- drawing explicit attention of the syntactic features of pupils' writing can increase pupils' awareness of how language works; this may in turn increase their control over their writing.

The Grammar Papers also note that many teachers are not confident in their knowledge of grammar that is so helpful in developing systematic and incidental teaching. Sustained use of frameworks like Katharine Perera's, which informed **Chapter 6**, may help to remedy this.

Figure 7.1 The historical development of grammar studies

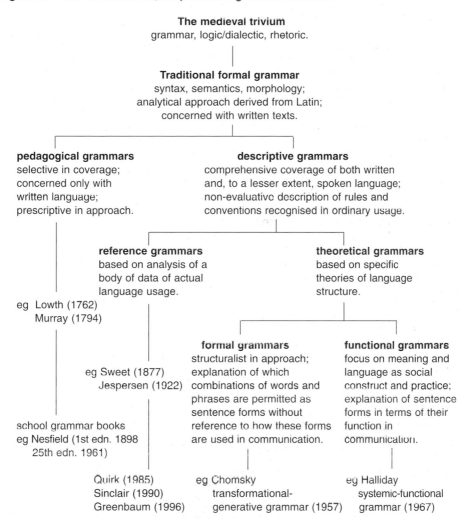

The medieval trivium
grammar, logic/dialectic, rhetoric.

Traditional formal grammar
syntax, semantics, morphology;
analytical approach derived from Latin;
concerned with written texts.

pedagogical grammars
selective in coverage;
concerned only with
written language;
prescriptive in approach.

descriptive grammars
comprehensive coverage of both written
and, to a lesser extent, spoken language;
non-evaluative description of rules and
conventions recognised in ordinary usage.

reference grammars
based on analysis of a
body of data of actual
language usage.

theoretical grammars
based on specific
theories of language
structure.

eg Lowth (1762)
Murray (1794)

formal grammars
structuralist in approach;
explanation of which
combinations of words and
phrases are permitted as
sentence forms without
reference to how these forms
are used in communication.

functional grammars
focus on meaning and
language as social
construct and practice;
explanation of sentence
forms in terms of their
function in
communication.

eg Sweet (1877)
Jespersen (1922)

school grammar books
eg Nesfield (1st edn. 1898
25th edn. 1961)

Quirk (1985)
Sinclair (1990)
Greenbaum (1996)

eg Chomsky
transformational-
generative grammar (1957)

eg Halliday
systemic-functional
grammar (1967)

The Grammar Papers also point out that the routine discussion and teaching of language is something that seems to have been lost. This loss includes discussion of syntactic structure and rules, as part of preparation for and feedback from writing. The National Literacy Strategy *Framework for Teaching* has many useful suggestions for linking text-level and word-level teaching to the grammar and punctuation details of sentence-level work. The NLS also has a substantial commitment to extended direct teaching in a daily Literacy Hour. The rolling programme of NLS objectives and plenary reviews may create the kind of interactive context in which grammar can be more consistently explored and reflected upon.

Dimensions of Writing Development

I found that by writing things down I could learn and remember much more.
(Gerald Durrell)[1]

This chapter
- explores different ways of analysing the development of writing
- outlines some ways of promoting spelling, vocabulary and grammar
- makes some suggestions for classroom assessment.

From the discussions in the previous chapters, it will be clear that the development of children's writing can be assessed along a number of different dimensions. It may appear that the most obvious way of assessing writing is to inspect its basic linguistic features, such as spelling, vocabulary and sentence structure. These features do indeed play a prominent part in some dimensions that are dealt with in this chapter.

Spelling, vocabulary and sentence structure, however, are part of a bigger picture. The significance of these features has to be considered in the light of what the writer is trying to achieve in writing, whom the writing is for and the genre that the writer is adopting. These considerations are part of the social context of the writing. All this has implications for day-to-day classroom assessment.

Implications for Classroom Assessment

Figure 8.1 sets out some of the main links between the points that are raised above and which have been discussed in the previous chapters.

This framework provides prompts for three levels of assessment, put crudely, 'the What?' 'the How?' and 'the What Now?' All three build on 'the Why?' and 'Who for?' As was shown in **Chapter 5**, there are various ways of considering range in writing, including 'the Why?' and 'the Who for?' James Kinneavy, at the University of Texas, is one of the most influential writers on the aims of writing. He has identified some key criteria related to the four basic aims of discourse that were outlined in **Chapter 5**: to share news, to entertain, to inform and to persuade. These aims are based on the communication triangle, which is set out opposite.

Figure 8.1

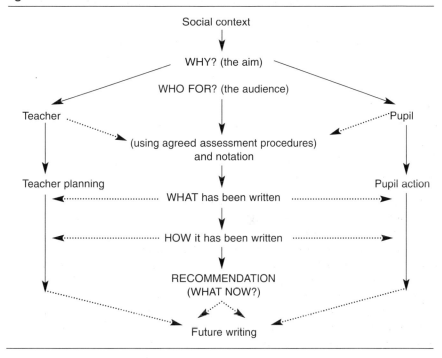

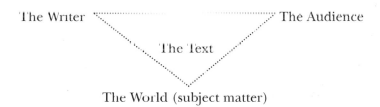

Different aims have different emphases within the triangle. These emphases give rise to different kinds of criteria, as shown in Figure 8.2.

Figure 8.2

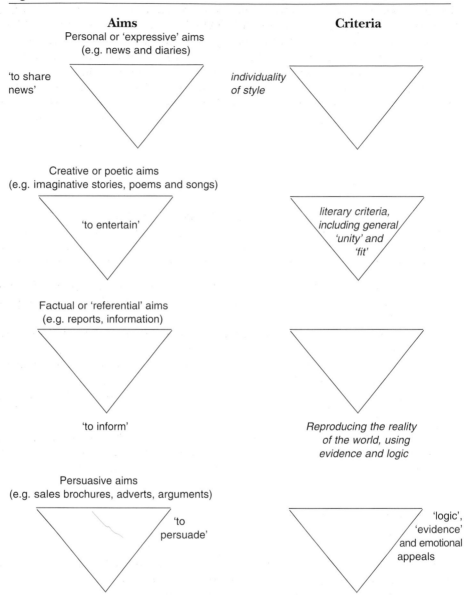

| **Aims** | **Criteria** |

Personal or 'expressive' aims
(e.g. news and diaries)

'to share news'   *individuality of style*

Creative or poetic aims
(e.g. imaginative stories, poems and songs)

'to entertain'   *literary criteria, including general 'unity' and 'fit'*

Factual or 'referential' aims
(e.g. reports, information)

'to inform'   *Reproducing the reality of the world, using evidence and logic*

Persuasive aims
(e.g. sales brochures, adverts, arguments)

'to persuade'   *'logic', 'evidence' and emotional appeals*

Any judgements of success in writing have to be related to what the writing is trying to achieve, its basic aim. Aims in writing may be achieved by adopting specific genre features or modes of organisation. Genres and modes may in turn be structured by adopting specific syntactical features, vocabulary or layout. As was shown in **Chapter 5**, there has been much recent interest in factual and non-fiction genres. It is also important to take note of the genre features that are used in literary and more personal or 'expressive' writing. Success in writing will depend on the convincing use of these features. Writers of any age may benefit from taking note of what these features are. Inexperienced writers may benefit from practising the use of these features and perhaps from having some features explained and modelled.

In this way the global assessment of writing will benefit from linking 'the What?' and 'the How?' to 'the Why?' The associated criteria show how authenticity can be added to a teacher's feedback when responding to children's writing.

The Importance of Feedback

Feedback from an audience is an important part of writing development. The response of the audience may indicate whether the original aim of the writing has been achieved (even when writing a memo to yourself). Taking the four aims set out in Figure 8.2, audience response might include the following:

- appreciating the sharing of a personal anecdote ('That happened to me once...'; 'What an amazing coincidence...'; 'Fancy that happening to you...');
- expressing pleasure at a poem or imaginative story ('I love that phrase...'; 'What a character she was...');
- being grateful for the information provided by the text ('Now I know how that was built'; 'Thanks for explaining that to me.');
- changing behaviour or belief ('OK, I'll do that instead..'; 'Yes, I can see that is a good idea...').

For some kinds of writing, audience feedback may include writing back, perhaps beginning some sustained correspondence. Feedback is often an integral part of the social context in which the writing is undertaken.

The Importance of 'Feedforward'

Effective teaching means engineering opportunities for children to write in a variety of contexts. It also means switching roles in order to respond in kind to the kinds of writing being undertaken in the classroom. As was shown in **Chapter 1**, inspection evidence suggests that more might also be done to 'feed forward' from the assessment of writing to subsequent practice. This assessment is likely to be better informed if attention is first given to the 'why' and the 'who for' of the writing. Such attention provides a more secure basis for assessing and promoting spelling, vocabulary and sentence structure.

Understanding Spelling Development

One of the most influential publications on spelling in recent years has come from Richard Gentry in North Carolina.[2] Gentry outlines a five-stage model of spelling development, using data from *GNYS AT WRK*, a case study by Glenda Bissex of her own son's early writing, which was mentioned in **Chapter 4**.[3] Table 8.1 sets out these stages and provides examples of each. The examples come from the attempts of a class of 4–5 year olds to spell the word 'school'.

Table 8.1

Stage	Features	Examples
1.'Pre-Communicative': using symbols from the alphabet to represent words.	The learner shows some alphabetic knowledge through production of letter forms to represent messages, but there may be a random stringing together of upper and lower case letters and the speller may or may not use left–right direction.	*SS HO*
2. 'Semi-phonetic': first attempts to use an alphabetic system.	The writing is generally set out left–right and letters begin to be used to represent sounds, although spelling may be 'abbreviated' (one letter representing a longer word).	*Scllhol*
3. 'Phonetic': complete mapping of sounds and letters.	The writing maps sounds to symbols in a systematic way, but the speller concentrates on sounds rather than the spelling system, using acceptable letter sequences.	*Snoll*
4. 'Transitional': some phonetic and some conventional spelling.	Basic spelling conventions are generally followed, e.g. a vowel in every syllable and all necessary letters are often included, although there may be some reversals.	*SCOL*
5. 'Conventional': the basis of a knowledge of English orthography is firmly established.	The learner uses knowledge of word structure, including prefixes, suffixes and compound words, and shows growing accuracy in using silent and double consonants etc. The learner can think of alternative spellings, can use visual identification of misspelled words for corrections, and continues to learn uncommon and irregular spellings.	*School*

As mentioned in **Chapter 4**, there are several cautions about such stage models.

- It is not always possible to place a child at a stage on the basis of a small sample of writing.

- Features of more than one stage may be found in a piece of writing as a child's spelling moves from one stage to the next, although there is little evidence that spelling development substantially regresses once one stage of development is reached.
- Development is fostered by purposeful writing, sustained reading and sympathetic adult support.
- The use of swift, well-formed handwriting contributes to success in spelling, as it assists children in learning common letter strings.

Some of the most searching critiques have come from Rebecca Treiman at Wayne State University in the USA and Margaret Snowling at York University in England.[4] Their findings suggest that children's early spelling is more influenced by graphic knowledge (letter strings) than some stage models would suggest. Children's early unaided spelling is far more likely to contain letter groups like <ee> and <ll> (which are common in English) than *<uu> or *<hh> which do not occur. Likewise, if children use <bb> or <ck>, they rarely place them at the beginning of words.

There is also evidence that children use grammatical strategies in spelling at an earlier stage than is indicated by the Gentry model. For instance, studies of 6 and 7 year olds show that children are more likely to misspell the second consonant sound in 'duty' as a /d/ than the second consonant sound in 'dirty'. The finding indicates that children were assisted by their sense of the /t/ in 'dirty' acting as a morpheme boundary: *dirt* + *y*.[5]

Phonological knowledge is a very helpful resource in learning to spell. Some authorities suggest that learning to draw upon this knowledge is a watershed, because it reveals that children are becoming sensitive to written English as an alphabetic system, in which the alphabet letters represent the phonemes of speech. The insights that it provides into the spelling system are also likely to benefit reading development as well. Many children may intuitively draw upon their phonological knowledge in their early spelling more than upon other sources of knowledge. This may be because the sounds of words are more accessible to them. However, as was discussed in **Chapter 3**, the spelling system is really a system of systems. Letters have a sound value by being linked to phonemes. In turn, letter-sound correspondences are part of other vocabulary and grammatical (morphemic) relationships, in overlapping sets.[6]

Learning to spell involves learning to use the relationships that exist between these sets. The National Literacy Strategy in England draws attention to these overlapping relationships in its training pack. The NLS also provides for recurrent systematic teaching of the links between words, meanings and grammar in its Literacy Hour.

Assessing and Developing Spelling

Margaret Peters and Bridget Smith have shown how an awareness of spelling development can be adapted to the task of assessing children's spelling.[7] Peters and Smith have devised dictation passages for the 7–11 age-range in order to plot significant spelling errors. This kind of assessment can provide insights for assessing spelling when children are writing any kind of text, provided that their age and the task are taken into consideration.

As Figure 8.3 shows, errors can be grouped in several ways. The following example is taken from the Peters and Smith assessment materials. It is based on the Y4 (8—9 year olds) dictation passage attempted by Josh.

Figure 8.3

a

Dictation Two

(may be suitable for children in Year 4 – P4 in Scotland)

One day, as I was walking down Bridge Street I heard the sound of trotting. I turned and saw behind me the shaggy dark hair of a frightened little horse. I knew where he belonged. I looked in my lunch box for an apple and gave it to him. I searched for a piece of rope to tie around his neck. Then I led him back. I opened the gate of his own field and he galloped in. I laughed with pleasure for I had been very worried until he was safe, far away from the noisy and dangerous traffic.

b

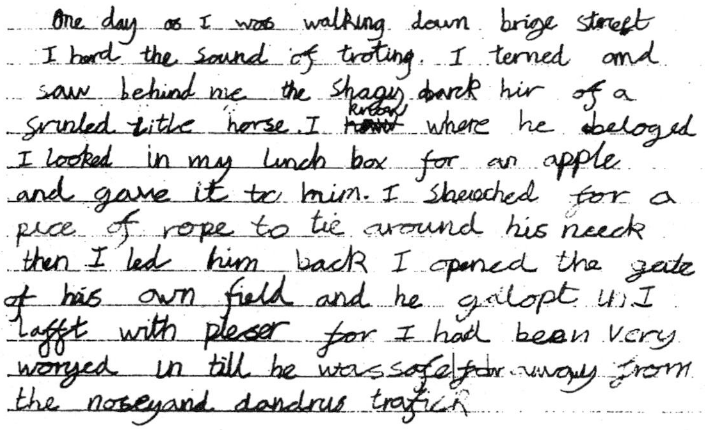
One day as I was walking down brige street
I herd the sound of troting. I terned and
saw behind me the Shagy darck hir of a
frinted litle horse. I know where he beloged
I looked in my lunch box for an apple
and gave it to him. I sherched for a
pice of rope to tie around his neeck
then I led him back I opened the gate
of his own field and he galopt in I
lafft with pleser for I had bean very
woryed in till he was safe far away from
the noseyand dandrus trafick

Diagnostic grid for Josh's dictation

PLAUSIBLE		INVENTED	RANDOM
Readable Words conforming to English spelling which are readable in the context of the passage.	**Unreadable** Words with some structural resemblance to the stimulus word, which may not be readable in the context of the passage.	Words invented from the sound of the word, with little or no reference to letter sequences in English.	Words that bear no resemblance, either in sound or structure, to English.
herd troting terned shagy darck hir trafick	brige frinted litle beloged sherèched pice neeck galopt pleser woryed in till nosey know	lafft dandrus	

Peters and Smith suggest the following kind of analysis. The last row in Table 8.2 includes a variety of general suggestions drawn from several sources.

Table 8.2

Random	Invented	Weaker plausible	Stronger plausible
No apparent use of phonology or knowledge of English letter groups (graphic knowledge).	Using phonology, but little graphic knowledge.	Using graphic knowledge, but not following spelling precedent (and perhaps showing little understanding of lexical and morphological structure).	Following spelling precedent (and perhaps showing understanding of lexical and morphological structure).
	lafft	*brige*	*herd*
	dandrus	*frinted*	*troting*
		litle	*terned*
		beloged	*shagy*
		shrereched	*darck*
		pice	*hir*
		neeck	*trafick*
		galopt	
		pleser	
		woryed	
		intill	
		nosey	
		know	
Learning needs – establishing directionality and phonological knowledge:	**Learning needs – building up graphic knowledge:**	**Learning needs – noting graphic and morphemic connections:**	**Learning needs – making associations with related words:**
• Setting out writing left–right; • Setting out writing top–bottom down the page; • Identifying the phonemes in words; • Attributing single letters, digraphs and trigraphs to phonemes.	• Looking at words; • Saying words; • Covering words; • Writing words;. • Checking the spelling	• *bridge*: ridge, porridge etc; • *frightened*: bright and brightened; light and lightened; • *little*: -attle, -ettle, -ittle, -ottle, and -uttle words; • *belong*: long and wrong; • *noisy*: noise; etc.	• *herd* c.f. hear, hearing • *troting* c.f. blotting • *terned* c.f. burn, turn • *shagy* c.f. baggy • *trafick*: the origin of the word is obscure, so it may need to be learned by rote.

This kind of assessment can easily produce an overfacing amount of information. The information needs to be used strategically. Children may also need to tackle the following:

- continuing to write for a variety of purposes;
- proof-reading and indicating spelling uncertainties (see the proof-reading symbols listed in **Chapter 3**);

- giving priority to learning irregular high-frequency words (e.g. 'are' or 'said') and by adding finger tracing to 'look, say, cover, write, check';
- learning spelling analogies (especially for 'weaker plausible' misspellings);[8]
- being encouraged to read widely in shared, guided and independent sessions;
- taking an interest in words, their origins and their meanings.

Such suggestions will bring direction and a sense of proportion to the learning and development of spelling.

Words and Word Order

One of the largest investigations into the linguistic features of writing development was undertaken at the University of Nottingham. William Harpin investigated the development of writing in a sample of nearly 300 Key Stage 2 school children.[9] The children completed several creative and factual writing tasks and the research concentrated on an analysis of the following:

word counts
vocabulary
syntactical structures   } sentence length
                            clause length
                            type and number of subordinate units.

Harpin goes to great lengths to point out the difficulties in trying to describe or analyse language development in general terms. He emphasises the need to view each child as an individual. Children progress in their uniquely individual ways, at their own speeds, first in accomplishing the physical skill of writing and then in exploring its potential.[10] Yet he also argues that, in order to explain and discuss what happens when children write and to be able to follow development, there is a need for a method of systematically describing the writing. He also cautions that such analyses may not always provide direct indices of writing quality.

As Harpin acknowledges, the design and administration of any measures of writing are beset with difficulties (e.g. 'St Francis got back and he had some followers as well' – one sentence or two?). Yet, despite such cautions, he reports some distinct patterns of syntactical development in children's writing.

Research Findings on Word Counts

Harpin looked at samples of creative and factual writing of 290 children over the 7–11 age-range (four pieces per term, over six terms). He found a huge range. In the 7,000 texts and 800,000 words, the shortest text was seven words

and the longest 1,100. Total output per pupil ranged from 500 to 8,000 words. There were several notable findings:

- a clear increase year on year;
- over the four years of schooling, output doubled;
- children wrote substantially more if the teacher provided full verbal preparation;
- the 11 year olds (Year 6) were beginning to reduce the rate of advance;
- together with other evidence, this suggested a stage of consolidation in Year 6, in which there was greater economy and more deliberate shaping of the writing.

Counting the number of words in children's completed texts is perhaps the crudest indicator of development. Such indicators have been used by large-scale longitudinal studies of school effectiveness[11] and of individual families and children.[12] There are obvious limitations of word counts as an index of writing development. However, as Catherine Snow and her colleagues found, these counts do often correlate highly with holistic ratings and even with measures of the sophistication of the vocabulary used.[13]

Research Findings on Vocabulary

Harpin's research did not deal directly with vocabulary because of the kinds of difficulty in assessing vocabulary growth that were dealt with in **Chapter 2**. Instead he used a measure to indicate range and the flexibility of vocabulary use. This measure involves expressing the number of different words (types) in a piece of writing as a proportion of the total number of words (tokens), to give a type–token ratio (TTR).

$$\frac{\text{number of different words (types)}}{\text{total number of words (tokens)}} = \text{type–token ratio}$$

Comparisons can be made between succeeding segments of 50 or 100 words from a piece of writing. Harpin's review of available evidence suggests that, for children aged 7–11, ratios for the first 100 words range from 0.45–0.70. The sharper the drop in TTR after the first 100 words, the more limited a child's written vocabulary is likely to be.[14] A low TTR will suggest that children are tending to use the same words over and over again.

Promoting Vocabulary Development

Findings such as the one summarised above raise the question of how vocabulary development is promoted. In one of the finest books on the teaching of writing, frank, analytical and enriched with many examples, Myna

Shaughnessy suggests three specific approaches to the teaching of vocabulary.[15] She also notes that little is known about how individuals acquire new words. Most studies have concentrated on concept formation among children and on the relationship of concepts to word meanings. Performance in vocabulary tests is highly predictive of educational performance and yet learning to pass a vocabulary test is not the same as learning to use the academic vocabulary in writing. There are degrees of difficulty with words, depending on everything from the physical characteristics of words to the complexity of their meaning. An important part of the task of teaching vocabulary is to decide what realistically can be done to help pupils cope with the language demands of schools. At least three kinds of learning are involved:

1. LEARNING ABOUT WORDS: AS PHYSICAL, GRAMMATICAL, AND SEMANTIC ITEMS

Certain general insights about words may have a direct bearing on a student's vocabulary development, but such insights are more likely to come about inductively, through specific encounters with words, rather than through formal explanations. Some pupils tend to mistake words for the things words refer to. Some pupils tend to think of words as having meanings that are not affected by shifts in time or situation. Widening vocabulary in school is probably as much a task of learning specialised meanings for familiar words as it is of learning completely new words (e.g. *solution* in science, or *set* in mathematics). Education itself might be described as the process whereby students learn to associate new concepts with familiar words or familiar concepts with new words.

2. LEARNING WORDS: ABSORBING SPECIFIC WORDS INTO OUR VOCABULARY

Some pupils are at a great disadvantage in school because they do not know many of the words their teachers assume they know. This difficulty shows up most clearly in pupils' writing, where words outside the basic vocabulary are usually either missing or erroneously used. The vocabulary of general literacy includes both various classes of words and various ways of using words. Within such a vocabulary there are:

- words that allude to events, places, and people that are assumed to be commonly, if but vaguely, known (*Gandhi*, *the French Revolution*, *the Nile*, etc.);
- words that serve as formal equivalents to concepts already familiar to the student in different words (as *atheist* is the equivalent to 'someone who doesn't believe in God').
- words that serve to identify complex historical movements (*Renaissance*, *Marxism*, *evolution*, etc.);
- words that, although part of a specific subject, are also used in the wider culture with variant meanings (in literature, for example, such terms as *fiction*, *drama*, or *novel*);

- words that are intended to initiate highly specific academic activities (*define, compare, generalise, document, illustrate, prove, summarise, interpret,* etc.);
- words that are used in deliberately ambiguous ways in order to enrich or refine meaning (irony, figures of speech, etc.);
- words that articulate relationships such as addition, negation, condition, or causation (*moreover, therefore, however,* etc.);
- words that represent Latin- or Greek-based synonyms for familiar words (e.g. *initiate* or *commence* for 'begin') and that tend to give an academic flavour to the writing and speech of teachers.

Shaughnessy reminds us that the writers of school texts and teachers who have spent years acquiring the language of their professions tend, like most people who have accomplished a skill, not to see the water they swim in.

3. LEARNING A SENSITIVITY TO WORDS: MAKING CONSCIOUS CHOICES IN WRITING

Writing is a process that gives us more time to form sentences than we have in speech. In fact, it greatly multiplies the number of choices we face. This is the beauty – and the pain – of writing. But as we write we are doing more than just retrieving words from memory; we are advancing our thoughts. As we discriminate among words, we discover the qualities of our ideas. This, Shaughnessy suggests, more than any improvement in style, is the value of attending to words.

The process whereby writers make conscious choices is, of course, not observable, but pupils can experience the process through activities such as the following:

- **Substitution practice**: taking words from the pupils' own writing and asking them to list as many alternatives for the word as they can suggest.
- **Looking at first drafts**: looking over original manuscripts (see Figure 8.4). These can show that the process that creates precise writing can sometimes be messy, with so many deletion marks and changes littering the page as to make some manuscripts almost indecipherable. The scrutiny of such manuscripts can be instructive. They provide a 'map' of the writer's internal debates. Such maps can, in turn, encourage pupils to hesitate in positive ways over their own words.
- **Reading what has been written**: trying to trace the thinking of the writer e.g. why the writer used this word instead of that, developed the text in this direction instead of that, or chose to expand upon one point and not another.

Finally, we should also note the challenge facing teachers in helping children to acquire vocabulary, these building blocks of the writing process. However 'real' and motivating the writing tasks which are provided, Shaughnessy's research indicates that there appear to be stubborn (and doubtless individually different) limits to the pace at which words can enter our active vocabularies.[16]

Figure 8.4

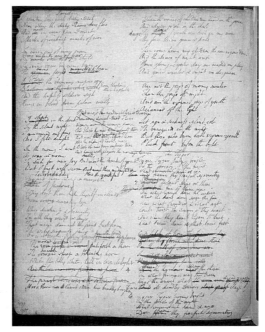

Annotations by William Blake to his 'Tyger' drafts

Research Findings on Word Order

In reporting his findings on the sentence structure of children's writing, Harpin draws upon grammatical terms that were discussed earlier in this book (see **Chapters 6** and **7**).

Table 8.3

Independent clause	Units of language which contain a finite verb or verb phrase	*The band began to play.* or *Everyone enjoyed the music.*
Simple sentence	A sentence with one independent clause	*The band began to play.*
Compound sentence	Two independent clauses joined by a conjunction	*The band began to play and everyone enjoyed the music.*
Subordinate or dependent clause	A clause that cannot act as a sentence on its own	*When the audience had arrived...*
Complex sentence	An independent clause and at least one subordinate clause	*When the audience had arrived, the band began to play.*

The Importance of Subordination

One of the most significant features in this development is the use of **subordinate clauses**. These allow far more variety than simple or compound sentences. They allow the work of nouns, adverbs and adjectives to be done by clauses. These clauses can be combined to show a variety of relationships of time, result, reason, condition and so on.

Subordinate clauses can be broadly classified according to their function:

- **Noun clauses** (e.g. 'He remembered *that he had left the door open.*')
- **Adverbial clauses** (e.g. '*When he got home,* he tried to close it.')
- **Adjectival (or relative) clauses** (e.g. 'He found that the door, *which had a broken catch,* would not shut easily.')

Harpin describes how the use of 'and' as a universal coordinator in the speech of young children is transferred to their writing in its early stages. He notes that, by the time children come to write, it is a powerful habit. It gives way only slowly and reluctantly to the very large number of different joining methods provided for in English.[17]

Part of the growing maturity of writing is to accommodate not only alternatives to 'and', but also to express the subtleties of meaning which other near-equivalents can allow.

Table 8.4

The wind blew *and* the snowflakes fell.	As the wind blew, the snow flakes fell.	additional, simultaneous detail
The autumn came *and* the leaves fell.	Because the autumn came, the leaves fell.	cause-effect relationship
He finished work *and* went to bed.	After he finished work, he went to bed.	time sequence

Harpin indicates the value of investigating the kinds of subordinate clauses used by children and of tracing their attempts to use less familiar kinds, such as relative clauses. He shows how studying such attempts can help to provide a portrait of the developing young writer. The ability to realise meaning is extended and assured through subordination.[18]

Research Findings on Subordination

The data collected over six terms from the 290 children showed the following:

- Nearly all the children used some subordinate clauses, although in a few cases they were used very infrequently.
- Far more adverbial and noun clauses were used than relative clauses.
- Adverbial clauses of time predominated throughout the 7–11 age-range.

- Other kinds of adverbial clause made up only 11 per cent of the total number of subordinate clauses, the most frequently used being clauses of cause, condition, place and result.
- Noun clauses decreased as a percentage of all subordination between 7 year olds (46 per cent) and eleven year olds (34 per cent).
- Within this range there was a definite shift from direct to indirect speech.
- Noun clauses were predominantly used as the objects of sentences (e.g. 'She said "I am going outside to play"').
- Noun clauses were very rarely used in other ways, such as subject (e.g. 'What he wants is help').
- There was increasing use of relative clauses in the 7–11 age-range ('The lady who was sitting in the bus' . . .). The increase was from 11 per cent (of the total number of clauses) in Year 3 to 22 per cent in Year 6.

Harpin suggests that this relative increase might be a reflection of children's increasing mastery of the use of potentially confusing relative pronouns (*who, whom, which, that*). It may also reflect a growing interest in the possibilities of additional, decorative structures, especially in descriptions.

William Harpin's study remains one of the largest and most robust investigations into children's writing development in the 3–13 age-range. Its strengths and limitations are revealed further when it is contrasted with other studies of writing development in the primary and middle years of schooling such as those that are discussed in **Chapter 9**.

Promoting Grammatical Development in Writing

It is understandable why parents and teachers may initially judge the quality of pupils' writing by its accuracy and neatness. Such features almost jump off the page in the way they conform to, or transgress, certain social conventions or values. A closer look may be needed in order to judge how the specific choice of words adds to the individuality of a text and the subtlety of its expressions.

Judging the grammar of a piece of writing, however, involves a different level of consciousness. It involves a particular kind of reading, reading between the words, to identify the grammatical constructions which are used to bind words together in particular orders. These word orders have then to be considered in relation to the clause elements which they express and to their appropriateness in the light of the kind of writing being undertaken. Such considerations are more demanding and time-consuming, but they do provide invaluable insights into how well a child's writing repertoire is being developed in readiness for the demands of the later years of schooling and for the world beyond school. In these later years, syntactical maturity and flexibility are likely to count for a great deal. So, how can these aspects be promoted? Katharine Perera provides many valuable suggestions from her analysis of data accumulated from research in Wales by Robin Fawcett and Michael Perkins.[19] Among the features of word order which repay encouragement in the 3–13 age-range are those outlined in the following section.

Development in Clause Structure

1. **Thoughtfully using adverbial elements**
   As their writing becomes more confident, children will begin to use more adverbial elements and to use them more flexibly, including between subject and verb, e.g. 'The gentle breathing of the night animals *suddenly* ceases.'
2. **Ensuring that the passive is used from time to time**
   There is evidence that the use of the passive can increase rapidly between the ages of 8 and 12, perhaps as much as three-fold.
3. **The recapitulatory pronoun, it is less often seen**
   Using a pronoun to recapitulate what has been already said is a common feature of speech. Its use declines rapidly after the age of 9, although it still may be appropriate in the use of authentic direct speech in personal narratives, creative writing or drama.
4. **Ensuring subject–verb agreement**
   The lack of appropriate subject–verb agreement (concord) is one of the few errors in clause structure to occur in children's speech after they begin school. Its occurrence in writing may be related to the use of non-standard dialect (see **Chapters 2** and **7**) or the lack of careful checking.

Development in Phrase Structure: the Noun Phrase

1. **Expanding the noun phrase**
   This is a well researched area and it has been shown that these types of noun phrase are used with increasing frequency during the school years.

   determiner – adjective – noun e.g. *the busy morn*
   noun phrase – preposition – noun phrase e.g. *the silence of the night's descent*
   noun phrases in apposition e.g. *our headteacher, Mr Jones*

   From the ages of 9–10, these structures are used more in writing than in speech.

2. **Using expanded noun phrases as subjects of sentences**
   Another related feature of writing development in the 3–13 age range is in the use of expanded noun phrases (see point 1 above) as the subjects of sentences. In early writing development, children tend to use simple noun phrases as subjects (pronouns, proper nouns and determiner-noun phrases). By the age of about 10, they use expanded noun phrases more in writing than in speech and increasingly these are used as sentence subjects
3. **Use of narrator pronouns**
   When children's writing has been studied over a period of time, shifts have been found in the way they narrate stories and factual writing.

When writing stories they tend to prefer using the third person for narrative, preferring the first person from about nine. With factual writing the opposite occurs.

Development in Phrase Structure: the Verb Phrase

1. **Beyond simple active verb forms**
   In early writing, children characteristically use simple, active verb forms e.g. *went, saw, did.* These forms can be developed in several ways when appropriate e.g:

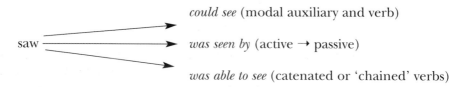

saw

could see (modal auxiliary and verb)

was seen by (active → passive)

was able to see (catenated or 'chained' verbs)

2. **Maintaining tense agreement**
   As children extend their writing into several clauses, an associated sign of growth is in children maintaining tense agreement between verbs, e.g. He *was getting* tired because he *had been working* most of the day without *having* a break.

This agreement is especially difficult to achieve when the writing refers to hypothetical situations, e.g. He decided that he *wouldn't* go even it if he *were* asked.

Development in the use of Compound Sentences

Compound sentences are a feature of early writing development ('*and... and... and*'). Maturity in style can be achieved in several ways:

1. Reducing the number of *and* conjunctions in a sentence. Just one may be all that is necessary to link two simple sentences together. After this, a more mature style may be achieved by beginning another sentence rather than adding another *and.*
2. Replacing *and* with other conjunctions where the kinds of relationships are not just the 'additions' e.g. 'I had an icecream and my sister had a lolly'.

Table 8.5

Different uses of *and*	Relationship	Alternative to *and*
'I picked up my toys and I put them away.'	sequence	*then, next...*
'I could not unlock the door and I went to get help.'	cause	*so...*
'I tried hard and I could not do it.'	adversative	*yet, but...*
'I watched tv and mummy went to sleep.'	simultaneous	*while...*

There is helpful evidence in the first three of Table 8.5 that the underlying relationships between clauses is not one of simple addition. The order of the two clauses in each sentence cannot be reversed without changing the meaning.

Development in the Use of Complex Sentences

As children's use of compound sentences decreases, so their use of complex sentences can increase. Between the ages of 8 and 10, the proportions of subordinate clauses in speech and writing are reversed. At 8 there is more subordination in speech; at 10 there is more in writing. The nature of this subordination can be heavily influenced by the nature of the writing task being undertaken, but it can include such growth points as:

- nominal clauses being used more as the subject element (as was mentioned earlier in the chapter, such clauses are used more as the object in early writing) e.g. '*The gentle breathing of the night animals suddenly ceases.*';
- using adverbial clauses other than those of time (which tend to be widely used in narrative writing), e.g. of

reason	*because*
condition	*if...*
place	*where...*
result	*so that...*
purpose	*so as to...*
manner	*like...*
concession	*even though...*

- different kinds of non-finite adverbial clauses, e.g. *Having finished this...*; *Knowing what I had to do..*; and more mature use of relative clauses.

Katharine Perera suggests four stages in the use of relative clauses:

1 Finite clauses in the **predicate** (the verb and complement), e.g. 'Mummy bought some sweets *that Jason would like.*'
2 a) finite clauses modifying the subject, e.g. 'The display *we put up* shows all our work on the topic.'
   b) non-finite clauses in the predicate, e.g 'He saw the puppy *sitting in the snow.*'

3 Clauses introduced by *whom, whose* or a preposition plus a relative pronoun, e.g. 'The first person I saw was my teacher, *whose name is Miss Jones.*' or '...the shop *in which I lost my purse*'.

4 a) Non-finite clauses modifying the subject, e.g. 'The tramp, *feeling very cold*, found it hard to sleep.'

b) Several relative clauses in one sentence.

Development in Connections between Sentences

There are several 'within sentence' features which are equally important to maintain 'between sentences' in order for writing to flow in a convincing and satisfying way. Chief among these is **consistent agreement of tenses**. In attending to so many aspects of writing (meaning, word order, punctuation, spelling and so on) it is easy for any writer to lose track of a particular tense form used in an earlier clause of a complex sentence. This may be even more likely between sentences.

As was outlined earlier, though, there are specific cohesive devices which need to be handled consistently. This is especially important for reference, which is the most commonly used cohesive device in the 3–13 age-range.

REFERENCE

- Using pronouns to avoid repetition of the same noun, e.g. 'I went looking for the key. I was really pleased when I found *it.*'
- Using **pro-forms** to avoid repetition of the same noun/pronoun sequence, e.g. 'I really wanted to go on the trip and I was really pleased when mummy said I *could.*'
- Maintaining agreement between nouns and pronouns, e.g. *dogs – they; the lake –* it; *I – me.*
- Avoiding ambiguity, especially in the use of the pronouns *it* or *they/them.*

SUBSTITUTION

This is not a widely used device in writing in the 3–13 age-range. It is relatively rare up to the age of 16. There is, then, a problem of under-use rather than misuse. Much may be gained in encouraging pupils to improve the economy of links between sentences by checking for:

- Nominal substitution, e.g. 'I saw the car. It was the same *one* as before.'
- Clausal substitution, e.g. 'Could I get there? I thought *so.*'
- Verbal substitution, e.g. 'Our class cheered. All the other classes *did*, as well.'

ELLIPSIS

Again, this device is not widely used by 3–13 year olds, but its use can add interest to writing, even adding a little tension, e.g. 'He tried to move. He *couldn't [ ].*'

SENTENCE CONNECTIVES

There is a curious irony in the use of sentence connectives in children's writing. The most widely used connectives are time-related ones (the ubiquitous 'and' and 'then') and yet in some ways these are the least needed. In the absence of explicit connectives, the reader will assume that events relayed in a text are following a time-order. In contrast, it is non-chronological writing which requires clear connectives to convey relationships between ideas in the text and between sentences. Yet these kinds of connectives are least widely used in children's writing.

So there is a strong case for drawing children's attention to the distinctive sentence connectives in non-chronological texts and for encouraging them to use these kinds of connectives in their writing. The increase in direct teaching of literacy in England through the Literacy Hour approach will provide opportunities for such links to be more strategically forged between reading and writing. This kind of teaching may be especially helpful in texts that are concerned with causal or 'adversative' (opposing) relationships, as these have their own distinctive connectives:

- increasing the use of causal connectives, e.g. *so, therefore, as a result, as a consequence, consequently.*
- increasing the use of opposing connectives, e.g. *and yet, but, however, in contrast, nevertheless, on the other hand, though, yet.*

This chapter has shown how the basic model of classroom assessment set out at the beginning can be developed in several ways to provide structure and guidance in assessing children's writing. The amended model is set out in Figure 8.5.

It cannot be stressed too strongly that frameworks such as this are provisional ones. The framework above can be developed in a variety of ways. The aspects dealing with 'the Why', 'the Who for' and 'the What' can be amended, according to the context in which the writing is undertaken and the content which is drawn upon. 'The How?' is likely to include spelling, vocabulary and word order as these represent the main strands of language outlined in **Chapter 2**. The inclusion of sentence connectives will depend on whether the text contains prose. The framework may be used to record distribution of some features (e.g. spelling errors, sentence types or connectives). Its advantage is that it can represent these features within specific genres.

In this way the interdependency of aims, audiences, genre and form can be linked to the linguistic strands in the text. It is essential that any assessment takes account of the aim and the audience of the writing and the social context that brought it about. It is equally important to consider the writing holistically, its final form and its use of particular genre features. This consideration can then lead on to the words themselves: the words that are used, how these words are spelled and how the words are ordered and punctuated. Judging writing also involves reading between the words in order to consider the syntactical patterns that contribute to the effectiveness of the text. Assessing writing is a multi-layered process. Done well, it can shed light on why texts succeed and where young writers need to devote their future attention when communicating in written language.

Figure 8.5

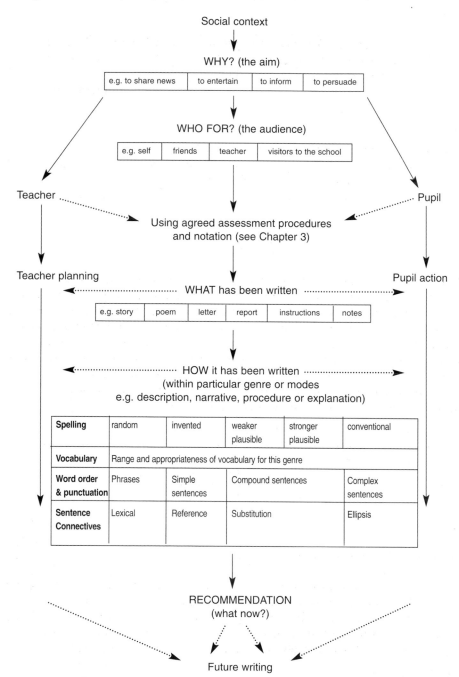

Broader Issues in Writing Development

Writing skill will grow with practice, but if there are no guiding principles informing the setting and the response, any growth will depend for its speed and strength on the uncertain operations of our intentions as teachers.

(William Harpin)[1]

This chapter

- explores broader dimensions of writing development
- discusses how gender and information technology affect writing development
- comments on recent debates about the nature of literacy and 'literacies'.

Broader Dimensions of Writing Development

There are several ways in which the development of children's writing can be studied. These ways are more tacit than those discussed in the previous chapter. They include the level of abstraction in the writing, the kind of cognitive development that is indicated and the way the writing may indicate the personal development of the writer. Each of these dimensions has been the focus of major British and North American research studies in the 3–13 age-range. References to this research may be useful in off-setting any preoccupation with more superficial judgements of the surface features of a text. The studies are set out in Table 9.1 below and each is then discussed in turn.

Table 9.1

Dimension	Researcher
levels of abstraction	James Moffett[2]
personal development	Andrew Wilkinson[3]
cognitive stages	Carl Bereiter[4]

Development in Levels of Abstraction

The developmental model of James Moffett contrasts with Harpin's framework in that it does not deal with any specifically linguistic aspects of writing. Moffett, who taught at Phillips Exeter Academy and served on the faculties of Harvard and the University of California at Berkeley, developed a model to account for the levels of abstraction that writing reveals:

- Recording
- Reporting
- Generalising
- Theorising

The focus on abstraction is useful to Moffett because he can apply it equally well to mental development and to the structure of discourse.[5] Moffett argues that differentiating among modes of discourse, registers of speech or kinds of audiences is essentially a matter of decentering. This involves seeing alternatives, of standing in others' shoes, of knowing that one has a private or local point of view and knowledge structure.[6]

Moffett assumes that generalising and theorising are more difficult for children to deal with in writing. These levels lack the time-related organisation that is often so helpful in, for example, the writing of stories, autobiographical writing and reports of visits or experiments.[7]

Dimensions of Personal Development in Writing

Andrew Wilkinson and his colleagues at the University of Exeter adopted Moffett's model in their research on the writing of 7–13 year old children in Crediton, Devon. They examined development in style and also affective, moral, and cognitive development (the latter incorporating Moffett's levels). Wilkinson *et al.* argue that examining writing development by counting words, sentence length or clause type neglects personal development and the construction of meaning. At the centre of this research is the recognition of the child as the communicating being. Consequently, the researchers in the Crediton Project established and applied models in additional areas. The principal features of the models are as follows in Table 9.2:

Table 9.2

cognitive	affective	moral	style
description	awareness of self	anomy	simple literal affirmative sentences
interpretation generalisation speculation	awareness of others empathy with reader sense of environment awareness of reality	heteronomy socionomy autonomy	growth in syntax, verbal competence, organisation, cohesion, reader awareness, appropriateness, effectiveness

These models were then selectively used in a study of the writing of 150 children aged 7, 10 and 13 on four written tasks:

- an autobiographical narrative
- an explanation
- a fictional story
- a persuasive argument.

The authors also warn of the provisional nature of such models, particularly models concerned with affect and style. There was very little previous research work to draw upon but there was generally a good deal of evidence to support the four models.[8]

The Crediton Project was an unusually wide-ranging investigation, going far beyond the more traditional focus of vocabulary, spelling, or punctuation. Andrew Wilkinson also provides a thoughtful caveat on possible responses to children's stock expressions and over-writing. He points out that the young writer's very eagerness to write well can produce an impression of insincerity where the language seems second-hand and the emotions expressed exaggerated. Sometimes the reaching out for metaphorical language seems to result in exaggerated or melodramatic emotion. Wilkinson suggests, however, that young writers can work through the stock language and the stereotypes associated with it to reach an individual perception expressed in their own terms. This is a hard-won end and we can scarcely expect children to have gone through the process by the age of 13.[9]

Cognitive Stages in Writing Development

The third longitudinal framework to be discussed here is that of Carl Bereiter at the Institute for Studies in Education in Ontario. Bereiter sets out five basic 'stages' of writing. He uses the term *stage* in a limited way to help emphasise that writing development may involve successively discrete forms of cognitive organisation. Each stage will require some readjustment of the process used, rather than the mere addition of new skills to it. Bereiter warns that his suggested stages from a series of research studies may not be universal or have a necessary order. Nevertheless, making one stage automatic greatly facilitates progress to the next stage.[10]

Figure 9.1

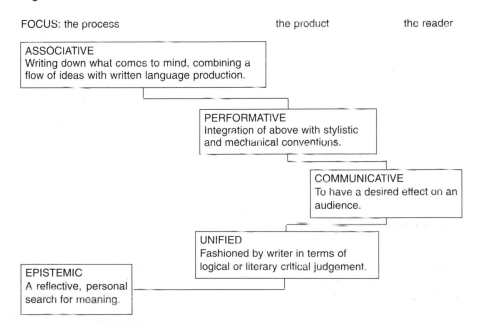

FOCUS: the process   the product   the reader

ASSOCIATIVE
Writing down what comes to mind, combining a flow of ideas with written language production.

PERFORMATIVE
Integration of above with stylistic and mechanical conventions.

COMMUNICATIVE
To have a desired effect on an audience.

UNIFIED
Fashioned by writer in terms of logical or literary critical judgement.

EPISTEMIC
A reflective, personal search for meaning.

As was mentioned in **Chapter 4**, the Beginning Writing group at the University of East Anglia constructed a model that explored development before the associative stage. They settled on three phases:

1. orientation towards writing scribble text (with or without illustration);
2. early text-making (which the child can read and which includes some conventional letters);
3. simple texts that can be read, at least in part, by others.

One particularly interesting feature of Carl Bereiter's model is that it allows for differing emphases of conscious focus. **Associative** and **epistemic** writing are focused on the process of writing. **Performative** and **unified** writing are focused on the product. **Communicative** writing is focused on the reader. Bereiter suggests that traditional teaching methods that concentrate on setting writing and teacher correction (what George Hillocks refers to as presentational writing — see **Chapter 3**) are devoted to moving students from **associative** to **performative** writing. Such a narrow focus neglects a number of valuable possibilities, which are embodied in the later stages.

- As pupils attain a degree of mastery over conventions they realise that writing can be used to affect the reader – that it can direct, inform, amuse, move emotionally and so on. From that point, emerges the **communicative** stage.
- Once pupils start writing for readers, it becomes a natural next step for them to start reading their own writing. This sets in motion the writing-reading feedback loop on which the stage of **unified** writing depends.
- Once this feedback loop is functioning well, it will be natural to discover that it leads to improved writing and to improved understanding. The feedback loop is a kind of dialogue with oneself. From the internal dialogue the final, **epistemic** stage of writing development may emerge.[11]

Issues in Writing Development

The study of writing development is a complex area. It is beset with many issues connected to the validity of any judgements that are made. Several strands of language can be used as dimensions of development. Yet development along one dimension may not necessarily be accompanied by development along another. For instance, the increase in vivid vocabulary that can be such a feature of creative writing in the 3–13 age-range may not be accompanied by growth in subordination. On the other hand, consciously crafted changes along some dimensions may not be stylistically or socially appropriate. For instance, some genres may be more successfully accomplished if vocabulary and sentence structure are relatively shorter or simpler. Then again, development along a certain dimension may be a relatively unreliable criterion of an individual's understanding or personal growth.[12]

Basic Issues in Assessing Writing

Of the two main facets of literacy, writing is more difficult to assess on a large scale than reading. In contrast, reading fluency and comprehension can be related to the original text and the author's intended meaning. The lack of this basic reference point undermines efforts to establish the validity of writing assessment when one text is compared with another. Validity is the extent to which assessment procedures actually assess what they purport to assess. The same is true of reliability, the consistency between the assessments that are made. Questions of reliability arise when the same text is assessed by different people. Such questions also arise when similar texts written by different people are assessed by one person.

These broader approaches to writing assessment include the three listed below, which are used in many research studies and national assessment programmes.

- **Holistic assessment** allows the text to be considered as a whole.
- **Primary trait scoring** specifies key features in advance, with teacher and pupils agreeing the purpose, audience and subject matter of the text. These features might be, for example, 'Write a letter to your headteacher to say how your school might be improved'.[13]
- **Portfolio assessment** allows a sample of different texts to be built up over time.

Table 9.3 below sums up the advantages and disadvantages of each. Some of the ways of redressing the disadvantages are listed in the final column.

Table 9.3

	Advantages	Disadvantages	Redress
Holistic assessment	Focuses on text as whole and the way the text conveys meaning. Relatively quick to administer.	Lacks specificity and reliability may suffer.	Use exemplar texts to illustrate range of performance; or agree an assessment guide with criteria for high, middle and low quality levels.
Primary trait scoring	Allows assessors to agree in advance the features that they are looking for.	Attention to specific traits may distract from the text as whole. Primary trait scoring is generally more time consuming than holistic assessment.	Collect supplementary information on pupils' experience of tackling this kind of task as a whole.

Portfolio assessment	Provides evidence of writing over time. May include more than one genre.	Very time-consuming. May be difficult to reach a generalised assessment.	Select one or more texts from larger sample as representative or most successful.

If specific criteria are agreed and balanced with some holistic, 'text-level' considerations, valid judgements may be made on pupil attainment. These judgements may in turn have implications for teaching provision. Validity and reliability will be higher if the holistic criteria and trait details are agreed at the outset by everyone who is involved.[14] This is the kind of thinking behind many national testing programmes.

National Testing Programmes

National Testing Programmes can only take into account some of the dimensions discussed in this chapter. The scale of their enterprise is such that the design of reliable measures is given priority. High reliability is achieved by using observable indicators and unambiguous criteria. The validity of the tests is circumscribed by their arbitrary nature. Considerations of the writing as an authentic, personal act of communication have to be given lower priority. At the same time, the existence of some kind of National Curriculum means there is plenty of scope for devising assessment tasks that have some interest and relevance for the pupils who take them.

This is the case with the Standard Assessment Tasks that have been used in England and Wales since 1991. Varieties of narrative and non-narrative tasks are set. Since 1996, a 'best fit' approach has been taken in assessment, replacing the statements of attainment approach of previous years. Judgements of 'best fit' are related to level descriptions devised by a central government agency. By the end of the 1990s, the assessment criteria were based partly on genre features ('purpose and organisation') and partly on linguistic features ('grammar'). Grammar was in turn subdivided into 'punctuation' and 'style' (including syntax and vocabulary).

The extracts on page 197 show how these genre and linguistic features can be used to indicate 'national expectations' for 11 year olds in the writing of a newsletter about a future school outing. Other tasks on this occasion were composing an interview and the choice from two narratives.[15]

The use of any dimension of writing development raises questions about the validity of the assessments made. Questions are always worth asking about the subject matter and the purpose of writing. These issues are central elements of the construct validity of writing assessment. The grades, scores or levels derived from national assessment programmes, for example, need to be balanced by information from how pupils perform in other contexts, with different subject matter and alternative purposes. This complementary information may also shed light on the internal, 'psychodynamic' development of individuals[16] and the part that writing plays in their lives.

Table 9.4

Purpose and Organisation	Grammar	
L E V E L 4	Punctuation	Style
There is some use of the conventions appropriate to newsletters, such as relevant introduction, series of logically ordered points and suitable concluding phrase and sentence which may make a direct appeal to the reader (*if you have any questions about the trip, ask Mrs Grant*). The writer seeks to inform the reader by presenting information clearly, and there is some attempt to engage the reader, for example by mentioning the attractions or advantages of the trip. Ideas are sustained and developed in a logical way. The writing is coherent and well paced, with adequate coverage of a range of aspects of the trip. Layout is mainly appropriate, and may include lists or timetables, or sub-headings.	Most sentences are correctly demarcated by full stops, capital letters and question marks. Within sentences, there is some evidence of the correct use of commas to separate elements of a sentence such as short phrases, clauses, or items in a list.	The use of some complex sentences helps to extend meaning. For example, there may be expansion (*modern coaches with seatbelts*) or use of subordinate clauses (*the trip which is on...*) to express information accurately to convey an authoritative tone, for example through impersonal constructions, or through the use of adverbs for emphasis (*definitely not...*). Connectives give order and emphasis (*if... then, [so as] to*). Some words or phrases are particularly well-chosen for interest or precision. Pronouns and tenses are generally consistent throughout.

Boys and Writing

The outcomes from national assessment programmes in turn raise their own questions, for instance about the relative performance of different groups. In England and Wales in recent years, there has been increasing concern about the underachievement of boys. Extracts from National Curriculum Assessment Reports give a flavour of the concern:

'"Boys' performance in seven year olds is lower than that of girls in all tasks and tests".[17]

'The results [for 11 year olds] show a 2% improvement, but that of boys has remained static...the number of boys achieving level 5 is approximately half that of girls'.[18]

'This year 73% of [14 year old] girls achieved level 5 or above compared to 57% of boys'.[19]

This gender difference in literacy attainment and attitude can be traced back over many years. It was reported in the early survey reports of the Assessment of Performance Unit.[20] A decade later it was the subject of an Ofsted publication based on inspection findings, *Boys and English*.[21] In the late 1990s the gap appeared to widen, causing extensive debate within the education service and media generally.

The gender issue has attracted a good deal of attention in the educational press and a variety of explanations have been put forward. Some explanations have focused on boys' greater vulnerability to the distractions of wider social change. Others have focused more on the culture of primary schools and the kinds of literacy practice that are valued in them. Others again have pointed to differences in developmental patterns and suggested that boys in particular may require greater systematic teaching in early reading, including a greater emphasis in decoding.

Closing the Gender Gap

What might be done to close the gender gap? In the absence of any kind of consensus, it may be safer to keep a variety of additional provisions in mind. These provisions may need to include not only strategies for teaching reading and writing. Broader patterns of classroom organisation and curriculum presentation may require attention too.

Several authors have set out strategies to help reduce the gender gap, including the three whose suggestions are summarised below. Elaine Millard, who has thoroughly explored the gender issue in her work at Sheffield University, has stressed the importance of the provision for reading, including the following:[22]

- **Redress imbalances**: introduce pupils to a wide range of genres and formats in the 7–11 age-range and audit individual pupils' reading. Build a picture of what influences pupils' reading and what they can draw on in their writing.
- **Improve book provision**: keep book stocks lively and up-to-date and work with parents in recommending and promoting books, including annotated lists for family presents.
- **Carefully plan shared reading activities**: pay careful attention to books chosen for reading together in class, including the interrogation of non-fictional topical forms of popular culture.

What Else Might be Done?

Other sources have taken broader views. Table 9.5 compares the suggestions from the Basic Skills Agency and the Qualifications and Curriculum Authority, suggestions that effectively complement those of Elaine Millard.

Table 9.5

Basic Skills Agency[23] Whole school	Qualifications and Curriculum Authority[24] Whole school
Reviewing and developing appropriate ethos and expectations.	*Highly valuing* language and literacy for all sorts of purposes.
Baseline testing at 11 (comparing non-verbal test performance and reading attainment). Ensuring that book collections and libraries include material that reflects boys' interests and preferences.	*Headteacher and senior staff committing time and resources* to identifying issues and focusing work on boys' achievement. *Valuing* expectations of progress and access for all.
Targeting, monitoring, mentoring individuals: • sharing assessment data with pupils and parents; • discussions of individual pupils' achievements at staff meetings; • using mentors for individuals (e.g. staff or sixth formers).	*Linking* assessment to planning. *Setting* and monitoring targets. *Keeping* parents informed.
Setting up homework and revision clubs etc. *Reviewing* how pupils are grouped, e.g. balancing the advantages of setting by ability with the need to keep low achievers in touch with good role models, e.g. by 'broad band' setting.	

Specific lesson organisation	**Specific lesson organisation**
Generally *using a specific, brisk approach* including: • *sharing objectives* with pupils; • *maintaining* a brisk pace; • *ending lessons* with a review; • *clearly phasing* stages; • *varying seating* arrangements; • *keeping high* expectations; • *using non-confrontational approach* to discipline; • *'jig-sawing'* (sharing tasks between groups, with reporting back).	*Identifying* good quality teaching and helping all teachers to achieve it. *Providing* clear structure, short-term goals and feedback. *Extending* the range of oral work to collaboration and role play. *Monitoring* the attention given to boys and girls and the consistency of responses to their contributions.

Literacy teaching and learning	**Literacy teaching and learning**
Systematically dealing with texts e.g.: • *using graphic aids* to thinking, e.g. grids, columns, flow charts, spider diagrams, etc.; • *providing effective models* for written assignments and examples of task, style, genre etc.; • *sharing headings and structures* for note-taking, but avoiding copying; • *using short, structured sessions* with clear targets and deadlines; • *using film/video scenes* as a way into studying texts; • *making prominent use of non-literary materials* (especially newspapers);	*Valuing boys'* voluntary reading and encouraging boys to extend it. *Increasing* the number and range of non-fiction texts used in English teaching. *Explicitly teaching* the features of different kinds of texts and strategies for reading and writing them. *Increasing* the use of drama, especially at Key Stage 2. *Ensuring* that literacy is associated with

- *using a variety of support activities*, e.g. group prediction, group cloze procedure, SQ3R, sequencing, highlighting and writing frames.

getting things done as well as expressing thoughts and feelings

Using diagnostic assessment to target action and support.

Special Needs Provision
Intensive teaching in the 11–14 age-range:
- *providing for the reading practice* which pupils may have missed through a slow start in primary school;
- *frequent contact with parents* if possible;
- *multi-layered support* (various combinations of withdrawal teaching, in-class support, paired/parent/peer reading, computer software, clinics and clubs);
- *intensive teaching*, using small group teaching, a balance of decoding and comprehension work and target-setting.

In the final SATs of the twentieth century, it was reported that 11 year old boys had closed the gap somewhat in their performance in English. However, this was more related to their reading than in their writing. The 1999 reading assessment involved a text on spiders, which was laid out in short sections. Some commentators suggested that this was the kind of text that appealed more to boys than previous SATs texts had done.[25] If this were the case, then it raises further questions about the socially derived context of school writing. Would boys be more motivated to improve their writing if the tasks and subject matter were more to their liking? Similar questions were raised some years earlier in connection with the advent of word processing in schools. So far, the outcomes from this have not generally fulfilled many of the early expectations.

The Word Processing Issue in Writing Development

Of all the developments in the literacy field in recent years, the increase of word processing has been one of the most disappointing. The disappointment has been related to the gap between the promise that this new technology originally seemed to offer and what subsequent research has indicated. Recent research reviews may have been a little more encouraging. Overall, though, the sense of unfulfilled promise – or even of false promise – remains in many recent research studies, from the case studies written by practising teachers to the reports of carefully controlled quasi-experimental research.

When microcomputers were first introduced into British schools in the early 1980s, there was much excitement about how their use might revolutionise how writing was taught and how it could improve the quality of pupil writing. The influential writer Seymour Papert was quoted as saying that he had seen a child move from total rejection of writing to an intense involvement (accompanied by rapid improvement of quality) within a few weeks of beginning to write with a computer.[26]

Many publications of that time speculated on what word processing in schools offered the teaching and learning of writing. The central government Kingman Report of 1988 outlined the gains as follows: 'the word processor, with its ability to shape, delete and move text around, provides the means by which pupils can achieve a satisfactory product...the process of writing – redrafting through editing to proof-reading and publishing – is one which children take to with enjoyment'.[27] This sense of optimism was fuelled by references to anecdotal evidence. Even before then, however, doubts were already being expressed by both teachers and researchers. Sue Robson, an English primary school teacher working in north London, reported in 1988 some of the pragmatic difficulties of using word processors with 6 and 7 year olds. The pupils preferred to use the technology to transcribe stories already written (which took longer than writing the originals and led to more errors). Class size meant that the teacher had to encourage the pupils to compose joint texts in twos and threes. This was something which they at first resisted. Even when the children were settled to a task, they need to spend three or four sessions of 30 minutes on a text before it was finished.[28]

Earl Woodruff, Carl Bereiter and Marlene Scardamalia were one of the first research teams formally to report inconclusive findings on the effect of word processing on the quality of the writing of 11–13 year olds.[29] By the end of the decade, successive research findings were confirming these more circumspect conclusions. For instance, as part of his doctoral research at the University of Leeds, Michael Peacock reviewed over 50 research projects, covering the age-range from primary school to higher education in the UK, USA, and Australia.[30] The large majority found no difference in the writing quality of writers using word processors when compared to the writing quality of writers using pen and paper.

Only when some other factor was present, for instance, detailed response of a teacher to an early draft, coupled with the use of word processors,[31] did the researchers begin to get significant findings. Details of studies comparing the use of typewriters and word processors, and braille writers and word processors, reported similarly inconclusive findings. Several of the researchers displayed a hint of bafflement in the conclusions they had been forced to draw. One put it this way: 'the anticipated focus on development and elaboration of texts did not occur', and the results seemed 'largely determined by the assignments' rather than attributable to the word processor.[32]

The conclusions from Peacock's literature review were similar to those of Annie Piolat in her French-based review of research findings. She concluded that, despite its history extending over a ten-year period, the study of whether and how word processing can improve writing still appears to be walking 'on rough ground'.[33] Sources like Dissertation Abstracts International are littered with reports which scarcely conceal surprise and dismay at the findings being relayed. At the USA International University, Janet Hall-Molina compared the writing quality, attitude towards writing and problem solving ability of elementary pupils using pencil and paper with pupils using a word processor.[34] Fifty-five 10 and 11 year olds each completed fifty hours of writing time. Pre- and post-tests of reasoning, silent reading, writing attitude and holistic scoring of writing failed to establish any significant differences between the groups.

The findings of Teresa Van Haalen at the University of Houston were even more disappointing.[35] Forty-two 11 year olds, half of whom were bilingual (English-Spanish), each wrote two compositions using pencil and paper and then two more using a word processor. Van Haalen analysed the types of revision the pupils reported making, their writing strategies and the holistic qualities of the final texts. Intriguingly, the pupils reported making more revisions when using pencil and paper. The quality of the compositions was judged to be higher when pencil and paper were used as well. Inevitably such reported findings raise questions on how far the pupils were trained in the use of word processors and how far they were aware of the facilities that the technology offered. Pupils' responses might also have been influenced by the nature of the task and how motivated they were by it. Nevertheless the above findings are broadly representative of many other findings of recent years.

A meta-analysis of 32 research studies by Robert Bangert-Drowns at the University of Albany in New York also failed to demonstrate that word processing improves the quality of pupils' writing. The only gains in 'before and after' studies of the effects of helping primary pupils become reasonably proficient at word processing skills have been where pupils' pencil and paper skills were initially low.[36]

Re-appraising ICT and Writing Development

So, what kind of conclusion is to be drawn from such recurrent findings in the research literature? Perhaps some kind of reappraisal is needed of the role of ICT in developing writing in the primary and middle years. The reappraisal could include the following questions:

1   *Is the potential of word processors being properly recognised?*
    A major feature of word processed text is its provisionality. It simplifies editing and it facilitates experimentation. As computers become more readily available in schools and as shared and guided writing become more established, the full potential of word processing in schools may become more widely understood. Robert Bangert-Drowns suggests that the key to increasing pupils' appreciation of word processing may simply lie in more sustained experience of what it can offer.[37] Only experience of editing, addition and deletion, re-arrangement and re-writing can help pupils to learn about the fluidity of text in ICT. As Angela McFarlane points out, inspection evidence suggests that word processors are still being widely used in schools as an amanuensis to help produce more presentable end products.[38]

2   *Is it being recognised that word processing can create new social contexts in schools?*

Peter Scrimshaw at the Open University sees the increasing availability of word processors in classrooms as creating new social contexts for teachers and children to work together.[39] For example, greater collaborative writing may be promoted through the following:

- divisions of labour – individuals taking responsibility for parts of the overall task;
- serial working – individuals working at the same task in turn;
- peer tutoring – one more skilled pupil helping another.

These strategies in turn may lead to genuine collaboration – the joint negotiation and completion of the task. After studying writing in five classrooms in Pennsylvania over two years, Marilyn Cochran-Smith reaches similar conclusions. In the new contexts that she observed, children learned new strategies and, more particularly, greater efficiency in using the strategies they already had. These new strategies may be linked to the multiple representations which ICT enables teachers and learners to share.[40]

The 'Literacies' Issues in Writing Development

Some writers have recently begun to argue against treating literacy as a single thing.[41] They have rejected this 'autonomous' model of literacy and have referred instead to 'literacies', in recognition of the fact that literacy practices are always embedded in social and cultural contexts.

Other writers, however, have pointed out that the word 'literacy' has developed two meanings: 'the ability to read and write' and 'competence' or 'knowledge'.[42] The latter meaning has been stretched in recent years to include 'computer literacy', 'historical literacy', 'musical literacy' and even 'emotional literacy'.[43] It is helpful to keep this distinction clear by referring to literacy (ability to read and write, or 'Literacy 1') and our account of reading and writing (or 'Literacy 2').[44]

According to this counter-argument, there may be different 'Literacies' (accounts of how reading and writing are used and of their significance in different settings). However, it is argued, there may not be substantively different kinds of 'Literacy 1', in terms of the decoding and encoding of text. Indeed, the decoding aspects of literacy involve universal features that provide texts with independent meanings in terms of what texts 'say' (as they are translated from symbol to sound). The relativity comes in the meaning that is constructed from the text and the implications that are drawn.[45]

One way of dealing with the question of whether there are 'literacies' comes from studies which have adopted the notion of 'vernacular literacies'.[46] This term refers to literacy practices which are not regulated or systematised by formal rules or procedures of social institutions. It contrasts these practices with the dominant practices of formal organisations (schools, churches, work places etc.).

The idea of vernacular literacies underpins studies of the ways reading and writing are used in private, informal or everyday purposes. These studies have revealed various kinds of expertise that have been created in the multiple and shifting purposes of individual citizens and their communities. Some of these vernacular literacies are humorous or disrespectful. It is interesting to note, though, that some of the people studied in the research did not see these literacy practices as 'real' reading or writing.

It remains a matter of debate whether there are multiple literacies. The accounts of vernacular literacies could also be interpreted as providing evidence of different accounts or social uses using the same core of skills. There are linguistic difficulties in treating a non-count noun like literacy as a count noun (see **Chapter 6**). There are conceptual difficulties in deciding where these different 'literacies' begin and end. It is also difficult to decide upon their precise nature, scope and number. Making a plural of the word literacy, when referring to the same language, assists communication similarly to such plurals as 'healths' or 'wealths' or 'happinesses'. It is an open question whether the insights provided by unqualified use of these plurals really repay their use.

Nevertheless, the literacies debate reminds us of the many distinctive literacy practices in everyday life, across a variety of cultures. It reminds us of the importance of keeping under careful review the nature and range of writing tasks undertaken in school in order to reflect real-world demands. It draws attention to the kinds of experience in reading and writing which children and their families bring to school and which can be used as resources for discussing and planning writing in the curriculum. Like much of this chapter, an awareness of the broader issues in writing development helps to bring a sense of proportion to the significance of written language in enhancing our lives.

10 | # Final Words

Writing not only helps us remember what was thought and said but also invites us to see what was thought and said in a new way.

(David Olson)[1]

This book began with a look back and it ends in a similar way. This time, however, the retrospective view takes account of the research and publications discussed in the book. This final chapter uses the look back to suggest some implications for the future, in teaching and teacher training.

Consolidated Gains: Range

The book has outlined how, in recent years, earlier understanding of range in writing has been consolidated. The book has also shown how the notion of range can be applied to several aspects of writing. These aspects can interact in numerous ways. Writing can be for various aims and audiences. It can draw on specific real-world or imaginative content. It can be organised in different ways and it can end up in various forms. The challenge for schools and homes is to provide the opportunity and support for writing competence to develop on several fronts. Well-roundedness in writing is unlikely to develop otherwise. Genre theory has connected older notions of range to a more recent recognition of how certain types of text are linked to educational success and to social mobility. The key to understanding range in writing lies in considering the contextual factors that influence specific communicative aims. These factors can then be linked to the distinctive features of the types of text likely to achieve these aims.

A Reappraisal: Process

This book has also shown how recent research and publications have built on the pioneering work of the 1970s on the processes of writing. There is now a clearer understanding of the cognitive processes involved in what is done before, during and after the text is written or typed. There is greater awareness of the influence of social context and of the parts played by layout and illustration. In other respects, the process of writing has undergone something of a reappraisal. The notion of drafting has been clarified. It now includes the production of outlines, lists of words, bunches of ideas and other outcomes from composing and planning. The term is now less used to refer exclusively to the production of several versions of the full text. It has been increasingly realised that this interpretation of 'process writing' can be tedious and counter-reproductive for many young writers. Process writing has also been subjected to a reappraisal regarding its effectiveness. There has been increasing recognition of the role of the teacher in pupils' writing development. This role includes forging productive links between children's reading and writing. It includes the value of modelling, explaining and synthesising the structure of texts, for classes and groups of children. Perhaps most importantly, research has revealed the values of 'guided writing', if this term is taken to mean specific, structured, problem solving activities, based on clear objectives and productive teacher–pupil interaction.

Technical Issues: Skills in Context

There have been significant advances in the general understanding of how spelling develops in children. Its nature as a visual-motor ('eye-hand') skill was established over 30 years ago. Subsequent publications have identified the assistance given to spelling by early phonological development. Through learning to hear sounds in words, children are able to map letters on to the phonemes that they represent. There is now an increasing awareness of how children need also to be helped to use the other two strands of language, grammar and vocabulary, in developing conventional spelling. Spelling development also reflects the interconnectedness of language learning in other ways. Spelling is supported by a wide experience of reading – and by being read to, if shared reading of large format texts is used. Handwriting supports spelling as well. Swift, economical letter formation assists the eye-hand aspects.

   However, various authorities argue that all this is best done in context. Spelling and handwriting are most effectively developed as part of a commitment to improving communicative competence. Children benefit from being taught about words that they need when they are writing with intent. Spelling is the servant of the author.[2]

Practical Implications: The Role of Feedback

Spelling and handwriting are good examples of where intervention by teachers and parents has a key influence. There has been much interest in recent years in children's emergent or developmental writing. The emphasis has been on early mark-making and on young children constructing continuous text from an early age. This is an enlightened development in the field of literacy education. Children often come to school seeing themselves as writers. Schools can build productively on this, but it is also important that adult intervention is strategic and well informed. International comparisons suggest that British schools have a long tail of under-achievement. The need for intervention programmes such as reading recovery is testimony to the need for strategic intervention if emergent literacy is not to become submergent literacy and if developmental writing is not to stall. Another finding from international effectiveness research is the significance of feedback to learners. Feedback in turn can help structure and shape the direction of future teaching, as the discussions in **Chapters 4** and **8** show. A key implication for early years educators is to identify the nature and extent of spelling and handwriting difficulties and the kinds of teaching that are needed. As children become more able to structure and shape their texts, there is a similar need to attend to sentence structure. It is, of course, important to read the lines and between the lines, to respond to the writing in terms of its communicative intent. It is also important to read between the words in order to consider the sentence structure. **Chapter 6** provides many insights for assessing the structure and variety of word order. **Chapter 7** indicates how responsive teaching can help enlighten young minds on the ways in which syntax can be manipulated to add interest and variety within various contexts and genres.

Current Issues: Professional Knowledge

Much of what has been discussed in this final chapter underlines the importance of professional knowledge in educational provision. Many issues demand that implicit knowledge is made explicit between educators, although the relationship between professional knowledge and teacher effectiveness is a complex one.[3] It is difficult enough to plan for children's writing development and to reach judgements on how well spelling, vocabulary and syntax are integrated within particular genres and contexts. The detection of strengths and weaknesses makes considerable demands on our abilities to make our knowledge of language explicit. Many technical terms provide an unambiguous short-hand for this professional communication. The linguistic terminology used in this book adds precision and focus to the discussion of many aspects of the second R. This terminology also provides for productive communication between researchers and teachers. Without access to this specialised language, teachers are in danger of being isolated from, and disempowered within, the community of research and practice.

Promising Futures

Overall, though, writing is an area of literacy education that has much promise for the future. Despite the disappointments from research into word processing that are discussed in **Chapter 9**, the electronic medium will offer increasing opportunities for exploiting the immediacy and flexibility that ICT brings to written communication. The new medium also provides unique opportunities for designing and integrating illustrations and other graphic features to support and enhance written text. This integration may be an even more important skill in the new millennium than when Janet White reported its rarity in school writing in the 1980s.[4] These opportunities are likely to bring about new relationships between teachers, pupils, texts and the wider community. Motivation and communicative self-esteem may be similarly enhanced. The needs of underachieving groups are being increasingly recognised. Central government initiatives are helping to share and disseminate more effective practices. Such developments add a new gloss to the following final recommendations. These recommendations are not new, but they have an enduring quality.

Cultivate an Interest in Language

Underlying the whole of this book is an assertion of the importance of a professional understanding of the nature and growth of language. It is an understanding that can have far-reaching ramifications. Attempts to develop components of children's writing are likely to be more effective if they are based on an appreciation of the patterned nature of language. Teachers need to be aware of the ways in which the use of language can foster thinking. A major factor in school performance is often the quality of dialogue that a child has with others.

Consider the Context of Children's Writing

There is a dynamic relationship between what children bring to a writing task, the context in which the writing is done and the principal dimensions of the writing, its aim, audience, content and organisation. Children are sometimes encouraged to put pen or pencil to paper for an unrealistic amount of the time. They may need to give more time to planning and composing. Writing is an 'abstract, deliberate activity'.[5] Classroom conditions need to help children to 'learn to be alone' in the special, psychological sense that is needed for many of the writing tasks in which they engage.

Provide Support for Children Writing

Inspection and research evidence suggests that teachers generally provide support for children writing in a good number of ways. But there are two possibilities that may be under-exploited. One is to make more of what children write available for other children to read. Writing for others is a well-known slogan that has not been translated into practice as widely as it might have been. The techniques of book production in itself can provide a natural consolidation of such work, techniques that have been very effectively conveyed by Paul Johnson.[6]

Children seem to write in some genres more readily than in others and this may be related to a lack of available models. It is certainly worth reviewing what range of texts is read aloud to and with children and modelled for them. Such reading aloud might help to provide a broader background of experience and opportunities for teaching and discussion, on which children can draw in the development of their own writing. The teaching approaches of the National Literacy Strategy in England will help to shed more light on how shared reading and writing can support guided and independent writing in subjects across the curriculum.

Plan Interventions

An understanding of the nature of language, a realistic context and sympathetic support may still not be enough. Many children will need carefully planned interventions by teachers to encourage practice and growth in aspects of writing identified by well-founded diagnostic assessment. **Chapter 8** includes a provisional framework for assessment and intervention. There is also much to be done to encourage children to assess their own writing, by looking back over what they have written with a writer's alertness to technique – and then thinking on.

Write Yourself, with the Children

Writing yourself, with the children, can provide many insights into how writing is composed, transcribed and reviewed. It can also bring home to us the complexity of the interrelationships between these aspects of written communication. Shared writing does more than model the processes of writing. Guided writing does more than engage pupils with these processes. Shared and guided teaching approaches help to confront the essence of creating meaning through the written word. They help us to take an authentic view of what is involved, and of what is at stake, in developing writing 3–13.

Bibliography
(author index in bold)

ADAMS, M.J. (1990) *Beginning to Read: Thinking and Learning about Print.* Cambridge, Mass.: The MIT Press. **44, 75, 81, 83, 231, 234, 235**

ADAMS, M.J. (1991) 'Why not phonics *and* whole language?', in ELLIS, W. (Ed.) *All Language and the Creation of Literacy.* Baltimore, Maryland: The Orton Dyslexia Society. **44, 231**

ALEXANDER, J. and CURRIE, A. (1998) '"I Normally Just Ramble On" – Strategies to Improve Writing at Key Stage 3', *English in Education,* 32, 2, 36–43. **231**

ALEXANDER, R.J. (1992) *Policy and Practice in Primary Education.* London: Routledge. **15, 227**

ALSTON, J. and TAYLOR, J. (Eds.) (1987) *Handwriting: Theory, Research and Practice.* London: Croom Helm. **234**

ANDREWS, R. (1997) 'Reconceiving Argument', *Educational Review,* 49, 3, 259–269. **237**

APPLEBEE, A.N. and LANGER, J.A. (1983) 'Instructional Scaffolding: Reading and writing as natural language activities', *Language Arts,* 60, 168–175. **54, 233**

ARNOLD, R. (1991) *Writing Development.* Milton Keynes: Open University Press. **245, 246**

ASSESSMENT OF PERFORMANCE UNIT (1981) *Language Performance in Schools: Primary Survey Report No. 1.* London: HMSO. **198, 246**

ATWELL, N. (1986) *In the Middle: Writing, reading and learning with adolescents.* Portsmouth, N.H.: Heinemann. **231**

BAIN, A. (1887) *English Composition and Rhetoric* (Enlarged Edition) London: Longmans, Green and Co. **90, 237**

BANGERT-DROWNS, R.L. (1993) 'The Word Processor as an Instructional Tool: A Meta-Analysis of Word Processing in Writing Instruction', *Review of Educational Research,* 63,1, 69–93. **202, 247**

BARBER, M. (1997) *The Learning Game: Arguments for An Education Revolution.* London: Indigo. **1, 226**

BARRON, I. (1996) 'Emergent Writing and the Teacher', *Journal of Teacher Development,* 5, 2, 41–8. **87, 236**

BARRS, M. (1983) 'Born Again Teachers' (Review of Graves, D.H. *Writing: Teachers and Children at Work*), *The Times Educational Supplement.* 24 June, p. 23. **51, 232**

BARTON, D. and HAMILTON, M. (1998) *Local Literacies: Reading and Writing in One Community.* London: Routledge. **203–4, 247**

BATES, R.G. (1992) *Children's Writing Strategies in the Early Years of Schooling* (Unpublished Ph.D. thesis). Leeds: University of Leeds School of Education. **77, 235**

BEALE, W. (1977) 'On the Classification of Discourse', *Rhetoric Society Quarterly,* 7, 31–40. **238**

BEAN, M.A. and WAGSTAFF, P. (1991) *Practical Approaches to Writing in the Primary School.* London: Longman. **237**

BEARD, R. (1984) *Children's Writing in the Primary School.* Sevenoaks: Hodder and Stoughton. **2, 3, 226**

BEARD, R. (1990) 'Children's Composing and Comprehending of Text' in WRAY D. (Ed.) *Emerging Partnerships: Current Research in Language and Literacy*, Clevedon: Multilingual Matters Ltd. (British Education Research Association Dialogue Series, No.4). **230**

BEARD, R. (1990) *Developing Reading 3–13 (2E)*. London: Hodder and Stoughton. **17**

BEARD, R. (1991) 'Learning to Read like a Writer', *Educational Review*, 43, 1, 17–24. **42, 231**

BEARD, R. (1994) 'Lessons from Reading Recovery', *Child Education*, August, 14–15. **235**

BEARD, R. (1995b) 'The National Curriculum in English', in ANNING, A. (Ed.) *The National Curriculum at Key Stage One: Five Years On*. Milton Keynes: Open University Press. **5, 226**

BEARD, R. (1999a) *The National Literacy Strategy: Review of Research and Other Related Evidence*. London: DfEE. **16, 227, 229**

BEARD, R. (1999b) 'English: Range, Key Skills and Language Study' in RILEY J. and PRENTICE, R. (Eds.) *The Curriculum for 7–11 year olds*, pp. 47–66, London: Paul Chapman. **8, 226**

BEARD, R. (Ed.) (1993) *Teaching Literacy: Balancing Perspectives*. London: Hodder and Stoughton. **228**

BEARD, R. (Ed.) (1995a) *Rhyme, Reading and Writing*. London: Hodder and Stoughton. **35, 229**

BEARD, R. and WILLCOCKS, J. (1997) 'Terms for Teaching Phonic Knowledge: A Legacy of Confusion'. Paper presented at the International Seminar on *Literacy. Integrating Research and Practice*, University of London Institute of Education, December. **123, 240**

BEARNE, E. (1998) *Making Progress in English*. London: Routledge. **230**

BEREITER, C. (1980) 'Development in writing', in GREGG, L. W. and STEINBERG, E. R. (Eds.) *Cognitive Processes in Writing*. Hillsdale, New Jersey: Lawrence Erlbaum Associates. **191, 193–4, 244, 245**

BEREITER, C. and SCARDAMALIA, M. (1982) 'From conversation to composition: the role of instruction in a developmental process', in GLASER, R. (Ed.) *Advances in Instructional Psychology*, Vol 2. London: Lawrence Erlbaum Associates. **40, 230**

BEREITER, C. and SCARDAMALIA, M. (1987) *The Psychology of Written Composition*. Hillsdale, New Jersey: Lawrence Erlbaum. **40, 54, 230, 233**

BETTELHEIM, B. (1977). *The Uses of Enchantment: the Meaning of Importance of Fairy Tales*. London: Thames and Hudson. **104, 239**

BISSEX, G.L. (1980) *GNYS AT WRK*. Cambridge, Mass.: Harvard University Press. **77–9, 175, 235, 243**

BLATCHFORD, P. (1991) 'Children's Handwriting at 7 Years: Associations With Handwriting on School Entry and Pre-School Factors', *British Journal of Educational Psychology*, 61, 73–84. **72, 234**

BLATCHFORD, P. and PLEWIS, I. (1990) 'Pre-School Reading-related Skills and Later Reading Achievement: further evidence', *British Educational Research Journal*, 16, 4, 425–428. **75, 234**

BLATCHFORD, P., BURKE, J., FARQUHAR, C., PLEWIS, I., and TIZARD, B. (1987) 'Associations between Pre-School Reading Related Skills and Later Reading Achievement', *British Educational Research Journal*, 13, 1, 15–23. **75, 234**

BOARD OF EDUCATION (1931) *Report of the Consultative Committee on the Primary School* (The Hadow Report). London: H.M.S.O. **90, 237**

BOWMAN, M. (1999) 'Children, Word Processors and Genre', *Scottish Educational Review*, 31, 1, 66–83. **247**

BRITTON, J. (1970) *Language and Learning*. Harmondsworth: Penguin. **51, 232**

BRITTON, J. *et al.* (1975) *The Development of Writing Abilities (11–18)*. Basingstoke: Macmillan. **90, 94, 237**

BROWN, A.L. and PALINSCAR, A.S. (1989) 'Guided, Cooperative and individual Learning Acquisition', in RESNICK, L.B. (Ed.) *Knowing, Learning and Instruction*. Hillsdale, N.J.: Lawrence Erlbaum. **233**

BROWN, R. (1968) 'Introduction' in MOFFETT, J. *Teaching the Universe of Discourse*. Boston, Mass.: Houghton Mifflin. **37, 229**

BROWNE, A. (1993) *Helping Children to Write*. London: Paul Chapman. **54, 233**

BROWNJOHN, S. (1994) *To Rhyme Or Not To Rhyme?* London: Hodder and Stoughton. **239**

BRUNER, J. (1964) 'The Course of Cognitive Growth', *American Psychologist*, 19, 1–15. **18, 227**

BRUNER, J. (1972) *The Relevance of Education*. London: Allen and Unwin. **38, 230**

BRUNER, J. (1985) 'Vygotsky: a historical and conceptual perspective', in WERTSCH,. J.V. (Ed.) *Culture, Communication and Cognition: Vygotskyan Perspectives*. Cambridge: Cambridge University Press.**19, 228**

BRYANT, P. and BRADLEY, L. (1980) 'Why children sometimes write words which they cannot read' in Frith, U. (1980) *Cognitive Processes in Spelling*. London: Academic Press. **80, 235**

BRYANT, P., DEVINE, M., LEDWARD, A. and NUNES, T. (1997) 'Spelling with apostrophes and understanding possession', *British Journal of Educational Psychology*, 67, 91–120. **84, 235**

BRYANT, P., NUNES, T. and BINDMAN, M. (1998) 'Awareness of Language in Children Who Have Reading Difficulties: Historical Comparisons in a Longitudinal Study', *Journal of Child Psychology and Psychiatry*, 39, 4, 501–510. **84, 238**

CALKINS, L. M. (1986) *The Art of Teaching Writing*. Portsmouth, N.H.: Heinemann. **53**

CALKINS, L.M. (1983) *Lessons From a Child*. Exeter, New Hampshire: Heinemann. **52, 233**

CAMBOURNE, B. (1988) *The Whole Story: Natural Learning and the Acquisition of Literacy in the Classroom*. Gosford, NSW: Aston Scholastic. **85, 236**

CARNEY, E. (1994) *A Survey of English Spelling*. London: Routledge. **32–3, 228**

CATO, V., FERNANDES, C., GORMAN, T., KISPAL, A. with WHITE, J. (1992) *The Teaching of Initial Literacy: How do teachers do it?* Slough: NFER. **236**

CHALL, J., JACOBS, V.A. and BALDWIN, L.E. (1990) *The Reading Crisis: Why Poor Children Fall Behind*. Cambridge, Mass.: Harvard University Press. **86, 236**

CHRISTIE, F. (1996) 'Review of Freedman, A. and Medway, P. (Eds.) (1994) *Genre and the New Rhetoric*', *Language and Education*, 10, 1, 71–75. **111, 239**

CLARK, M.M. (1974) *Teaching Left-Handed Children.* London: Hodder and Stoughton.**74, 234**

CLARKE, L.K. (1988) 'Invented Versus Traditional Spelling in First Graders' Writings: Effects on Learning to Spell and Read', *Research in the Teaching of English.* 22, 3, 281–309. **83, 235**

CLAY, M.M. (1975) *What Did I Write? Beginning Writing Behaviour.* Portsmouth, N.H.: Heinemann. **67–8, 234**

CLAY, M.M. (1987) *Writing Begins at Home.* Auckland: Heinemann. **63, 233**

CLAY, M.M. (1993) *Reading Recovery: A guidebook for teachers in training.* Auckland, New Zealand: Heinemann Education. **82, 235**

CLEGG, A. (1964) *The Excitement of Writing.* London: Chatto and Windus. **92, 237**

COCHRAN-SMITH, M., PARIS, C.L. and KAHN, J.L. (1991) *Learning to Write Differently.* Hove: Ablex Pub. Co. **48, 203, 232, 247**

COOPER, C. R. (1977) 'Holistic Evaluation of Writing', in COOPER, C. R. and ODELL, L. (Eds.) *Evaluating Writing: Describing, Measuring, Judging.* State University of New York at Buffalo: National Council of Teachers of English. **245**

COPE, B. and KALANTZIS, M. (1993) *The Powers of Literacy: A Genre Approach to Teaching Writing.* London: The Falmer Press. **107, 109, 239**

CORBETT, P. and MOSES, B. (1986) *Catapults and Kingfishers: teaching poetry in primary schools.* Oxford: Oxford University Press. **109, 239**

COWIE, H. (Ed.) (1984) *The Development of Children's Imaginative Writing.* London: Croom Helm. **104, 239**

CREEMERS, B.P.M. (1994) *The Effective Classroom.* London: Cassell. **15, 227**

CRYSTAL, D. (1979) *Working With LARSP.* London: Edward Arnold. **149, 241**

CRYSTAL, D. (1987a) *Child Language, Learning and Linguistics* (2E). London: Edward Arnold. First chapter reprinted in BEARD, R. (Ed.) (1993) *Teaching Literacy: Balancing Perspectives.* London: Hodder and Stoughton.**23, 28, 228, 229**

CRYSTAL, D. (1987b) *The Cambridge Encyclopedia of Language.* Cambridge: Cambridge University Press. **31, 229**

CRYSTAL, D. (1988) *Rediscover Grammar.* London: Longman. **129, 240**

CRYSTAL, D. (1990) *The English Language.* Harmondsworth: Penguin. **30, 154, 229, 242**

CRYSTAL, D. (1995) *The Cambridge Encyclopedia of the English Language.* Cambridge: Cambridge University Press.**155, 156, 242**

CRYSTAL, D., FLETCHER, P. and GARMAN, M. (1976) *The Grammatical Analysis of Language Disability.* London: Edward Arnold.**29, 229**

CZERNIEWSKA, P. (1992) *Learning About Writing: the early years.* Oxford: Blackwell. **67, 234**

CZERNIEWSKA, P.(1992) 'Review of Nicholls, J. *et al.* (1989) *Beginning Writing,' Language and Education,* 6, 1, 76–77.**77, 235**

D'ANGELO, F.D. (1976) 'Modes of Discourse', in TATE, G. (Ed.) *Teaching Composition: Ten Bibliographical Essays.* Fort Worth, Texas: Christian University Press.**90, 237**

DAHL, K.L. and FARNAN, N. (1998) *Children's Writing: Perspectives From Research.* Newark, Delaware and Chicago, Ill: International Reading Association and National Reading Conference. **41, 230**

DALE, P. S. (1976) *Language Development: Structure and Function* (2E). New York: Holt, Rinehart and Winston. **26, 228**

DAVIES, J. and BREMBER, I. (1997) 'Monitoring reading standards in Year 6: A seven-year cross-sectional study', *British Educational Research Journal*, 23, 5, 615–622. **9, 227**

DAVIES, J. and BREMBER, I. (1998) 'Standards of Reading at Key Stage 1: A cause for celebration? A seven-year cross-sectional study', *Educational Research*, 40, 2, 153–160. **9, 227**

DAY, T. (1997) 'The Role of Children's Informal Talk in Their Writing', *Irish Educational Studies*, 16, 97, 223–234. **228**

DEPARTMENT FOR EDUCATION (1995) *English in the National Curriculum.* London: HMSO. **4, 5, 6, 7, 226**

DEPARTMENT FOR EDUCATION AND EMPLOYMENT (1998a) *The National Literacy Strategy: Framework for Teaching.* London: DfEE. **4, 5, 13, 81, 169, 226, 227, 235, 241**

DEPARTMENT FOR EDUCATION AND EMPLOYMENT (1998b) *The National Literacy Strategy: Literacy Training Pack.* London: DfEE. **4, 13, 175**

DEPARTMENT FOR EDUCATION AND EMPLOYMENT (1999a) *English: The National Curriculum for England Key Stages 1–4.* London: DfEE and QCA. **4, 5, 6, 7–8, 90, 102, 200, 226, 236, 238, 247**

DEPARTMENT FOR EDUCATION AND EMPLOYMENT (1999b) *The National Curriculum: Handbook for Primary Teachers in England*, Key Stages 1 and 2. London: DfEE and QCA. **4, 5, 6, 7–8, 100, 151, 226, 238, 241**

DEPARTMENT OF EDUCATION AND SCIENCE (1959) *Primary Education.* London: HMSO. **92**

DEPARTMENT OF EDUCATION AND SCIENCE (1975) *A Language for Life* (The Bullock Report). London: HMSO. **18, 51, 94, 227, 229, 237**

DEPARTMENT OF EDUCATION AND SCIENCE (1985) *Education for All* (The Swann Report). London: HMSO. **30, 229**

DEPARTMENT OF EDUCATION AND SCIENCE (1988) *Report of the Committee of Inquiry into the Teaching of the English Language* (The Kingman Report). London: HMSO. **4, 8, 43, 150, 201, 226, 231, 241, 246**

DEPARTMENT OF EDUCATION AND SCIENCE (1978) *Primary Education in England.* London: HMSO. **3, 226**

DEPARTMENT OF EDUCATION AND SCIENCE AND THE WELSH OFFICE (1989) *English in the National Curriculum.* London: HMSO. **4, 5, 6–7, 226**

DEPARTMENT OF EDUCATION NORTHERN IRELAND (1996) *English Programmes of Study and Attainment Targets: Key Stages 1,2 and 3* (3 vols.) Bangor, Co. Down: DENI. **5, 100, 102, 226, 238**

DIRINGER, D. (1968) *The Alphabet* (3E). London: Hutchinson. **30, 229**

DONALDSON, M. (1989) *Sense and Sensibility: Some thoughts on the teaching of literacy* (Occasional Paper No. 3). Reading: Reading and Language Information Centre, University of Reading. Reprinted in BEARD, R. (Ed.) (1993) *Teaching Literacy: Balancing Perspectives.* London: Hodder and Stoughton. **39, 230**

DUGUID, L. (1988) 'The art of conversation: A profile of Jan Mark'. *Times Educational Supplement*, 3 June. **52, 123, 233, 240**

DYER, B. (1996) 'L1 and L2 composition theories: Hillocks' "environmental mode" and task-based language teaching', *English Language Teaching Journal*, 50, 4, 312–317. **53, 233**

DYSON, A. (1982) 'The Emergence of Visible Language: Interrelationships between Drawing and Early Writing', *Visible Language*, XVI, 4, 360-381. **63–4, 233**

DYSON, A. H. (1989) *Multiple Worlds of Child Writers*. New York: Teachers College Press. **231**

DYSON, A.H. (1997) *Writing Superheroes: contemporary childhood, popular culture and classroom literacy*. New York: Teachers College Press. **238**

EDWARDS, V. and CHESHIRE, J. (1989) 'The survey of British dialect grammar', in CHESHIRE, J., EDWARDS, V., MUNSTERMANN, H. and WELTENS, B. (Eds.) *Dialect and Education: Some European Perspectives*. Clevedon: Multilingual Matters. **150, 151, 241**

EDWARDS, V.K. (1979) *The West Indian Language Issue in British Schools: Challenges and Responses*. London: Routledge and Kegan Paul. **30, 229**

EHRI, L. (1997) 'Learning to read and learning to spell are one and the same, almost', in PERFETTI, C., RIEBEN, L. and FAYOL, M. (Eds.) *Learning to Spell: Research, Theory and Practice Across Languages*. Mahwah, N.J.: Lawrence Erlbaum. **235**

ELDREDGE, J.L., REUTZEL, D.R. and HOLLINGSWORTH, P.M. (1996) 'Comparing the Effectiveness of Two Oral Reading Practices: Round-Robin Reading and the Shared Book Experience', *Journal of Literacy Research*, 28, 2, 201–225. **43, 231**

ELLEY, W.B. (1989) 'Vocabulary acquisition from listening to stories', *Reading Research Quarterly*, 24, 174-187. **43, 231**

ELLIS, S., HUGHES, A. and MACKAY, R. (1997) 'Writing Stories 5–14: What must teachers teach?' *Scottish Educational Review*, 29, 1, 56 65. **238**

FERREIRO, E. (1997) 'What does it mean to study children's theories about the writing system?'. Paper presented at International Symposium on *Integrating Research and Practice in Literacy*. University of London Institute of Education, March. **234**

FERREIRO, E. and TEBEROSKY, A. (1982) *Literacy Before Schooling*. London: Heinemann.**64–7, 233, 234**

FITZGERALD, J. (1987) 'Research on revision in writing', *Review of Educational Research*, 57, 481–506. **232**

FOX, R. (1999) 'Rewriting the literacy hour', *Times Educational Supplement Primary Magazine*, 25.6.99, p.6. **236**

FRANK, L.A. (1992) 'Writing to be read: Young writers' ability to demonstrate audience awareness when evaluated by their readers', *Research in the Teaching of English*, 26, 3, 277–298. **238**

FRATER, G. (1997) *Improving Boys' Literacy: a survey of effective practice in secondary schools*. London: Basic Skills Agency. **199–201, 246**

FREEDMAN, A. and MEDWAY, P. (Eds.) (1994) *Genre and the New Rhetoric*. London; Taylor and Francis. **110, 239**

FRISCH, K. von. (1953) *The Dancing Bees: an account of the life and senses of the honey bee* (translated by Dora Ilse) San Diego: Harcourt Brace Jovanovich. **18, 227**

FRITH, U. (1985) 'Beneath the surface of developmental dyslexia', in PATTERSON, K.E., MARSHALL, J.C. and COLTHEART, M. (Eds.) *Surface Dyslexia.* Hillsdale, N.J.: Lawrence Erlbaum. **79, 235**

GALBRAITH, D. and RIJLAARSDAM, G. (1999) 'Effective strategies for the teaching and learning of writing', *Learning and Instruction*, 9, 93–108. **230**

GANNON, P. and CZERNIEWSKA, P. (1980) *Using Linguistics: An Educational Focus.* London: Edward Arnold. **27, 229**

GARTON, A. and PRATT, C. (1998) *Learning to be Literate* (2E). Oxford: Blackwell. **230**

GENTRY, J.R. (1982) 'An analysis of developmental spelling in *GNYS AT WRK*', *The Reading Teacher*, 36, 192–200. **78, 174, 235, 243**

GIBSON, H. and ANDREWS, R. (1993) 'A Critique of the Chronological/Non-chronological Distinction in the National Curriculum for English', *Educational Review.* 45, 3, 239–249. **91, 111, 237, 239, 244**

GILBERT, P. (1989) 'Student Text as Pedagogical Text', in CASTELL, S. de, LUKE, A. and LUKE, C. (Eds.) (1989) *Language, Authority and Criticism.* London: Falmer Press. **51–2, 232**

GIPPS, C., BROWN, M., MCCALLUM, B. and MCALISTER, S. (1995) *Intuition or evidence?: Teachers and national assessment of seven year olds* Buckingham: Open University Press. **9, 227**

GOLDSTEIN, A.A. and CARR, P.G. (1996) 'Can students benefit from process writing?' *National Assessment of Educational Progress Facts 1. Report No. NCES-96–845. ED 395 320.* Washington, D.C.: US Dept. of Education, National Center for Educational Statistics. **40, 230**

GOMBERT, J.E. and FAYOL, M. (1992) 'Writing in Pre-Literate Children', *Learning and Instruction*, 2, 23–41. **64, 233**

GOMBERT, M., BRYANT, P. and WARRICK, N. (1997) 'Children's Use of Analogy in Learning to Read and to Spell', in PERFETTI, C.A., RIEBEN, L. and FAYOL, M. (Eds.) *Learning to Spell: Research, Theory and Practice Across Languages.* Mahwah, N.J.: Lawrence Erlbaum. **244**

GORMAN, T. and BROOKS, G. (1996) *Assessing Young Children's Writing: A Step-by-Step Guide.* London: The Basic Skills Agency. **65, 69, 71, 234**

GOSWAMI, U. (1999) 'Phonological Development and Reading by Analogy: Epilinguistic and Metalinguistic Issues', in OAKHILL, J. and BEARD, R. (Eds.) *Reading Development and the Teaching of Reading: a psychological perspective.* Oxford: Blackwell. **35, 229**

GOSWAMI, U. and BRYANT, P. (1990) *Phonological Skills and Learning to Read.* Hove: Lawrence Erlbaum. **35, 229**

GOUGH, P. (1999) 'The New Literacy: *Caveat Emptor*' in OAKHILL, J. and BEARD, R. (Eds.) (1999) *Reading Development and the Teaching of Reading.* Oxford: Blackwell. **203–4, 247**

GRAHAM, J. and KELLY, A. (Eds.) (1998) *Writing Under Control.* London: David Fulton in association with Roehampton Institute. **246**

GRAVES, D. (1983) *Writing: Teachers and Children at Work.* Portsmouth, N.H.: Heinemann. **50, 53, 232**

GRAVES, D.H. (1975) 'An examination of the writing processes of seven-year-old children', *Research in the Teaching of English*, 9, 227–241. **51, 232**

GRAVES, D.H. (1994) *A Fresh Look at Writing*. Portsmouth, N.H.: Heinemann. **50, 232**

GREENBAUM, S. (1991) *An Introduction to English Grammar*. Harlow: Longman. **163, 229, 242**

GREGORY, E. (1996) *Making Sense of a New World*. London: Paul Chapman. **69, 234**

GREGORY, R. L. (1977) 'Psychology: towards a science of fiction', in MEEK, M. *et al.* (Eds.) *The Cool Web*. London: The Bodley Head. **104, 238**

GROSSMAN, A. N. (1988) 'Writing and using a word processor in an LD resource room: case studies of five minimally handicapped high school students', *Dissertation Abstracts International*, 50/1, 113. **201, 246**

GRUGEON, E., HUBBARD, L., SMITH, C. and DAWES, L. (1998) *Teaching Speaking and Listening in the Primary School*. London: David Fulton. **22, 228**

HALL-MOLINA, J. M. (1990) 'A comparison of writing quality, attitude towards writing, and problem solving ability of elementary students who use a word processor and those who use the paper pencil method of composition', *Dissertation Abstracts International*, 51/7, 2263A. **201–2, 247**

HALL, N. (1998) 'Young children and resistance to punctuation', *Research in Education*, 60, 29–39. **48, 232**

HALL, N. and ROBINSON, A. (Eds.) (1994) *Keeping in touch: using interactive writing with young children*. London: Hodder and Stoughton. **238**

HALL, N. and ROBINSON, A. (Eds.) (1996) *Learning About Punctuation*. Clevedon: Multilingual Matters. **47, 232**

HALLIDAY, M.A.K (1975) *Learning How to Mean*. London: Edward Arnold. **27, 229**

HALLIDAY, M.A.K. and HASAN, R. (1976) *Cohesion in English*. Harlow: Longman. **144, 154, 241, 242**

HARPIN, W (1976) *The Second 'R' : Writing Development in the Junior School*. London: Allen and Unwin. **178–9, 182–4, 191, 244**

HARTHILL, R. (1989) *Writers Revealed*. London: B.B.C. Books. **52, 233**

HARTOG, P.J. (1908) *The Writing of English* (2E). Oxford: Clarendon Press. **88, 236**

HARVEY, C. and HENDERSON, S. (1997) 'Children's handwriting in the first three years of school: consistency over time and its relationship to academic achievement', *Handwriting Review*, 11, 8–25. **234**

HAWKINS, E. (1987) *Awareness of Language: An Introduction* (Revised Edition) Cambridge: Cambridge University Press. **166, 243**

HAYES, J.R. (1996) 'A New Framework for Understanding Cognition and Affect in Writing' in LEVY, C.M. and RANSDELL, S. (Eds.) *The Science of Writing: Theories, Methods, Individual Differences, and Applications*. Mahwah, N.J.: Lawrence Erlbaum Associates. **39, 230**

HAYES, J.R. and FLOWER, L.S. (1980) 'Writing as Problem Solving', *Visible Language*, 14, 4, 388–399. **40, 230**

HENDERSON, E. (1985) *Teaching Spelling*. Boston: Houghton Mifflin. **243**

HER MAJESTY'S INSPECTORATE (1991) *English Key Stage 1: A Report by HM Inspectorate on the First Year, 1989–90*. London: HMSO. **11**

HER MAJESTY'S INSPECTORATE (1992) English Key Stages 1, 2 and 3: A *Report by HM Inspectorate on the Second Year 1990–91*, London: HMSO. **11**

HILLOCKS, G. (1986) *Research on Written Composition*. Urbana, Il.: National Conference on Research in English/ERIC Clearinghouse on Reading and Communication Skills. **53, 194, 233**

HILLOCKS, G. (1995) *Teaching Writing as Reflective Practice.* New York: Teachers College Press. **53, 194, 233**

HONEY, J. (1997) *Language is Power.* London: Faber. **151, 241**

HUDSON, R. (1992) *Teaching Grammar.* Oxford: Blackwell. **241**

HUDSON, R. and HOLMES, J. (1995) *Children's Use of Standard Spoken English.* London: School Curriculum and Assessment Authority. **151, 164, 241, 243**

HUGHES, T. (1976) 'Myth and Education', *Children's Literature in Education 1,1.* Reprinted in FOX, G. (Ed.) (1995) *Celebrating Children's Literature in Education.* London: Hodder and Stoughton.**104, 239**

HUGHES, T. (1987) 'To parse or not to parse: the poet's answer', *The Sunday Times.* 22 November. **52, 123, 149, 233, 240, 241**

HURFORD, J.R. (1994) *Grammar: A Student's Guide.* Cambridge: Cambridge University Press. **229**

JACKSON, H. (1988) *Words and Their Meaning.* London: Longman. **228**

JOHNSON, P. (1990) *A Book of One's Own: developing literacy through making books.* London: Hodder and Stoughton. **208, 247**

KEITH, G. (1990) 'Language Study at Key Stage 3', in CARTER, R. (Ed.) *Knowledge about Language and the Curriculum: The LINC Reader.* London: Hodder and Stoughton. **8, 123, 226, 240**

KELLOGG, R. (1970) *Analysing Children's Art.* Palo Alto, California: Mayfield Pub. Co. **58–63, 233**

KING, M. L. and RENTEL, V. (1979) 'Toward a theory of early writing development', *Research in the Teaching of English,* 13, 3, 243–253. **85, 236**

KINNEAVY, J. L. (1971) *A Theory of Discourse.* Englewood Cliffs, New Jersey: Prentice Hall. **90, 97, 237**

KINNEAVY, J. L. (1983) 'A pluralistic synthesis of four contemporary models for teaching composition', in FREEDMAN, A. *et al.* (Eds.) *Learning to Write: First Language/Second Language.* London: Longman. **237**

KINNEAVY, J. L., COPE, J.Q. and CAMPBELL, J.W. (1976) *Writing: Basic Modes of Organisation.* Dubuque, Iowa: Kendall Hunt Pub. Co. **90, 237**

KINNEAVY, J.L (1991) 'Rhetoric', in FLOOD, J. et al. (Eds.) *Handbook of Research on Teaching the English Language Arts.* New York: Macmillan. **237**

KRESS, G. (1994) *Learning to Write* (2E). London: Routledge.**46, 109, 231, 239**

KRESS, G. (1999) *Early Spelling.* London: Routledge. **78, 235**

KROLL, B. (1985) 'Rewriting a complex story for a younger reader: The development of audience-adapted writing skills, *Research in the Teaching of English,* 19, 2, 120–139. **238**

LANE, S. M. and KEMP, M. (1967) *An Approach to Creative Writing in the Primary School.* London: Blackie. **92, 237**

LANGER, J. (1986) *Children Reading and Writing: Structures and Strategies.* Norwood, N.J. : Ablex. **231**

LENSMIRE, T. (1994) *When Children Write: Critical re-visions of the writing workshop.* New York: Teachers College Press. **232**

LEWIS, M. and WRAY, D. (1995) *Developing Children's Non-Fiction Writing: working with writing frames.* Leamington Spa: Scholastic. **109, 113, 239**

LITERACY TASK FORCE (1997a) *A Reading Revolution: How We Can Teach Every Child to Read Well*. London: The Literacy Task Force c/o University of London: Institute of Education. **13, 227**

LITERACY TASK FORCE (1997b) *The Implementation of the National Literacy Strategy*. London: Department for Education and Employment. **13, 227**

LITTEN, C. L. (1989) 'The effects of word processing and peer review on the revision process of freshman composition students', *Dissertation Abstracts International*, 51/4, 1101A. **201, 246**

LITTLEFAIR, A.B. (1991) *Reading All Types of Writing*. Milton Keynes: Open University Press. **239**

LLOYD-JONES, R. (1977) 'Primary trait scoring', in COOPER, C. R. and ODELL, L. (Eds.) *Evaluating Writing: Describing, Measuring, Judging*. State University of New York at Buffalo: National Council of Teachers of English. **99, 238, 245**

LUMBELLI, L., PAOLETTI, G. and FRAUSIN, T. (1999) 'Improving the ability to detect comprehension problems: from revising to writing', *Learning and Instruction*, 9, 2, 143–166. **232**

LURIA, A. R. (1959) 'The directive function in speech in development and dissolution', *Word*, 15, 3, 341–52. Reprinted in OLDFIELD, R. C. and MARSHALL, J. C. (Eds.) (1968) *Language*, Harmondsworth: Penguin Books. **19, 228**

MACKAY, D., THOMPSON, B. and SCHAUB, P. (1979) *Breakthrough to Literacy: Teacher's Manual (2E.)*. London: Longman, for the Schools Council. **232**

MARTIN, J.R. (1989) *Factual Writing: exploring and challenging social reality (2E)*. Oxford: Oxford University Press. **53, 108, 239**

MARZANO, R. (1976) 'The Sentence Combining Myth', *English Journal*, 65, 57–59. **242**

MASONHEIMER, P.E., DRUM, P.A. and EHRI, L.C. (1984) 'Does environmental print identification lead children into word reading?' *Journal of Research Behaviour*, 16, 257–271. **71, 234**

MAYBURY, B. (1967) *Creative Writing for Juniors*. London: Batsford. **92, 237**

MCARTHUR, T. (Ed.) (1992) *The Oxford Companion to the English Language*. Oxford: Oxford University Press. **28, 34, 229, 239, 240**

MCFARLANE, A. (Ed.) (1997) *Information Technology and Authentic Learning*. London: Routledge. **202, 247**

MCNAUGHTON, M.J. (1997) 'Drama and Children's Writing: a study of the influence of drama on the imaginative writing of primary school children', *Research in Drama Education*, 2, 1, 55–85. **103, 238**

MEDWELL, J., WRAY, D., POULSON, L. and FOX, R.(1998) *Effective Teachers of Literacy* Exeter: University of Exeter School of Education. **247**

MERCER, N. (1995) *The Guided Construction of Knowledge: talk amongst teachers and learners*. Clevedon: Multilingual Matters. **22–3, 228**

MERCER, N. (1996) 'The quality of talk in children's collaborative activity in the classroom', *Learning and Instruction*, 6, 359–379. **22–3, 228**

MERCER, N., WEGERIF, R. and DAWES, L.(1999) 'Children's Talk and the Development of Reasoning in the Classroom', *British Educational Research Journal*, 25, 1, 95–111. **23, 228**

MILLARD, E. (1997) *Differently Literate: Boys, Girls and the Schooling of Literacy.* London: The Falmer Press. **198, 246**

MINISTRY OF EDUCATION (1954) *Language: Some Suggestions for Teachers of English and others.* London: HMSO. **92, 237**

MINSKY, M. (1985) 'A Framework for Representing Knowledge', in WINSTON, P.H. (Ed.) *The Psychology of Computer Vision.* New York: McGraw-Hill. **113, 239**

MOFFETT, J. (1968) *Teaching the Universe of Discourse.* Boston, Massachusetts: Houghton Mifflin. **191–2, 244**

MORTIMORE, P. (1991) 'The nature and findings of school effectiveness research in the primary sector', in RIDDELL, S. and BROWN, S. (Eds.) *School Effectiveness Research: Its Messages for School Improvement.* London: HMSO. **14, 227**

MORTIMORE, P., SAMMONS, P., STOLL, L., LEWIS, D. and ECOB, R. (1988) *School Matters: The Junior Years.* Wells: Open Books. **14, 179, 227, 244**

MOUNTFORD, J. (1998) *An Insight into English Spelling.* London: Hodder and Stoughton. **45. 231**

MUDD, N. (1994) *Effective Spelling: A practical guide for teachers.* London: Hodder and Stoughton. **243**

MURRAY, D. M. (1990) *Shoptalk: Learning to write with writers.* Portsmouth, N.H.: Boynton/Cook. **229**

NICHOLLS, J., BAUERS, A., PETTITT, D., REDGWELL, V., SEAMAN, E. and WATSON, G. (1989) *Beginning Writing.* Milton Keynes: Open University Press. **76, 235, 245**

NUNES, T., BRYANT, P. and BINDMAN, M. (1997) 'Morphological Spelling Strategies: Developmental Stages and Processes', *Developmental Psychology,* 33, 4, 637–649. **84, 236**

NUTBROWN, C. (1999) 'Baseline assessment of writing: the need for reconsideration', *Journal of Research in Reading,* 22, 1, 37–44. **87, 236**

O'HARE, F. (1973) *Sentence-Combining: Improving Student Writing without Formal Grammar Instruction.* Illinois: National Council of Teachers of English. **160, 242**

ODELL, L. *et al.* (1978) 'Discourse theory: implications for research in composing', in COOPER, C. R. and ODELL, L. *Research on Composing: Points of Departure.* Urbana, Illinois: National Council of Teachers of English. **99, 237**

OFFICE FOR STANDARDS IN EDUCATION (1993a) *English: Key Stages, 1, 2 and 3: Third Year 1991–2.* London: HMSO. **11**

OFFICE FOR STANDARDS IN EDUCATION (1993b) *English: Key Stages, 1, 2, 3 and 4: Fourth Year 1992–3.* London: HMSO. **11**

OFFICE FOR STANDARDS IN EDUCATION (1993c) *Boys and English.* London: Ofsted. **198, 246**

OFFICE FOR STANDARDS IN EDUCATION (1995) *English: A review of inspection findings 1993/94.* London: HMSO. **11**

OFFICE FOR STANDARDS IN EDUCATION (1996a) *The Annual Report of Her Majesty's Chief Inspector of Schools: Standards and Quality in Education 1994/95.* London: HMSO. **11**

OFFICE FOR STANDARDS IN EDUCATION (1996b) *Subjects and Standards: Issues for school development arising from OFSTED inspection findings 1994–5: Key Stages 1 & 2.* London: HMSO. **12**

OFFICE FOR STANDARDS IN EDUCATION (1996c) *Subjects and Standards: Issues for school development arising from OFSTED inspection findings 1994–5: Key Stages 3 & 4 and Post-16* . London: HMSO. **12**

OFFICE FOR STANDARDS IN EDUCATION (1997a) *The Annual Report of Her Majesty's Chief Inspector of Schools: Standards and Quality in Education 1995/6.* London: The Stationery Office. **12**

OFFICE FOR STANDARDS IN EDUCATION (1997b) *Standards in English 1995–6: Primary Schools.* London: Ofsted. **12**

OFFICE FOR STANDARDS IN EDUCATION (1998a) *The Annual Report of Her Majesty's Chief Inspector of Schools: Standards and Quality in Education 1996/97.* London: The Stationery Office. **12**

OFFICE FOR STANDARDS IN EDUCATION (1998b) *Standards in Primary English.* London: Ofsted. **12**

OFFICE FOR STANDARDS IN EDUCATION (1999) *The Annual Report of Her Majesty's Chief Inspector of Schools: Standards and Quality in Education 1997/98.* London: The Stationery Office. **12**

OLSON, D.R. (1994) *The World on Paper.* Cambridge: Cambridge University Press. **205, 247**

PAPERT, S. (1980) *Mindstorms.* Brighton: Harvester Press. **200–1, 246**

PEACOCK, C. (1986) *Teaching Writing.* London: Croom Helm. **230**

PEACOCK, M. (1992) *Evaluating word processed pupil writing* (Unpublished PhD thesis). Leeds: University of Leeds School of Education. **201, 246**

PERERA, K. (1984) *Children's Writing and Reading: Analysing Classroom Language.* Oxford: Basil Blackwell, in Association with Andre Deutsch Ltd. **91, 99, 128, 184–8, 237, 240, 242, 244**

PERERA, K. (1993) 'The "Good Book": linguistic aspects', in BEARD, R. (Ed.) *Teaching Literacy: Balancing Perspectives.* London: Hodder and Stoughton. **46, 231**

PERERA, K. (1996) 'Who Says What? Learning to "Read" the Punctuation of Direct Speech', in HALL, N. and ROBINSON, A. (Eds.) *Learning About Punctuation.* Clevedon: Multilingual Matters. **46, 231**

PERFETTI, C. (1995) 'Cognitive research can inform reading education', *Journal of Research in Reading,* 18, 2, 106–115. Reprinted in OAKHILL, J. and BEARD, R. (Eds.) (1999) *Reading Development and the Teaching of Reading: a psychological perspective.* Oxford: Blackwell. **203, 247**

PETERS, M.L. (1985) *Spelling: Caught or Taught? A New Look.* London: Routledge.

PETERS, M.L. (1970) *Success in Spelling.* Cambridge: Cambridge Institute of Education. **44, 79, 230, 235**

PETERS, M.L. and SMITH, B. (1993) *Spelling in Context: Strategies for Teachers and Learners.* Windsor: NFER-Nelson. **175–7, 243**

PIAGET, J. (1959) *The Language and Thought of the Child* (revised edition). New York: Harcourt Brace and World. **19, 228**

PIOLAT, A. (1991) 'Effects of word processing on text revision', *Language and Education,* 5, 4, 255–272. **201, 246**

POWLING, C. (1985) *Roald Dahl.* Harmondsworth: Penguin (Puffin Books). **52, 233**

PUMFREY, P.D. and ELLIOTT, C.D. (Eds.) (1990) *Children's Difficulties in Reading, Writing and Spelling.* Basingstoke: Falmer Press. **235**

PURVES, A.C. (Ed.) (1992) *The IEA Study of Written Composition II: Education and Performance in Fourteen Countries.* Oxford: Pergamon. **9–10, 227**

QUALIFICATIONS and CURRICULUM AUTHORITY (1998a) *Standards at Key Stage 1: English and Mathematics. Report of the 1998 National Curriculum Assessments for 7 year olds.* London: QCA. **9–10, 152, 197, 227, 242, 246**

QUALIFICATIONS and CURRICULUM AUTHORITY (1998b) *Standards at Key Stage 2: English, Mathematics and Science. Report of the 1998 National Curriculum Assessments for 11 year olds.* London: QCA. **9–10, 152, 197, 227, 242, 246**

QUALIFICATIONS and CURRICULUM AUTHORITY (1998c) S*tandards at Key Stage 3: English. Report of the 1998 National Curriculum Assessments for 14 year olds.* London: QCA. **9, 152, 197, 227, 242, 246**

QUALIFICATIONS and CURRICULUM AUTHORITY (1998d) *The Grammar Papers.* London: QCA. **123, 167–9, 240, 243**

QUALIFICATIONS AND CURRICULUM AUTHORITY (1998e) *Can Do Better: Raising Boys' Achievement in English.* London: QCA. **198–201, 246**

QUALIFICATIONS AND CURRICULUM AUTHORITY (1998f) *Key Stage 2 English Tests Mark Schemes* London: QCA/DfEE. **196–7, 246**

QUALIFICATIONS and CURRICULUM AUTHORITY (1999a) *Early Learning Goals.* London: QCA/DfEE. **87, 236**

QUALIFICATIONS AND CURRICULUM AUTHORITY (1999b) *Not whether but how.* London: QCA. **123, 240**

QUIRK, R., GREENBAUM, S., LEECH, G. and SVARTVIK, J. (1985) *A Comprehensive Grammar of the English Language.* Harlow: Longman. **122, 128, 240**

READ, C. (1971) 'Pre-school children's knowledge of the English orthography', *Harvard Educational Review,* 41, 1–34. **243**

READ, C. (1975) Children's Creative Spelling. London: Routledge and Kegan Paul. **243**

REES, F. (1996) *The Writing Repertoire: Developing Writing at Key Stage 2.* Slough: National Foundation for Educational Research. **90, 236**

REID, J. F. (1974) *Breakthrough in Action.* London: Longman, for the Schools Council. **232**

RICHARDS, C. (Ed.) (1982) *New Perspectives on Primary Education.* Lewes: The Falmer Press. **3, 226**

RILEY, J. and REEDY, D. (2000) *Developing Writing for Different Purposes: Teaching about Genre in the Early Years.* London: Paul Chapman. **239**

RILEY, J. (1996) *The Teaching of Reading: The Development of Literacy in the Early Years of School.* London: Paul Chapman. **75, 234, 235**

ROACH, P. (1991) *English Phonetics and Phonology: A Practical Course* (2E) Cambridge: Cambridge University Press. **228**

ROBSON, S. (1986) '"No one can see the awful mistakes you've made": Word processing with six and seven year olds', *Primary Teaching Studies,* 1, 2, 62–79. **201, 246**

ROSEN, M. (1989)*Did I Hear You Write?* London: Andre Deutsch. **51, 232**

RUTH, L. and MURPHY, S. (1988) *Designing Writing Tasks for the Assessment of Writing.* Norwood, N.J.: Ablex. **245**

SAINSBURY, M., SCHAGEN, I., WHETTON, C. and CASPALL, L. (1999) 'An investigation of hierarchical relationships in children's literacy attainments at baseline', *Journal of Research in Reading*, 22, 1, 45–54. **87, 236**

SAINSBURY, M., SCHAGEN, I., WHETTON, C., with HAGUES, N. and MINNIS, M. (1998) *Evaluation of the National Literacy Project: Cohort 1, 1996–98.* Slough: NFER. **16, 227**

SASSOON, R. (1990a) *Handwriting: The Way to Teach it.* Cheltenham: Stanley Thornes. **48, 69, 232, 234**

SASSOON, R. (1990b) *Handwriting: A New Perspective.* Cheltenham: Stanley Thornes. **48, 73–4, 232, 234**

SASSOON, R. (1995a) *The Acquisition of a Second Writing System.* Oxford: Intellect Books. **69–71, 234**

SASSOON, R. (1995b) *The Practical Guide to Children's Handwriting.* London: Hodder and Stoughton. **48, 232**

SCARDAMALIA, M., BEREITER, C. and FILLION, B. (1981) *Writing for Results: A Sourcebook of Consequential Composing Activities.* Ontario: OISE Press. **53, 55, 116, 233, 237, 239**

SCHEERENS, J. (1992) *Effective Schooling: Research, Theory and Practice.* London: Cassell. **14, 227**

SCHOOL CURRICULUM and ASSESSMENT AUTHORITY (subsequently the Qualifications and Currriculum Authority) (1997) *Use of Language; a common approach,* London: SCAA. **103, 238**

SCOTTISH OFFICE EDUCATION DEPARTMENT (1991) *National Guidelines: English Language 5–14.* Edinburgh: SOED. **5, 8, 100, 226, 238**

SCRIMSHAW, P. (Ed.) (1993) *Language, classrooms and computers.* London: Routledge. **203, 247**

SHARPLES, M. (1999) *How We Write: Writing as Creative Design.* London: Routledge. **50, 232**

SHAUGHNESSY, M. P. (1977) *Errors and Expectations: A guide for the teacher of basic writing.* New York: Oxford University Press. **42, 43, 165–6, 179–181, 231, 243, 244**

SMAGORINSKY, P. (1987) 'Graves Revisited: A Look at the Methods and Conclusions of the New Hampshire Study', *Written Communication*, 4, 4, 331–342. **51, 232**

SMIT, M.G. (1992) *The Teaching of English in the Primary School with particular reference to the development of children's imaginative writing* (unpublished MEd thesis). Leeds: University of Leeds School of Education. **104, 238**

SMITH, F. (1994) *Writing and the Writer* (2E). Hillsdale, New Jersey: Lawrence Erlbaum Associates. **38, 42, 230, 231**

SMITH, J. and ELLEY, W. (1997) *How Children Learn to Write.* London: Paul Chapman. **236**

SMITH, N. and WILSON, D. (1979) *Modern Linguistics.* Harmondsworth: Penguin. **29, 229**

SNOW, C., BARNES, W.S., CHANDLER, J., GOODMAN, I.F. and HEMPHILL, L. (1991) *Unfulfilled Expectations: Home and School Influences on Literacy.* Cambridge, Mass.: Harvard University Press. **3, 86, 179, 231, 236, 244**

SNOWLING, M.J. (1994) 'Towards a Model of Spelling Acquisition: The Development of Some Component Skills', in BROWN, G.D.A. and ELLIS, N.C. (Eds.) *Handbook of Spelling: Theory, Process and Intervention.* Chichester: John Wiley and Sons. **78, 175, 235, 243**

STREET, B.V. (1984) *Literacy in Theory and Practice.* Cambridge: Cambridge University Press. **203, 247**

STREET, B.V. (1995) 'The new literacy studies: guest editorial', *Journal of Research in Reading.* 16, 2, 81–97. **203, 247**

STRONG, W. (1976) 'Back to basics and beyond', *English Journal,* 65, 56 and 60–64. **242**

STUBBS, M. (1980) *Language and Literacy: The Sociolinguistics of Reading and Writing.* London: Routledge and Kegan Paul. **243**

STUBBS, M. (1992) 'Who Climbs the Grammar-Tree?' in *Sonderdruck aus LA 381.* Tübingen: Max Niemeyer Verlag, 221–234. **243**

SUTCLIFFE, D. (1982) *British Black English.* Oxford: Basil Blackwell. **30, 229**

SUTTON-SMITH, B. (1988) 'In Search of the Imagination', in EGAN, K. and NADANER, D. (Eds.) *Imagination and Education.* Milton Keynes: Open University Press. **104, 238**

TEACHER TRAINING AGENCY (1998) *Teaching: High Status, High Standards: Requirements for Courses of Initial Teacher Training.* London: DfEE. **123, 240**

TEMPLE, C., NATHAN, R., TEMPLE, F. and BURRIS, N.A. (1993) *The Beginnings of Writing* (3E), Boston, Mass.: Allyn and Bacon. **67, 72, 94, 234, 237**

THARP, R.G. and GALLIMORE, R. (1988) *Rousing Minds to Life: Teaching, learning and schooling in social context.* Cambridge: Cambridge University Press. **233**

TOMLINSON, D. (1994) 'Errors in the research into the effectiveness of grammar teaching', *English in Education,* 28, 1, 20–26. **123, 167–8, 240**

TREIMAN, R and CASSAR, M. (1997) 'Spelling Acquisition in English', in PERFETTI, C.A., RIEBEN, L. and FAYOL, M. (Eds.) *Learning to Spell: Research, Theory and Practice Across Languages.* Mahwah, N.J.: Lawrence Erlbaum. **78, 175, 235, 243**

TREIMAN, R. (1993) *Beginning to Spell: A Study of First-Grade Children.* New York: Oxford University Press. **35, 229**

VAN HAALEN, T. G. (1990) 'Writing and revising: Bilingual students' use of word processing', *Dissertation Abstracts International,* 52/2, 418. **202, 247**

VYGOTSKY, L.S. (1962) *Thought and Language.* Cambridge , Mass.: M.I.T. Press. **19, 65, 208, 228, 233, 247**

VYGOTSKY, L.S. (1978) *Mind in Society* (Ed. M. Cole *et al.*) Cambridge, Mass: Harvard University Press. **19, 228**

WALSH, J. (1985) 'Monstrous Regimens', *Books and Bookmen.* December, pp. 6–7. **52, 233**

WANN, J., WING, A.M. and SOVIK, N. (Eds.) (1991). *Development of Graphic Skills: Research, Perspectives and Educational Implications.* London: Academic Press. **234**

WATERHOUSE, K. (1991) *English Our English.* Harmondsworth: Penguin Books. **46, 231**

WELLS, G. (1985) *Language, Learning and Education*. Windsor: NFER/Nelson. **37, 42, 230, 231**

WELLS, G. (1986) *The Meaning Makers*. London: Hodder and Stoughton. **20, 228**

WHITE, J. (1986) *The Assessment of Writing: Pupils aged 11 and 15*. Windsor: NFER-Nelson. **207, 247**

WILKINSON, A (1971) *The Foundations of Language*. Oxford: Oxford University Press. **20, 167, 228, 243**

WILKINSON, A. (1986) *The Quality of Writing*. Milton Keynes: Open University Press. **105, 191–3, 239, 244**

WILKINSON, A. *et al.* (1980) *Assessing Language Development*. Oxford: Oxford University Press. **105, 191–3, 239, 244–5**

WILLIAMS, J.D. (1998) *Preparing to Teach Writing* (2E), Mahwah, N.J.: Lawrence Erlbaum. **232, 242**

WILLIAMSON, J. and HARDMAN, F. (1997) 'Those Terrible Marks of the Beast: Non-standard Dialect and Children's Writing', *Language and Education*, 11, 4, 287–299. **152, 242**

WINCH, C. and GINGELL, J. (1994) 'Dialect Interference and Difficulties in Writing: An Investigation in St. Lucian Primary Schools', *Language and Education*, 8, 3, 157–182. **152–3, 242**

WOLFENDALE, S. and LINDSAY, G. (1999) 'Guest Editorial: Issues in baseline assessment', *Journal of Research in Reading*, 22, 1, 1–13. **87, 236**

WOODRUFF, E., BEREITER, C. and SCARDAMALIA, M. (1981) 'On the Road to Computer Assisted Compositions', *Journal of Educational Technology Systems*, 10, 2, 133–148. **201, 246**

WRAY, D (1994) *Literacy and Awareness*. London: Hodder and Stoughton. **243**

WRAY, D. and LEWIS, M. (1997) *Extending Literacy*. London: Routledge. **102, 238**

WRAY, D. and MEDWELL J. (Eds.) (1994) *Teaching Primary English: The State of the Art*. London: Routledge. **229**

WYATT-SMITH, C. (1997) 'Teaching and Assessing Writing: An Australian Perspective', *English in Education*, 31, 3, 8–22. **239**

WYLIE, R.F. and DURRELL, D.D. (1970) 'Teaching Vowels Through Phonograms', *Elementary English*, 47, 787–791. **35, 229**

WYSE, D. (1998) *Primary Writing*. Buckingham: Open University Press. **52, 233**

Footnotes

Chapter 1 Notes

[1] *Four Quartets*, Faber & Faber.

[2] It has been common in Britain to refer to 'basic subjects' in primary schools as the 'three Rs': reading, (w)riting and (a)rithmetic. In the National Curriculum, there are now three 'core' subjects: English, Mathematics and Science.

[3] BARBER, M. (1997) *The Learning Game: Arguments for An Education Revolution*. London: Indigo, p. 174.

[4] Information and Communication Technology.

[5] BEARD, R. (1984) *Children's Writing in the Primary School*. Sevenoaks: Hodder and Stoughton.

[6] See, for example, DEPARTMENT OF EDUCATION AND SCIENCE (1978) *Primary Education in England*. London: HMSO.

[7] RICHARDS, C. (Ed.) (1982) *New Perspectives on Primary Education*. Lewes: The Falmer Press.

[8] DEPARTMENT FOR EDUCATION AND EMPLOYMENT (1998a) *The National Literacy Strategy: Framework for Teaching*. London: DfEE.

[9] SCOTTISH OFFICE EDUCATION DEPARTMENT (1991) *National Guidelines: English Language 5–14*. Edinburgh: SOED.

[10] DEPARTMENT OF EDUCATION AND SCIENCE AND THE WELSH OFFICE (1989) *English in the National Curriculum*. London: HMSO.

[11] See BEARD, R. (1995b) 'The National Curriculum in English', in Anning, A. (Ed.) *The National Curriculum at Key Stage One: Five Years On*, pp.18–32. Milton Keynes: Open University Press.

[12] DEPARTMENT FOR EDUCATION (1995) *English in the National Curriculum*. London: HMSO; DEPARTMENT OF EDUCATION NORTHERN IRELAND (1996) *English Programmes of Study, Attainment Targets and Level Descriptions: Key Stages 1–4*. Bangor, Co. Do.: DENI.

[13] DEPARTMENT FOR EDUCATION AND EMPLOYMENT (1999a) *English: The National Curriculum for England Key Stages 1–4*. London: DfEE and QCA.

[14] DEPARTMENT FOR EDUCATION AND EMPLOYMENT (1999b) *The National Curriculum: Handbook for primary teachers in England Key Stages 1 and 2*. London: DfEE and QCA.

[15] DEPARTMENT OF EDUCATION AND SCIENCE (1988) *Report of the Committee of Inquiry into the Teaching of the English Language* (The Kingman Report). London: HMSO.

[16] See KEITH, G. (1990) 'Language Study at Key Stage 3', in Carter, R. (Ed.) *Knowledge about Language and the Curriculum: The LINC Reader*. London: Hodder and Stoughton.

[17] DES (1988) p.19.

[18] This is discussed in greater detail in BEARD, R. (1999b) 'English: Range, Key Skills and Language Study' in Riley, J. and Prentice, R. (Eds.) *The*

Curriculum for 7–11 year olds, pp. 47–66. London: Paul Chapman.

[19] LITERACY TASK FORCE (1997b) *The Implementation of the National Literacy Strategy*. London: Department for Education and Employment.

[20] PURVES, A.C. (Ed.) (1992) *The IEA Study of Written Composition II: Education and Performance in Fourteen Countries*. Oxford: Pergamon.

[21] See DAVIES, J. and BREMBER, I. (1997) 'Monitoring reading standards in Year 6: a 7-year cross-sectional study', *British Educational Research Journal*, 23, 5, 615–622; and also DAVIES, J. and BREMBER, I. (1998) 'Standards of Reading at Key Stage 1: a cause for celebration? A seven-year cross-sectional study', *Educational Research*, 40, 2, 153–160.

[22] GIPPS, C. *et al.* (1995) *Intuition or evidence?: teachers and national assessment of seven year olds*. Buckingham: Open University Press.

[23] QUALIFICATIONS AND CURRICULUM AUTHORITY (1998a, b and c) *Standards at Key Stages 1, 2 and 3 English: Reports of the 1998 National Curriculum Assessments for 7, 11 and 14 year olds* (in three volumes). London: QCA.

[24] LITERACY TASK FORCE (1997a) *A Reading Revolution: How We Can Teach Every Child to Read Well*. London: The Literacy Task Force c/o University of London: Institute of Education.

[25] LITERACY TASK FORCE (1997b) *The Implementation of the National Literacy Strategy*. London: Department for Education and Employment.

[26] DfEE (1998a).

[27] MORTIMORE, P., SAMMONS, P., STOLL, L., LEWIS, D. and ECOB, R. (1988) *School Matters: The Junior Years*. Wells: Open Books

[28] MORTIMORE, P. (1991) 'The nature and findings of school effectiveness research in the primary sector' in Riddell, S. and Brown, S. (Eds.) *School Effectiveness Research: Its Messages for School Improvement*. London: HMSO.

[29] SCHEERENS, J. (1992) *Effective Schooling: Research, Theory and Practice*. London: Cassell.

[30] CREEMERS, B.P.M. (1994) *The Effective Classroom*. London: Cassell.

[31] ALEXANDER, R.J. (1992) *Policy and Practice in Primary Education*. London: Routledge.

[32] See, for example, Mortimore (1988).

[33] BEARD, R. (1999a) *The National Literacy Strategy: Review of Research and other related evidence*. London: DfEE.

[34] SAINSBURY, M., SCHAGEN, I., WHETTON, C., with HAGUES, N. and MINNIS, M. (1998) *Evaluation of the National Literacy Project: Cohort 1, 1996–98*. Slough: NFER.

Chapter 2 Notes

[1] *Lives of the English Poets: Cowley*.

[2] FRISCH, KARL VON (1953) *The Dancing Bees: an account of the life and senses of the honey bee* (translated by Dora Ilse). San Diego: London : Harcourt Brace Jovanovich.

[3] BRUNER, J. (1964) 'The Course of Cognitive Growth', *American Psychologist*, 19, 1–15.

[4] See DES (1975) *A Language for Life* (The Bullock Report). London: HMSO, p.47.

[5] LURIA, A. R. (1959) 'The directive function in speech in development and dissolution', *Word*, 15, 3, 341–52. Reprinted in OLDFIELD, R. C. and MARSHALL, J. C. (Eds.) (1968) *Language*, Harmondsworth: Penguin Books.

[6] PIAGET, J. (1959) *The Language and Thought of the Child* (revised edition). New York: Harcourt Brace and World.

[7] VYGOTSKY, L. S. (1962) *Thought and Language*. Cambridge, Massachusetts: MIT Press; VYGOTSKY, L. S. (1978) *Mind in Society* (Ed. M.Cole *et al.*) Cambridge, Massachusetts: Harvard University Press.

[8] BRUNER, J. (1985) 'Vygotsky: a historical and conceptual perspective', in Wertsch, J.V. (Ed.) *Culture, Communication and Cognition: Vygotskyan Perspectives.* Cambridge: Cambridge University Press.

[9] From Joan Tough's research at the University of Leeds into Communication Skills in Early Childhood.

[10] WILKINSON, A. (1965) *Spoken English*. University of Birmingham. Cited in WILKINSON, A. (1971) *The Foundations of Language*. Oxford: Oxford University Press.

[11] WELLS, G. (1986) *The Meaning Makers*. London: Hodder and Stoughton. For a recent study of the informal talk of 11–12 year old children while writing, see DAY, T. (1997) 'The Role of Children's Informal Talk in Their Writing', *Irish Educational Studies*, 16, 97, 223–234.

[12] GRUGEON, E. *et al.* (1998) *Teaching Speaking and Listening in the Primary School.* London: David Fulton.

[13] MERCER, N. (1995) *The Guided Construction of Knowledge: talk amongst teachers and learners.* Clevedon: Multilingual Matters; MERCER, N. (1996) 'The quality of talk in children's collaborative activity in the classroom', *Learning and Instruction*, 6, 359–379.

[14] MERCER, N., WEGERIF, R. and DAWES, L.(1999) 'Children's Talk and the Development of Reasoning in the Classroom', *British Educational Research Journal*, 25, 1, 95–111.

[15] CRYSTAL, D. (1987a) *Child Language, Learning and Linguistics* (2E). London: Edward Arnold. Reprinted in BEARD, R. (1993) *Teaching Literacy: Balancing Perspectives.* London: Hodder and Stoughton.

[16] See Crystal (1987a) p.41.

[17] I have indicated individual phonemes by following linguistic convention and placing them between pairs of oblique lines. I have tried to use letters that clearly indicate each phoneme. A more satisfactory way of doing this is to use the International Phonetic Association symbols (as in the book I draw heavily on later: CARNEY, E. (1994) *A Survey of English Spelling.* London: Routledge), but unfortunately IPA symbols are not widely used in education and are initially more difficult to read for anyone new to the field. For more on phonetics and phonology, see ROACH, P. (1991) *English Phonetics and Phonology: A practical course* (2E) Cambridge: Cambridge University Press.

[18] DALE, P. S. (1976) *Language Development: Structure and Function* (2E). New York: Holt, Rinehart and Winston, p. 192. For more on words and meanings, see JACKSON, H. (1988) *Words and Their Meaning.* London: Longman.

[19] FRIES, C.C. (1962) *Linguistics and Reading.* New York: Holt, Rinehart and

Winston. Cited in DES, (1975) *A Language for Life.* London: HMSO para. 6.35.
[20] HALLIDAY, M.A.K. (1975) *Learning How to Mean.* London: Edward Arnold.
[21] GANNON, P. and CZERNIEWSKA, P. (1980) *Using Linguistics: An Educational Focus.* London: Edward Arnold.
[22] MCARTHUR, T, (1992) *The Oxford Companion to the English Language.* Oxford: Oxford University Press, p.316
[23] SMITH, N. and WILSON, D. (1979) *Modern Linguistics.* Harmondsworth: Penguin, p.204
[24] Crystal (1987a).
[25] CRYSTAL, D., FLETCHER, P. and GARMAN, M. (1976) *The Grammatical Analysis of Language Disability.* London: Edward Arnold. For general introductions on grammar, see GREENBAUM. S. (1991) *An Introduction to English Grammar.* Harlow: Longman; and HURFORD, J.R. (1994) *Grammar: A Student's Guide.* Cambridge: Cambridge University Press.
[26] CRYSTAL, D. (1990) *The English Language.* Harmondsworth: Penguin.
[27] EDWARDS, V.K. (1979) *The West Indian Language Issue in British Schools: Challenges and Responses.* London: Routledge and Kegan Paul; SUTCLIFFE, D. (1982) *British Black English.* Oxford: Basil Blackwell.
[28] DES (1985) *Education for All* (The Swann Report). London: HMSO, p.422.
[29] Adapted from DIRINGER, D. (1968) *The Alphabet* (3E). London: Hutchinson; and CRYSTAL, D. (1987b) *The Cambridge Encyclopedia of Language.* Cambridge: Cambridge University Press.
[30] CARNEY, F. (1994) *A Survey of English Spelling.* London: Routledge.
[31] MCARTHUR (1992).
[32] e.g. GOSWAMI, U. and BRYANT, P. (1990) *Phonological Skills and Learning to Read.* Hove: Lawrence Erlbaum; TREIMAN, R. (1993) *Beginning to Spell: A Study of First-Grade Children.* New York: Oxford University Press, GOSWAMI, U. (1999) 'Phonological Development and Reading by Analogy: Epilinguistic and Metalinguistic Issues', in OAKHILL, J. and BEARD, R. (Eds.) *Reading Development and the Teaching of Reading: a psychological perspective.* Oxford: Blackwell.
[33] See also the section on the Reception age-range in BEARD, R. (1999a) *The National Literacy Strategy: Review of Research and other related evidence.* London: DfEE. For discussions of the linguistic, psychological and literary significance of rhyme in education, see BEARD, R. (Ed.) (1995a) *Rhyme, Reading and Writing.* London: Hodder and Stoughton.
[34] WYLIE, R.E. and DURRELL, D.D. (1970) 'Teaching Vowels Through Phonograms', *Elementary English,* 47, 787–791.

Chapter 3 Notes

[An earlier version of this chapter appeared in WRAY, D. and MEDWELL J. (Eds.) (1994) *Teaching Primary English: The State of the Art.* London: Routledge, pp. 99–111.]
[1] Cited in MURRAY, D. M. (1990) *Shoptalk: Learning to write with writers.* Portsmouth, N.H.: Boynton/Cook, p.101.
[2] BROWN, R. (1968) 'Introduction' in Moffett, J. *Teaching the Universe of*

Discourse. Boston, Massachusetts: Houghton Mifflin, p.v

[3] WELLS, G. (1985) *Language, Learning and Education.* Windsor: NFER/Nelson.

[4] SMITH, F. (1994) *Writing and the Writer* (2E). Hillsdale, New Jersey: Lawrence Erlbaum Associates, p.16.

[5] BRUNER, J. (1972) *The Relevance of Education.* London: Allen and Unwin, p.47.

[6] DONALDSON, M. (1989) *Sense and Sensibility: Some thoughts on the teaching of literacy* (Occasional Paper No. 3). Reading: Reading and Language Information Centre, University of Reading. Reprinted in BEARD, R. (Ed.) (1993) *Teaching Literacy: Balancing Perspectives.* London: Hodder and Stoughton, p.50: See also GARTON, A. and PRATT, C. (1998) *Learning to be Literate* (2E). Oxford: Blackwell.

[7] To be consistent, this book refers to 'composing' and 'planning' synonymously. Following the Chambers Dictionary, this book also refers to 'a plan' and 'a draft' synonymously. However, some other publications (e.g. DAHL and FARNAN, 1998) refer to planning only when written notes are produced. Some other publications (e.g. BEARNE, 1998) also refer to a draft as an initial version of a complete text, rather than as a plan or outline for it.

[8] HAYES, J.R. and FLOWER, L.S. (1980) 'Writing as Problem Solving', *Visible Language,* 14, 4, 388–399; HAYES, J.R. (1996) 'A New Framework for Understanding Cognition and Affect in Writing' in LEVY, C.M. and RANSDELL, S. (Eds.) *The Science of Writing: Theories, Methods, Individual Differences, and Applications.* Mahwah, N.J.: Lawrence Erlbaum Associates. One of the most concise but informative books of recent years on the processes of writing is set out in PEACOCK, C. (1986) *Teaching Writing.* London: Croom Helm.

[9] HAYES (1996). An overview of psychological research in writing appears in GALBRAITH, D. and RIJLAARSDAM, G. (1999) 'Effective strategies for the teaching and learning of writing', *Learning and Instruction,* 9, 93–108.

[10] GOLDSTEIN, A.A. and CARR, P.G. (1996) 'Can students benefit from process writing?' (National Assessment of Educational Progress Facts 1. Report No. 1. Report No. NCES-96-845. ED 395 320). Washington, D.C.: U.S. Dept. of Education, National Center for Educational Statistics.

[11] BEREITER, C. and SCARDAMALIA, M. (1982) 'From conversation to composition: the role of instruction in a developmental process', in GLASER, R. (Ed.) *Advances in Instructional Psychology,* Vol 2. London: Lawrence Erlbaum Associates.

[12] BEREITER, C. and SCARDAMALIA, M. (1987) *The Psychology of Written Composition.* Hillsdale, New Jersey: Lawrence Erlbaum.

[13] BEREITER and SCARDAMALIA (1987); also BEARD, R. (1990) 'Children's Composing and Comprehending of Text' in Wray D. (Ed.) *Emerging Partnerships: Current Research in Language and Literacy.* Clevedon: Multilingual Matters Ltd. (British Education Research Association Dialogue Series, No.4).

[14] DAHL, K.L. and FARNAN, N. (1998) *Children's Writing: Perspectives From Research.* Newark, Delaware and Chicago, Ill: International Reading Association and National Reading Conference. Dahl and Farnan draw heavily on Bereiter

and Scardamalia (1987). They also draw attention to the complementary studies of children's composing across the 3–13 age-range by Anne Dyson (1989), Judith Langer (1986) and Nancy Atwell (1986). Joy Alexander and Anne Currie report a classroom-based study of the composing strategies of 11–14 year olds in ALEXANDER, J. and CURRIE, A. (1998) '"I Normally Just Ramble On" – Strategies to Improve Writing at Key Stage 3', *English in Education*, 32, 2, 36–43.

[15] BEARD, R. (1991) 'Learning to Read like a Writer', *Educational Review*, 43, 1, pp. 17–24.

[16] Smith (1994).

[17] SHAUGHNESSY, M. P. (1977) *Errors and Expectations: A guide for the teacher of basic writing*. New York: Oxford University Press.

[18] WELLS, G. (1985) *Language, Learning and Education*. Windsor: NFER/Nelson.

[19] SNOW, C., BARNES, W.S., CHANDLER, J., GOODMAN, I.F. and HEMPHILL, L. (1991) *Unfulfilled Expectations: Home and School Influences on Literacy*. Cambridge, Mass.: Harvard University Press.

[20] ELLEY, W.B. (1989) 'Vocabulary acquisition from listening to stories', *Reading Research Quarterly*, 24, 174–187

[21] DEPARTMENT OF EDUCATION AND SCIENCE (1988) *Report of the Committee of Inquiry into the Teaching of the English Language* (The Kingman Report). London: HMSO.

[22] ELDREDGE, J.L., REUTZEL, D.R. and HOLLINGSWORTH, P.M. (1996) 'Comparing the Effectiveness of Two Oral Reading Practices: Round Robin Reading and the Shared Book Experience', *Journal of Literacy Research*, 28, 2, 201–225.

[23] Shaughnessy (1977) p.210.

[24] ADAMS, (1990) M.J. *Beginning to Read: Thinking and Learning about Print*. Cambridge, Mass.: The MIT Press; ADAMS, M.J. (1991) 'Why not phonics *and* whole language?', in Ellis, W. (Ed.) *All Language and the Creation of Literacy*. Baltimore, Maryland: The Orton Dyslexia Society.

[25] PETERS, M.L. (1970) *Success in Spelling*. Cambridge: Cambridge Institute of Education; PETERS, M.L. (1985) *Spelling: Caught or Taught? A New Look*. London: Routledge and Kegan Paul.

[26] MOUNTFORD, J. (1998) *An Insight into English Spelling*. London: Hodder and Stoughton.

[27] Strictly speaking, 'th' is a *graphophonemic* symbol, as the grapheme (or 'spelling unit') <th> represents a specific phoneme /ð / (using the international phonetic alphabet).

[28] WATERHOUSE, K. (1991) *English Our English*. Harmondsworth: Penguin Books.

[29] KRESS, G.R. (1994) *Learning to Write* (2E). London: Routledge.

[30] PERERA, K. (1993) 'The "Good Book": linguistic aspects', in BEARD, R. (Ed.) *Teaching Literacy: Balancing Perspectives* London: Hodder and Stoughton; PERERA, K. (1996) 'Who Says What? Learning to "Read" the Punctuation of Direct Speech', in HALL, N. and ROBINSON, A. (Eds.) *Learning About*

Punctuation. Clevedon: Multilingual Matters.

[31] HALL, N. and ROBINSON, A. (Eds.) (1996) *Learning About Punctuation.* Clevedon: Multilingual Matters.

[32] HALL, N. (1998) 'Young children and resistance to punctuation', *Research in Education,* 60, 29–39. The resources being used to teach the class included *Breakthrough to Literacy* (MacKay *et al.,* 1979) which includes a specific sentence maker. Similar points about the need for the writing of connected text were made in the original evaluation of the *Breakthrough* materials (Reid, 1974).

[33] From *In memoriam,* v. I am grateful to John Willcocks for drawing my attention to these words.

[34] SASSOON, R. (1990a) *Handwriting: the Way to Teach it.* Cheltenham: Stanley Thornes; SASSOON, R. (1990b) *Handwriting: a New Perspective.* Cheltenham: Stanley Thornes; SASSOON, R. (1995b) *The Practical Guide to Children's Handwriting.* London: Hodder and Stoughton.

[35] COCHRAN-SMITH, M. (1991) *Learning to Write Differently.* Hove: Ablex Pub. Co.

[36] SHARPLES, M. (1999) *How We Write: Writing as Creative Design.* London: Routledge.

[37] GRAVES, D. (1983) *Writing: Teachers and Children at Work.* Portsmouth, N.H.: Heinemann; GRAVES, D.H. (1994) *A Fresh Look at Writing.* Portsmouth, N.H.: Heinemann. A contrasting research perspective on revision in 11 year olds' writing can be seen in a recent Italian study: LUMBELLI *et al.* (1999). See also FITZGERALD (1987) for a helpful review.

[38] The workshop approach is discussed in helpful detail by James Williams of Governors State University in *Preparing to Teach Writing,* Lawrence Erlbaum, 1998. A critique of the workshop approach can be found in LENSMIRE, T. (1994) *When Children Write: Critical re-Visions of the writing workshop.* New York: Teachers College Press. Lensmire reports how fictionalised writing in writing workshops can be used for veiled attacks on unpopular students and can sometimes result in stories which are crudely stereotypical. Pam Gilbert (1989) raises similar concerns (see Note 45).

[39] GRAVES, D.H. (1975) 'An examination of the writing processes of seven-year-old children', *Research in the Teaching of English,* 9, 227–241.

[40] SMAGORINSKY, P. (1987) 'Graves Revisited: A Look at the Methods and Conclusions of the New Hampshire Study', *Written Communication.* 4, 4, 331–342.

[41] BARRS, M. (1983) 'Born Again Teachers' (Review of GRAVES, D.H. *Writing: Teachers and Children at Work*), *The Times Educational Supplement.* 24 June, p.23.

[42] Bereiter and Scardamalia (1982)

[43] ROSEN, M. (1989) *Did I Hear You Write?* London: Andre Deutsch.

[44] BRITTON, J. (1970) *Language and Learning.* Harmondsworth: Penguin; DES (1975) *A Language for Life* (The Bullock Report). London: HMSO.

[45] GILBERT, P. (1989) 'Student Text as Pedagogical Text', in CASTELL *et al.* (Eds.) *Language, Authority and Criticism.* London: Falmer Press. Gilbert raises similar concerns to LENSMIRE (1994): see Note 38 above.

[46] WYSE, D. (1998) *Primary Writing.* Buckingham: Open University Press.

[47] CALKINS, L.M. (1983) *Lessons From a Child.* Exeter, New Hampshire: Heinemann.

[48] HARTHILL, R. (1989) *Writers Revealed.* London: B.B.C. Books.

[49] WALSH, J. (1985) 'Monstrous Regimens', *Books and Bookmen.* December, pp. 6–7.

[50] HUGHES, T. (1987) 'To parse or not to parse: the poet's answer', *The Sunday Times*, 22 November; DUGUID, L. (1988) 'The art of conversation: A profile of Jan Mark', *Times Educational Supplement*, 3 June.

[51] e.g. POWLING, C. (1985) *Roald Dahl* Harmondsworth: Penguin (Puffin Books)

[52] e.g. Douglas Adams in WALSH (1985).

[53] HILLOCKS, G. (1986) *Research on Written Composition.* Urbana, Il.: National Conference on Research in English/ERIC Clearinghouse on Reading and Communication Skills; HILLOCKS, G. (1995) *Teaching Writing as Reflective Practice.* New York: Teachers College Press. Similar conclusions are reached in relation to the teaching and learning of writing in an additional language in DYER, B. (1996) 'L1 and L2 composition theories: Hillocks' "environmental mode" and task-based language teaching', *English Language Teaching Journal*, 50, 4, 312–317.

[54] Bereiter and Scardamalia (1987, pp. 362–3). Reprinted in BEARD, R. (Ed.) (1993) *Teaching Literacy: Balancing Perspectives.* London: Hodder and Stoughton.

[55] BROWNE, A. (1993) *Helping Children to Write.* London: Paul Chapman.

[56] APPLEBEE, A.N. and LANGER, J.A. (1983) 'Instructional Scaffolding: Reading and writing as natural language activities', *Language Arts*, 60, 168–175; BROWN, A. L. and PALINSCAR, A.S. (1989) 'Guided, Cooperative and individual Learning Acquisition', in RESNICK, L.B. *Knowing, Learning and Instruction.* Hillsdale, N.J.: Lawrence Erlbaum; THARP, R.G. and GALLIMORE, R. (1988) *Rousing Minds to Life: Teaching, learning and schooling in social context.* Cambridge: Cambridge University Press.

[57] SCARDAMALIA, M., BEREITER, C. and FILLION, B (1981) *Writing for Results: A Sourcebook of Consequential Composing Activities.* Ontario: OISE Press.

Chapter 4 Notes

[1] KELLOGG, R. (1970) *Analysing Children's Art.* Palo Alto, California: Mayfield Pub. Co. I am grateful to my colleague, Professor Angela Anning, for informing me of Rhoda Kellogg's work.

[2] CLAY, M.M. (1987) *Writing Begins at Home.* Auckland: Heinemann, p.12.

[3] DYSON, A. (1982) 'The Emergence of Visible Language: Interrelationships between Drawing and Early Writing', *Visible Language*, XVI, 4, 360–381.

[4] GOMBERT, J.E. and FAYOL, M. (1992) 'Writing in PreLiterate Children', *Learning and Instruction*, 2, 23–41.

[5] FERREIRO, E. and TEBEROSKY, A. (1982) *Literacy Before Schooling.* London: Heinemann.

[6] VYGOTSKY, L.S. (1962) *Thought and Language.* Cambridge, Mass.: M.I.T. Press.

234   *Developing Writing 3–13*

[7] GORMAN, T. and BROOKS, G. (1996) *Assessing Young Children's Writing: A Step by Step Guide.* London: The Basic Skills Agency.

[8] Ferreiro and Teberosky (1982); also FERREIRO, E. (1997) 'What Does it mean to study children's theories about the writing system?'. Paper presented at International Symposium on *Integrating Research and Practice in Literacy.* University of London Institute of Education, March.

[9] CZERNIEWSKA, P. (1992) *Learning About Writing: the early years.* Oxford: Blackwell.

[10] TEMPLE, C. *et al.* (1993) *The Beginnings of Writing* (3E), Boston, Mass.: Allyn and Bacon.

[11] CLAY, M.M. (1975) *What Did I Write? Beginning Writing Behaviour.* Portsmouth, N.H.: Heinemann.

[12] SASSOON, R. (1990a) *Handwriting: The Way to Teach it.* Cheltenham: Stanley Thornes. For a study of the link between handwriting and academic success, see HARVEY, C. and HENDERSON, S. (1997) 'Children's handwriting in the first three years of school: consistency over time and its relationship to academic achievement', *Handwriting Review, 11, 8–25.*

[13] SASSOON, R. (1995a) *The Acquisition of a Second Writing System.* Oxford: Intellect Books. This is a very helpful companion to Eve Gregory's excellent book on learning to read in a second language: GREGORY, E. (1996) *Making Sense of a New World.* London: Paul Chapman.

[14] MASONHEIMER, P.E., *et al.* (1984) 'Does environmental print identification lead children into word reading?' *Journal of Research Behaviour,* 16, 257–271.

[15] GORMAN and BROOKS (1996).

[16] TEMPLE *et al.* (1992).

[17] BLATCHFORD, P. (1991) 'Children's Handwriting At 7 Years: Associations With Handwriting on School Entry and Pre-School Factors', *British Journal of Educational Psychology,* 61, 73–84.

[18] The subsequent sample comprised 166 of the original 331 children.

[19] SASSOON (1990b) *Handwriting: A New Perspective.* Cheltenham: Stanley Thornes. Helpful collections of papers on handwriting can be found in ALSTON, J. and TAYLOR, J. (Eds.) (1987) *Handwriting: Theory, Research and Practice.* London: Croom Helm; and WANN, J., WING, A.M. and SOVIK, N. (Eds.) (1991). *Development of Graphic Skills: Research, Perspectives and Educational Implications.* London: Academic Press.

[20] e.g. CLARK, M. M. (1974) *Teaching Left-Handed Children.* London: Hodder and Stoughton.

[21] BLATCHFORD, P. *et al.* (1987) 'Associations between Pre-School Reading Related Skills and Later Reading Achievement', *British Educational Research Journal,* 13, 1, 15–23; BLATCHFORD, P. and PLEWIS, I. (1990) 'Pre-School Reading-related Skills and Later Reading Achievement: further evidence', *British Educational Research Journal,* 16, 4, 425–428.

[22] RILEY, J. (1996) *The Teaching of Reading: The Development of Literacy in the Early Years of School.* London: Paul Chapman.

[23] ADAMS, (1990) M.J. *Beginning to Read: Thinking and Learning about Print.* Cambridge, Mass.: The MIT Press.

[24] Bialystok (1991), cited in RILEY, 1996.

[25] NICHOLLS, J. *et al.* (1989) *Beginning Writing.* Milton Keynes: Open University Press.

[26] CZERNIEWSKA, P. (1992) 'Review of Nicholls, J. *et al.* (1989) *Beginning Writing.*', *Language and Education.* 6 , 1, 76–77.

[27] BATES, R.G. (1992) *Children's Writing Strategies in the Early Years of Schooling.* Unpublished PhD thesis, University of Leeds School of Education.

[28] See Chapter 3, note 14.

[29] BISSEX, G.L. (1980) *GNYS AT WRK.* Cambridge , Mass.: Harvard University Press.

[30] GENTRY, J.R. (1982) 'An analysis of developmental spelling in *GNYS AT WRK*', *The Reading Teacher,* 36, 192–200. An alternative approach to analysing early spelling can be found in KRESS, G. (1999) *Early Spelling,* London: Routledge.

[31] e.g. TREIMAN, R. and CASSAR, M. (1997) 'Spelling Acquisition in English' in Perfetti, C. *et al.* (Eds.) *Learning to Spell.: Research, Theory and Practice Across Languages.* Mahwah, N.J.: Lawrence Erlbaum; and SNOWLING, M.J. (1994) 'Towards a Model of Spelling Acquisition: The Development of Some Component Skills', in BROWN, G.D.A. and ELLIS, N.C. (Eds.) *Handbook of Spelling: Theory, Process and Intervention.* Chichester: John Wiley and Sons.

[32] PETERS, M.L. (1970) *Success in Spelling.* Cambridge: Cambridge Institute of Education.

[33] FRITH, U. (1985) 'Beneath the surface of developmental dyslexia', in Patterson, K.E. *et al.* (Eds.) *Surface Dyslexia.* Hillsdale, N.J.: Lawrence Erlbaum. For more recent thinking on stage models of reading and spelling, see EHRI, L. (1997) 'Learning to read and learning to spell are one and the same, almost', in PERFETTI, C., RIEBEN, L. and FAYOL, M. (Eds.) *Learning to Spell.; Research, Theory and Practice Across Languages.* Mahwah, N.J.: Lawrence Erlbaum.

[34] BRYANT, P. and BRADLEY, L. (1980) 'Why children sometimes write words which they cannot read', in Frith, U. (1980) *Cognitive Processes in Spelling.* London: Academic Press.

[35] DEPARTMENT for EDUCATION AND EMPLOYMENT (1998a) *The National Literacy Strategy: Framework for Teaching.* London: DfEE.

[36] from ADAMS (1990).

[37] CLAY, M.M. (1993) *Reading Recovery: A guidebook for teachers in training.* Auckland, New Zealand: Heinemann Education. See also BEARD (1994) for a short summary of the wider lessons which the programme offers. One of the most comprehensive books on spelling and writing difficulties in general is PUMFREY, P.D. and ELLIOTT, C.D. (Eds.) (1990) *Children's Difficulties in Reading, Writing and Spelling.* Basingstoke: Falmer Press.

[38] CLARKE, L.K. (1988) 'Invented Versus Traditional Spelling in First Graders' Writings: Effects on Learning to Spell and Read, *Research in the Teaching of English.* 22, 3, 281–309.

[39] ADAMS (1990) p.385.

[40] BRYANT, P. *et al.* (1997) 'Spelling with apostrophes and understanding

possession', *British Journal of Educational Psychology*, 67, 91–120; BRYANT, P. *et al.* (1998) 'Awareness of Language in Children Who Have Reading Difficulties: Historical Comparisons in a Longitudinal Study', *Journal of Child Psychology and Psychiatry*, 39, 4, 501–510; NUNES, T. *et al.* (1997) 'Morphological Spelling Strategies: Developmental Stages and Processes', *Developmental Psychology*, 33, 4, 637–649.

[41] KING, M. L. and RENTEL, V. (1979) 'Toward a theory of early writing development', *Research in the Teaching of English*, 13, 3, 243–253.

[42] CAMBOURNE, B. (1988) *The Whole Story: Natural Learning and the Acquisition of Literacy in the Classroom.* Gosford, NSW: Aston Scholastic. For a wide-ranging discussion of related issues, see SMITH, J. and ELLEY, W. (1997) *How Children Learn to Write.* London: Paul Chapman.

[43] There is a helpful discussion of the teaching of early writing in the NFER survey report, CATO, V. *et al.* (1992) *The Teaching of Initial Literacy: How do teachers do it?* Slough: NFER. Richard Fox at Exeter University has researched the way in which teachers of 5–7 year olds adapted the Literacy Hour approach. For short discussion of the research and the issues it raises, see FOX, R. (1999) 'Rewriting the literacy hour', *Times Educational Supplement Primary Magazine*, 25.6.99, p.6.

[44] CHALL, J. *et al.* (1990) *The Reading Crisis: Why Poor Children Fall Behind.* Cambridge, Mass.: Harvard University Press; SNOW, C. *et al.* (1991) *Unfulfilled Expectations: Home and School Influences on Literacy.* Cambridge, Mass.: Harvard University Press.

[45] See BARRON, I. (1996) 'Emergent Writing and the Teacher', *Journal of Teacher Development*, 5.2. 41–8.

[46] QUALIFICATIONS AND CURRICULUM AUTHORITY (1999a) *Early Learning Goals.* London: QCA/DfEE.

[47] NUTBROWN, C. (1999) 'Baseline assessment of writing: the need for reconsideration', *Journal of Research in Reading*, 22, 1, 37–44.

[48] SAINSBURY, M., SCHAGEN, I., WHETTON, C. and CASPALL, L. (1999) 'An investigation of hierarchical relationships in children's literacy attainments at baseline', *Journal of Research in Reading*, 22, 1, 45–54. The 'dependency indices' were as follows: print/pictures – letter shapes 0.63; letter shapes – own name 0.92; own name – words (with 3+ letters correct) 0.94.

[49] WOLFENDALE, S. and LINDSAY, G. (1999) 'Guest Editorial: Issues in baseline assessment', *Journal of Research in Reading*, 22, 1, 1–13.

Chapter 5 Notes

[1] *Essay on Criticism*

[2] HARTOG, P.J. (1908) *The Writing of English (Second Edition).* Oxford: Clarendon Press.

[3] Hartog (1908) p.61.

[4] The English National Curriculum for the year 2000 onwards explicitly links forms to purposes at Key Stage 3. In the earlier two key stages, forms and purposes are listed separately. A helpful book on range in forms of writing is REES, F. (1996) *The Writing repertoire: Developing Writing at Key Stage 2.* Slough: National Foundation for Educational Research.

[5] BAIN, A. (1887) *English Composition and Rhetoric* (Enlarged Edition) London: Longmans, Green and Co.

[6] D'ANGELO, F.D. (1976) 'Modes of Discourse', in TATE, G. (Ed.) *Teaching Composition: Ten Bibliographical Essays*. Fort Worth, Texas: Christian University Press

[7] BOARD OF EDUCATION (1931) *Report of the consultative committee on the primary school* (The Hadow Report). London: HMSO.

[8] BRITTON, J. *et al.* (1975) *The Development of Writing Abilities (11-18)*. Basingstoke: Macmillan.

[9] KINNEAVY, J. L. (1971) A *Theory of Discourse*. Englewood Cliffs, New Jersey: Prentice Hall; KINNEAVY, J. L. *et al.* (1976) *Writing: Basic Modes of Organisation*. Dubuque, Iowa: Kendall Hunt Pub. Co.; see also KINNEAVY, J. L. (1983) 'A pluralistic synthesis of four contemporary models for teaching composition', in Freedman, A. *et al.* (Eds.) *Learning to Write: First Language/Second Language*. London: Longman; KINNEAVY, J.L (1991) 'Rhetoric', in FLOOD, J. et al. (Eds.) *Handbook of Research on Teaching the English Language Arts*. New York: Macmillan. Similar approaches to range are found in BEAN, M.A. and WAGSTAFF, P. (1991) *Practical Approaches to Writing in the Primary School*. London: Longman.

[10] SCARDAMALIA *et al.* (1981) *Writing for Results: A Sourcebook of Consequential Composing Activities*. Ontario: OISE Press.

[11] PERERA, K. (1984) *Children's Writing and Reading: Analysing Classroom Language* Oxford; Basil Blackwell, in Association with Andre Deutsch Ltd. p.220.

[12] GIBSON, H. and ANDREWS, R. (1993) 'A Critique of the chronological/Non-chronological Distinction in the National Curriculum for English', *Educational Review*, 45, 3, 239–249. Richard Andrews' subsequent thinking on the writing of argument is set out in ANDREWS, R. (1997) 'Reconceiving Argument', *Educational Review* 49. 3, 259–269.

[13] MINISTRY OF EDUCATION (1954) *Language: Some Suggestions for Teachers of English and others*. London: HMSO. p.63.

[14] DEPARTMENT OF EDUCATION AND SCIENCE (1959) *Primary Education*. London: HMSO.

[15] CLEGG, A. (1964) *The Excitement of Writing*. London: Chatto and Windus: MAYBURY, B. (1967) *Creative Writing for Juniors*. London: Batsford; LANE, S. M. and KEMP, M. (1967) *An Approach to Creative Writing in the Primary School*. London: Blackie.

[16] DEPARTMENT OF EDUCATION AND SCIENCE (1975) *A Language for Life* (The Bullock Report). London: HMSO, p.163.

[17] Britton *et al.* (1975).

[18] TEMPLE, C., (1993) *The Beginnings of Writing* (3E), Boston, Mass.: Allyn and Bacon.

[19] Kinneavy (1971)

[20] Perera (1984) pp.216–221

[21] ODELL, L. *et al.* (1978) 'Discourse theory: implications for research in composing', in COOPER, C. R. and ODELL, L. *Research on Composing: Points of*

Departure. Urbana, Illinois: National Council of Teachers of English.
[22] LLOYD-JONES, R. (1977) 'Primary trait scoring', in COOPER, C. R. and ODELL, L. (Eds.) *Evaluating Writing: Describing, Measuring, Judging.* State University of New York at Buffalo: National Council of Teachers of English. Kinneavy's analysis is also subjected to close scrutiny in BEALE, W. (1977) 'On the Classification of Discourse', *Rhetoric Society Quarterly,* 7, 31–40.
[23] In LLOYD-JONES (1977) p.37.
[24] DEPARTMENT FOR EDUCATION AND EMPLOYMENT (1999b) *The National Curriculum: Handbook for primary teachers in England, Key Stages 1 and 2.* London: DfEE and DfEE.
[25] DEPARTMENT OF EDUCATION NORTHERN IRELAND (1996) English Programmes of Study and Attainment Targets: Key Stages 1, 2 and 3 (3 vols.) Bangor, Co. Down: DENI
[26] SCOTTISH OFFICE EDUCATION DEPARTMENT (1991) *English Language 5–14.* Edinburgh: SOED. The Scottish curriculum on writing has been discussed at length in ELLIS, S. *et al.* (1997) 'Writing Stories 5-14: What must teachers teach?' *Scottish Educational Review,* 29, 1, 56–65.
[27] DfEE (1999a)
[28] DENI (1996)
[29] SOED (1991), p. 10.
[30] There are helpful examples in WRAY, D. and LEWIS, M. (1997) *Extending Literacy.* London: Routledge.
[31] Age-specific studies of the influence of different audiences on children's writing include the following: KROLL, B. (1985) 'Rewriting a complex story for a younger reader: The development of audience-adapted writing skills, *Research in the Teaching of English,* 19, 2, 120–139; FRANK, L.A. (1992) 'Writing to be read: Young writers' ability to demonstrate audience awareness when evaluated by their readers', *Research in the Teaching of English,* 26, 3, 277–298; HALL, N. and ROBINSON, A. (Eds.) (1994) *Keeping in touch: using interactive writing with young children.* London: Hodder and Stoughton.
[32] Examples include SCHOOL CURRICULUM AND ASSESSMENT AUTHORITY (subsequently the QUALIFICATIONS AND ASSESSMENT AUTHORITY) (1997) *Use of language: a common approach,* London: SCAA; MCNAUGHTON, M.J. (1997) 'Drama and Children's Writing: a study of the influence of drama on the imaginative writing of primary school children', *Research in Drama Education,* 2, 1, 55–85.
[33] SUTTON-SMITH, B. (1988) in Egan, K. and Nadaner, D. (Eds.) *Imagination and Education.* Milton Keynes: Open University Press.
[34] SMIT, M.G. (1992) *The Teaching of English in the Primary School with particular reference to the development of children's imaginative writing.* Unpublished MEd. thesis. Leeds: University of Leeds School of Education.
[35] GREGORY, R. L. (1977) 'Psychology: towards a science of fiction', in MEEK, M. *et al.* (Eds.) *The Cool Web.* London: The Bodley Head, p.394. Anne Haas Dyson has explored how television and other visual media may influence children's writing in DYSON, A.H. (1997) *Writing Superheroes: contemporary childhood, popular culture on classroom literacy.* New York: Teachers College Press.

[36] HUGHES, T. (1976) 'Myth and Education', *Children's Literature in Education* 1,1. Reprinted in FOX, G. (Ed.) (1995) *Celebrating Children's Literature in Education*. London: Hodder and Stoughton.

[37] BETTELHEIM, B. (1977). *The Uses of Enchantment: The Meaning of Importance of Fairy Tales*. London: Thames and Hudson.

[38] COWIE, H. (Ed.) (1984) *The Development of Children's Imaginative Writing*. London: Croom Helm.

[39] WILKINSON, A. *et al.* (1980) *Assessing Language Development*. Oxford: Oxford University Press; see also WILKINSON, A. (1986) *The Quality of Writing*. Milton Keynes: Open University Press.

[40] Chambers English Dictionary, 1990.

[41] In FREEDMAN, A. and MEDWAY, P. (Eds.) (1994) *Genre and the New Rhetoric*. London; Taylor and Francis.

[42] COPE, B. and KALANTZIS, M. (1993) *The Powers of Literacy: A Genre Approach to Teaching Writing*. London: The Falmer Press.

[43] Cope and Kalantzis (1993) p.9.

[44] MARTIN, J.R. (1989) *Factual writing: exploring and challenging social reality* (2E). Oxford: Oxford University Press. A more recent paper summarising the influence of genre theory on the teaching of English in Australia is WYATT-SMITH, C. (1997) 'Teaching and assessing writing: an Australian perspective', *English in Education*, 31, 3, 8–22. Other helpful books on genre theory and writing include LITTLEFAIR, A.B. (1991) *Reading All Types of Writing*. Milton Keynes: Open University Press; RILEY J. and REEDY, D. (2000) *Developing Writing for Different Purposes: Teaching about Genre in the Early Years*. London: Paul Chapman.

[45] This definition of 'exposition' is different from that of Alexander Bain referred to earlier.

[46] LEWIS, M. and WRAY, D. (1995) *Developing Children's Non-Fiction Writing: working with writing frames*. Leamington Spa: Scholastic.

[47] COPE and KALANTZIS (1993) pp.12–14.

[48] KRESS, G. (1994) *Learning to Write* (2E). London: Routledge, p.126.

[49] COPE and KALANTZIS (1993) p.22.

[50] FREEDMAN and MEDWAY (1994) Chapter 1.

[51] CHRISTIE, F. (1996) 'Review of Freedman, A. and Medway, P. (Eds.) (1994) *Genre and the New Rhetoric*', *Language and Education*, 10, 1, 71–75.

[52] MCARTHUR, T. (Ed.) *The Oxford Companion to the English Language*. Oxford: Oxford University Press. For helpful advice on teaching poetry in primary schools, see CORBETT, P. and MOSES, B. (1986) *Catapults and Kingfishers: teaching poetry in primary schools*. Oxford: Oxford University Press; BROWNJOHN, S. (1994) *To Rhyme Or Not To Rhyme?* London: Hodder and Stoughton.

[53] GIBSON and ANDREWS (1993) p.245.

[54] LEWIS and WRAY (1995)

[55] MINSKY, M. (1985) 'A Framework for Representing Knowledge', in Winston, P.H. (Ed.) *The Psychology of Computer Vision*. New York: McGraw-Hill.

[56] SCARDAMALIA, M., BEREITER, C. and FILLION, B. (1981) *Writing for Results: A Sourcebook of Consequential Composing Activities*. Ontario: OISE Press.

Chapter 6 Notes

[1] Interview on the National Literacy Training Pack Video (DfEE, 1998b).

[2] QUIRK, R., GREENBAUM, S., LEECH, G. and SVARTVIK, J. (1985) *A Comprehensive Grammar of the English Language.* Harlow: Longman, pp.12–14.

[3] In order to avoid confusion between actual phrases and 'technical' phrases (which may only comprise a single word), PERERA (1984, pp. 36–37) suggests that the abbreviations NP, VP etc. are used to denote clause elements which actually comprise a group of words.

[4] I am grateful to George Keith for this example.

[5] e.g. Ted Hughes in HUGHES, T. (1987) 'To parse or not to parse: the poet's answer', *The Sunday Times.* 22 November; and Jan Mark in DUGUID, L. (1988) 'The art of conversation: A profile of Jan Mark'. *Times Educational Supplement,* 3 June.

[6] KEITH, G. (1990) 'Language Study at Key Stage 3', in CARTER, R. (Ed.) *Knowledge about Language and the Curriculum: The LINC Reader.* London: Hodder and Stoughton.

[7] TEACHER TRAINING AGENCY (1998) *Teaching: High Status, High Standards: Requirements for Courses of Initial Teacher Training.* London: DfEE.

[8] QUALIFICATIONS AND CURRICULUM AUTHORITY (1998d) *The Grammar Papers.* London: QCA; QUALIFICATIONS AND CURRICULUM AUTHORITY (1999b) *Not whether but how.* London: QCA.

[9] TOMLINSON, D. (1994) 'Errors in the research into the effectiveness of grammar teaching', *English in Education,* 28, 1, 20–26.

[10] BEARD, R. and WILLCOCKS, J. (1997) 'Terms for Teaching Phonic Knowledge: A Legacy of Confusion'. Paper presented at the International Seminar on *Literacy: Integrating Research and Practice,* University of London Institute of Education, December.

[11] From [abbrev. version] (1824) *The Infant's Grammar of a Picnic Party of the Parts of Speech.* London: Harris and Son.

[12] Following linguistic convention, the asterisk indicates a form of words that is grammatically unacceptable.

[13] See CRYSTAL, D. (1988) *Rediscover Grammar.* London: Longman, for more explanations and examples.

[14] Non-finite forms of the verb are not marked: the infinitive ('to sing'), the *-ing* participle ('singing') and the *-ed* participle. The verb 'to sing' has an irregular *-ed* participle ('sang', rather than *'singed'). In traditional grammar, the *-ing* participle is known as the present participle and the *-ed* participle is known as the past participle.

[15] The sentence 'The horses were neighing' shows how, if there is a series of verbs in the verb phrase, the finite verb is always the first.

[16] In some grammatical descriptions, the term 'complement' is used more broadly and can be found for every word class (see MCARTHUR, T. (Ed.) (1992) *The Oxford Companion to the English Language.* Oxford: Oxford University Press).

[17] 'Vocatives' are optional extras in some sentences. A vocative is an element which refers to the person(s) to whom the sentence is addressed. A name or a

noun phrase is used: 'Sydney, don't do that'; or 'Friends, Romans, countrymen, lend me your ears'.

[18] As was pointed out earlier, it is important to bear in mind that, in contemporary grammatical descriptions, the term 'phrase' is used a little differently from how it is used in everyday language. Common dictionary definitions often state that a 'phrase' is a group of words that does not contain a verb. However, in modern grammatical description, 'phrase' is used to refer to any word(s) that express a single clause element, including individual words and including verbs.

[19] 'Pleased' is an example of an adjective that only normally appears in the predicate (the verb and all the other clause elements that come after it). Other examples are 'afraid' and 'unwell'. Similarly some adjectives only appear as part of a noun phrase e.g. 'main' or 'utter'. Thus we do not say *'The pleased winner' or *'The reason was main'.

[20] Related to the overall meaning of the text.

[21] The rise and fall in the pitch of the voice.

[22] HALLIDAY, M. and HASAN, R. (1976) *Cohesion in English*. Harlow: Longman.

[23] The term used by the National Literacy Strategy *Framework for Teaching*.

Chapter 7 Notes

[1] HUGHES, T. (1987) 'To parse or not to parse: the poet's answer', *The Sunday Times*. 22 November.

[2] CRYSTAL, D. (1979) *Working With LARSP*. London: Edward Arnold.

[3] EDWARDS, V. and CHESHIRE, J. (1989) 'The survey of British dialects', cited in HUDSON, R. (1992) *Teaching Grammar*. Oxford: Blackwell. See also EDWARDS, V. and CHESHIRE, J. (1989) 'The survey of British dialect grammar', in CHESHIRE, J., EDWARDS, V., MUNSTERMANN, H. and WELTENS, B. (Eds.) *Dialect and Education: Some European Perspectives*. Clevedon: Multilingual Matters.

[4] DEPARTMENT OF EDUCATION AND SCIENCE (1988) *Report of the Committee of Inquiry into the Teaching of the English Language* (The Kingman Report). London: HMSO, p.14.

[5] HONEY, J. (1997) *Language is Power*. London: Faber.

[6] DEPARTMENT FOR EDUCATION AND EMPLOYMENT (1999b) *The National Curriculum: Handbook for Primary Teachers in England, Key Stages 1 and 2*. London: DfEE and QCA.

[7] EDWARDS and CHESHIRE (1989) p.201.

[8] HUDSON, R. and HOLMES, J. (1995) *Children's Use of Standard Spoken English*. London: School Curriculum and Assessment Authority. The tape-recordings used were from 1988 research undertaken by the National Foundation of Educational Research. These recordings had been originally undertaken as part of the Assessment of Performance Unit's monitoring of national standards.

[9] The percentage is based on the numbers who had a chance to use this form in the tape-recordings.

[10] Hudson and Holmes point out that SSE does allow '*There's hundreds* of people on the waiting list' and '*There's some people* I'd like you to meet'.

[11] This non-standard feature is widely used in the language of football ('We *got beat*').

[12] e.g. QUALIFICATIONS and CURRICULUM AUTHORITY (1998a) *Standards at Key Stage 1: English and Mathematics. Report of the 1998 national curriculum assessments for 7 year olds.* London: QCA; QUALIFICATIONS and CURRICULUM AUTHORITY (1998b) *Standards at Key Stage 2: English, Mathematics and Science. Report of the 1998 national curriculum assessments for 11 year olds.* London: QCA; QUALIFICATIONS and CURRICULUM AUTHORITY (1998c) *Standards at Key Stage 3: English. Report of the 1998 National Curriculum Assessments for 14 year olds.* London: QCA.

[13] WILLIAMSON, J. and HARDMAN, F. (1997) 'Those Terrible Marks of the Beast: Non-standard Dialect and Children's Writing', *Language and Education*, 11, 4, 287–299. There is also a helpful chapter on non-standard English and second language learning in Writing in WILLIAMS, J.D. (1998) *Preparing to Teach Writing* (2E), Mahwah, N.J.: Lawrence Erlbaum.

[14] WINCH, C. and GINGELL, J. (1994) 'Dialect Interference and Difficulties in Writing: An Investigation in St. Lucian Primary Schools', *Language and Education*, 8, 3, 157–182.

[15] HALLIDAY, M.A.K. HASAN, R. (1976) *Cohesion in English.* Harlow: Longman.

[16] CRYSTAL, D. (1990) *The English Language.* Harmondsworth: Penguin.

[17] Adapted from CRYSTAL, D. (1995) *The Cambridge Encyclopedia of the English Language.* Cambridge: Cambridge University Press, p.198.

[18] Adapted from CRYSTAL, D. (1995) *The Cambridge Encyclopedia of the English Language.* Cambridge: Cambridge University Press, p.128.

[19] The inclusion of a hyphen in many of these words seems increasingly to be a matter of style.

[20] See, for instance, O'HARE, F. (1973) *Sentence-Combining: Improving Student Writing without Formal Grammar Instruction.* Illinois: National Council of Teachers of English.

[21] William Strong (1976) has discussed the implications of sentence-combining research in 'Back to basics and beyond', *English Journal*, 65, 56 and 60–64. In the same edition of this journal (pp.57–59), Robert Marzano raises some questions about the paired rating procedures used by O'Hare, suggesting that it would have been more satisfactory to use ordinal scales on all scripts. Marzano also draws attention to another teaching technique, involving modifiers to a base clause, which might be equally as effective as sentence-combining and perhaps more efficient.

[22] This section owes much to the excellent discussion of written style in PERERA, K. (1984) *Children's Writing and Reading.* Oxford: Blackwell.

[23] Christopher, 10, cited in PERERA (1984) p.250.

[24] GREENBAUM, S. (1991) *An Introduction to English Grammar.* Harlow: Longman.

[25] HUDSON and HOLMES (1995).

²⁶ e.g. HAWKINS, E. (1987) *Awareness of Language: An Introduction* (Revised Edition) Cambridge: Cambridge University Press.

²⁷ David Wray (1994) has extended the language awareness perspective to focus primarily on literacy and to link with research in metacognition in *Literacy and Awareness*. The study of metacognition deals with our knowledge of our own thinking and the ways we monitor and refer to it.

²⁸ HAWKINS (1987) p.138.

²⁹ QUALIFICATIONS AND CURRICULUM AUTHORITY (1998d) *The Grammar Papers*. London: QCA.

³⁰ WILKINSON, A. (1971) *The Foundations of Language*. Oxford: Oxford University Press.

³¹ WILKINSON (1971) p.32.

Chapter 8 Notes

¹ *My Family and Other Animals*, Penguin

² GENTRY, J.R. (1982) 'An analysis of developmental spelling in *GNYS AT WRK*', *The Reading Teacher*, 36, 192–200. Gentry builds on the earlier research of Charles Read in Wisconsin. Read analysed the 2517 spellings for 1201 words created by 32 children in pre-schools and kindergartens. See READ, C. (1971) 'Pre-school children's knowledge of the English orthography', *Harvard Educational Review*, 41, 1–34; also READ, C. (1975) *Children's Creative Spelling*. London: Routledge and Kegan Paul. Similar stage models are used by other writers, including HENDERSON, E. (1985) *Teaching Spelling*. Boston: Houghton Mifflin.

³ BISSEX, G.L. (1980) *GNYS AT WRK: A Child Learns to Write and Read*. Cambridge, Mass.: Harvard University Press.

⁴ TREIMAN, R and CASSAR, M. (1997) 'Spelling Acquisition in English', in PERFETTI, C.A., RIEBEN, L. and FAYOL, M. (Eds.) *Learning to Spell: Research, Theory and Practice Across Languages*. Mahwah, N.J.: Lawrence Erlbaum; and SNOWLING, M.J. (1994) 'Towards a Model of Spelling Acquisition: The Development of Some Component Skills', in BROWN, G.D.A. and ELLIS, N.C. (Eds.) *Handbook of Spelling: Theory, Process and Intervention*. Chichester: John Wiley and Sons. Norma Mudd has written one of the most informative books on the teaching of spelling: MUDD, N. (1994) *Effective Spelling: A practical guide for teachers*. London: Hodder and Stoughton.

⁵ TREIMAN and CASSAR (1997)

⁶ Michael Stubbs has discussed the system of systems in English spelling in *Language and Literacy* Routledge and Kegan Paul (1980) and more recently in 'Who Climbs the Grammar-Tree?' in *Sonderdruck aus LA 381* Tübingen: Max Niemeyer Verlag, 221–234, 1992.

⁷ PETERS, M.L. and SMITH, B. (1993) *Spelling in Context: Strategies for Teachers and Learners*. Windsor: NFER-Nelson.

⁸ Margaret Peters' research suggests that words are best learned if they share the same letter strings, whether or not they sound the same. See PETERS, M. (1985) *Spelling: Caught or Taught? A new Look*. Routledge. For a paper on the significance

of analogy in spelling and reading, see GOMBERT, M., BRYANT, P. and WARRICK, N. (1997) 'Children's Use of Analogy in Learning to Read and to Spell', in PERFETTI, C.A., RIEBEN, L. and FAYOL, M. (Eds.) *Learning to Spell: Research, Theory and Practice Across Languages.* Mahwah, N.J.: Lawrence Erlbaum
[9] HARPIN, W. (1976) *The Second 'R': Writing Development in the Junior School.* London: Allen and Unwin.
[10] HARPIN (1976) p.50.
[11] MORTIMORE, P., SAMMONS, P., STOLL, L., LEWIS, D. and ECOB, R. (1988) *School Matters: The Junior Years.* Wells: Open Books.
[12] SNOW, C., BARNES, W.S., CHANDLER, J., GOODMAN, I.F. and HEMPHILL, L. (1991) *Unfulfilled Expectations: Home and School Influences on Literacy.* Cambridge, Mass.: Harvard University Press.
[13] SNOW et al.(1991) p.55.
[14] HARPIN (1976) p.56.
[15] SHAUGHNESSY, M. P. (1977) *Errors and Expectations: A guide for the teacher of basic writing.* New York: Oxford University Press.
[16] SHAUGHNESSY (1977) p.224.
[17] HARPIN (1976) p.68.
[18] HARPIN (1976) p.73.
[19] PERERA, K. (1984) *Children's Writing and Reading: Analysing Classroom Language.* Oxford: Basil Blackwell, in Association with Andre Deutsch Ltd.

Chapter 9 Notes

[1] *The Second* R , p. 156.
[2] MOFFETT, J. (1968) *Teaching the Universe of Discourse.* Boston, Massachusetts: Houghton Mifflin.
[3] WILKINSON, A. et al. (1980) *Assessing Language Development.* Oxford: Oxford University Press; also WILKINSON, A.(1986) *The Quality of Writing.* Milton Keynes: Open University Press.
[4] BEREITER, C. (1980) 'Development in writing', in GREGG, L. W. and STEINBERG, E. R. (Eds.) *Cognitive Processes in Writing* Hillsdale, New Jersey: Lawrence Erlbaum Associates
[5] MOFFETT (1968) p.18.
[6] MOFFETT (1968) p.57.
[7] The critique by Howard Gibson and Richard Andrews of the distinction between chronological and non-chronological writing was discussed in **Chapter 5**.
[8] The main conclusions included the following:
Cognitive development: 13 year olds were showing that they could abstract, summarise, evaluate and generalise, supporting generalisations with concrete evidence. Some were beginning to project hypotheses, something which none of the ten-year-old children were apparently doing in their writing.
Affective development: There was development from literal statements with no affective elements at 7 through to greater psychological authenticity at 13. At the age of 13 children used more realistic themes and introspection, which was not

found in 10 year olds' writing. At 10 there is greater explicitness of emotion to deepen the theme and the use of environmental details to intensify moods or attitudes. This was often accomplished through fantasy narratives with mass media-based themes. At 13, emotion was brought into writing more obliquely, through characters' behaviour.

Moral development: The findings on moral development needed to be interpreted with particular caution. They were based on inferences from verbal judgements and not from observed behaviour. With this reservation in mind, Wilkinson and his colleagues report that no evidence was found of judgements being made in terms of abstract universal principles, although this was to be expected, given the age-range studied. Generally the findings from earlier research by Lawrence Kohlberg were confirmed. At seven children tended to make moral judgements in terms of punishments or rewards (*heteronomy*). Ten year olds tended to judge in terms of the maintenance of good relationships (*socionomy*). Thirteen year olds were more likely to draw on principles of fairness and intention (*autonomy*).

Style: The findings on style confirmed the anticipated development outlined earlier in the chapter. There was increasingly growth from partial to complete organisation in terms of syntax and verbal competence; organisation and cohesion; reader awareness and appropriateness; and overall effectiveness.

[9] WILKINSON *et al* (1980) p.221.

[10] BEREITER (1980) p.84.

[11] BEREITER (1980) p.89; Bereiter's model was used in the Beginning Writing study at the University of East Anglia, which was referred to in **Chapter 4**: NICHOLLS, J. et al. (1989) *Beginning Writing*. Milton Keynes: Open University Press.

[12] The relationship between writing development and personal growth has been studied by Roslyn Arnold in an intervention project at Sydney University. Thirty-five 11 year olds in two schools were involved over a four-year period. Her framework included audience, creativity, thinking and language. The framework drew upon Moffett's and Wilkinson's work and also James Britton's model of language functions, discussed in **Chapter 5**. Arnold was particularly concerned with the 'psychodynamic' aspects of writing. By this she meant the ways in which inner speech is tapped, focused, selected, edited and ordered, in interaction with different tasks and readers (ARNOLD, R. (1991) *Writing Development*. Milton Keynes: Open University Press).

[13] See, for example, RUTH, L. and MURPHY, S. (1988) *Designing Writing Tasks for the Assessment of Writing*. Norwood, N.J.: Ablex. Holistic assessment of writing is discussed in COOPER, C. R. (1977) 'Holistic Evaluation of Writing', in COOPER, C. R. and ODELL, L. (Eds.) *Evaluating Writing: Describing, Measuring, Judging*. State University of New York at Buffalo: National Council of Teachers of English.

[14] LLOYD-JONES, R. (1977) 'Primary Trait Scoring' in COOPER, C. and ODELL, L. (Eds.) *Evaluating Writing: Describing, Measuring, Judging*. Urbana, Ill.: National Council for the Teaching of English.

[15] QUALIFICATIONS AND CURRICULUM AUTHORITY (1998f) *Key Stage 2 English Tests Mark Schemes.* London: QCA/DfEE. There is a useful chapter on using National Curriculum levels for assessing and planning for writing in GRAHAM, J. and KELLY, A. (Eds.) (1998) *Writing Under Control.* London: David Fulton in association with Roehampton Institute.

[16] ARNOLD (1991).

[17] QUALIFICATIONS AND CURRICULUM AUTHORITY (1998a) *Standards at Key Stage 1: English and Mathematics. Report of the 1998 national curriculum assessments for 7 year olds.* London: QCA. p.4.

[18] QUALIFICATIONS and CURRICULUM AUTHORITY (1998b) *Standards at Key Stage 2: English, mathematics and Science. Report of the 1998 national curriculum assessments for 11 year olds.* London: QCA. p.4.

[19] QUALIFICATIONS AND CURRICULUM AUTHORITY(1998c) *Standards at Key Stage 3: English. Report of the 1998 National Curriculum Assessments for 14 year olds.* London: QCA. p.4.

[20] ASSESSMENT OF PERFORMANCE UNIT (1981). *Language Performance in Schools: Primary Survey Report No. I.* London: HMSO.

[21] OFSTED (1993c) *Boys and English.* London: Ofsted.

[22] MILLARD, E. (1997) *Differently Literate: Boys, Girls and the Schooling of Literacy.* London: The Falmer Press.

[23] FRATER, G. (1997) *Improving Boys' Literacy: A survey of effective practice in secondary schools.* London: Basic Skills Agency.

[24] QUALIFICATIONS AND CURRICULUM AUTHORITY (1998e) *Can Do Better: Raising Boys' achievement in English.* London: QCA.

[25] DEPARTMENT OF EDUCATION AND EMPLOYMENT (1999a) *English: The National Curriculum for England Key stages 1–4.* London: DfEE/QCA.

[26] PAPERT, S. (1980) *Mindstorms.* Brighton: Harvester Press. p.30.

[27] DEPARTMENT OF EDUCATION AND SCIENCE (1988) *Report of the Committee of Inquiry into the Teaching of the English Language* (The Kingman Report). London: HMSO, p. 37.

[28] ROBSON, S. (1986) '"No one can see the awful mistakes you've made": Word processing with six and seven year olds', *Primary Teaching Studies*, 1, 2, 62–79.

[29] WOODRUFF, E., BEREITER, C. and SCARDAMALIA, M. (1981) 'On the Road to Computer Assisted Compositions', *Journal of Educational Technology Systems*, 10, 2, 133–148.

[30] PEACOCK, M. (1992) *Evaluating word processed pupil writing.* Unpublished PhD thesis, University of Leeds School of Education.

[31] LITTEN, C. L. (1989) 'The effects of word processing and peer review on the revision process of freshman composition students', *Dissertation Abstracts International*, 51/4, 1101A.

[32] GROSSMAN, A. N. (1988) 'Writing and using a word processor in an LD resource room: case studies of five minimally handicapped high school students', *Dissertation Abstracts International*, 50/1, 113.

[33] PIOLAT, A (1991) 'Effects of word processing on text revision', *Language and Education*, 5, 4, p.267.

[34] HALL-MOLINA, J. M. (1990) 'A comparison of writing quality, attitude towards writing, and problem solving ability of elementary students who use a word processor and those who use the paper pencil method of composition', *Dissertation Abstracts International*, 51/7, 2263A.

[35] VAN HAALEN, T. G. (1990) 'Writing and revising: Bilingual students' use of word processing', *Dissertation Abstracts International*, 52/2, 418.

[36] BANGERT-DROWNS, R.L. (1993) 'The Word Processor as an Instructional Tool: A Meta-Analysis of Word Processing in Writing Instruction', *Review of Educational Research*, 63,1, 69–93.

[37] BANGERT-DROWNS (1993).

[38] MCFARLANE, A. (Ed.) (1997) *Information Technology and Authentic Learning*. London: Routledge.

[39] SCRIMSHAW, P.(Ed.) (1993) *Language, classrooms and computers*. London: Routlege.

[40] COCHRAN-SMITH, M., *et al.* (1991) *Learning to Write Differently*. Hove: Ablex Pub. Co. A recent paper to explore the new kinds of context created by word processing is BOWMAN, M.(1999) 'Children, Word Processors and Genre', *Scottish Educational Review*, 31, 1, 66–83.

[41] e.g. STREET, B.V. (1984) *Literacy in Theory and Practice*. Cambridge: Cambridge University Press; STREET, B.V. (1993) 'The new literacy studies: guest editorial', *Journal of Research in Reading*. 16, 2, 81–97.

[42] e.g. GOUGH, P. (1999) 'The New Literacy: *Caveat Emptor*' in OAKHILL, J. and BEARD, R. (Eds.) (1999) *Reading Development and the Teaching of Reading*. Oxford: Blackwell.

[43] Shortly after the death of Diana, Princess of Wales, a report in a national newspaper, *The Independent*, suggested that the British royal family lacked 'emotional literacy'.

[44] This distinction is made by Phil Gough in GOUGH (1999).

[45] PERFETTI, C. (1995) 'Cognitive research can inform reading education', *Journal of Research in Reading*, 18, 2, 106–115. Reprinted in OAKHILL, J. and BEARD, R. (Eds.) (1999) *Reading Development and the Teaching of Reading: a psychological perspective*. Oxford: Blackwell.

[46] BARTON, D. and HAMILTON, M. (1998) *Local Literacies: Reading and Writing in One Community*. London: Routledge.

Chapter 10 Notes

[1] *The World on Paper*, Cambridge University Press, 1994, p.xv.

[2] Margaret Peters made recurrent use of these words in her many publications and broadcasts.

[3] See, for instance, MEDWELL, J., WRAY, D., POULSON, L. and FOX, R. (1998) *Effective Teachers of Literacy*. Exeter: University of Exeter School of Education.

[4] WHITE, J. (1986) *The Assessment of Writing: Pupils Aged 11 and 15*. Windsor: NFER-Nelson.

[5] VYGOTSKY, L. (1962) *Thought and Language*. Cambridge, Mass.: M.I.T. Press.

[6] JOHNSON, P. (1990) *A Book of One's Own: developing literacy through making books*. London: Hodder and Stoughton.

Index